BRIAN MOORE: THE AUTOBIOGRAPHY

THE AUTOBIOGRAPHY
BRIAN MOORE
— *With Stephen Jones* —

PARTRIDGE PRESS

LONDON · NEW YORK · TORONTO · SYDNEY · AUCKLAND

TRANSWORLD PUBLISHERS LTD
61–63 Uxbridge Road, London W5 5SA

TRANSWORLD PUBLISHERS (AUSTRALIA) PTY LTD
15–23 Helles Avenue, Moorebank, NSW 2170

TRANSWORLD PUBLISHERS (NZ) LTD
3 William Pickering Drive, Albany, Auckland

Published 1995 by Partridge Press
a division of Transworld Publishers Ltd
Copyright © Brian Moore & Stephen Jones 1995

A catalogue record for this book is available from the British Library.

ISBN 185225 2340

Typeset in 11/15pt Century Old Style by
Kestrel Data, Exeter, Devon.

Printed and bound in Great Britain by
Mackays of Chatham plc, Chatham, Kent.

To all those people who gave me so much help – even when I didn't deserve it.
And also to the happy memory of John Walsh

CONTENTS

BRIAN MOORE: THE AUTOBIOGRAPHY

PROLOGUE

Beware of the dog

IT IS DEFINITELY A MASOCHISTIC KIND OF LOVE, BUT LOVE IT IS. I love playing in Paris. There is nowhere in sport like the combined stadium, Coliseum and bearpit that is the Parc des Princes, home of the French team. I have never played anywhere with such an atmosphere – shrill, hostile, temperamental, overwhelming. To meet the French team there is, in the opinion of many people, one of the supreme physical tests in sport. Running through the list of the fierce French forwards I have met there, it is impossible to disagree.

When we went there in the quarter-finals of the World Cup

1

in 1991, all the stakes were raised even higher. It was sudden death, the winner went to the semi-finals, the loser went home. And since Serge Blanco, the great full-back, had announced that he would retire after the World Cup, there was the added drama, the overwhelming affection for the man in France, the knowledge of the lengths to which the French team and followers would go so that Serge would not have to bow out quite yet.

As we prepared for the match, even the undemonstrative, rock-like Peter Winterbottom, probably the hardest man I came across in rugby, was becoming agitated. 'This has really been getting to me for days,' he told me, quietly, 'I am so built up. We cannot lose, we cannot lose.'

The hype was massive and there was a crass error by some nameless World Cup official responsible for getting the teams out on the field. We assumed that we would go out first as the visiting team. France always station all their big men at the front of the queue to take the field, so we put all our big men in the lead and walked out of the dressing room into the glass-walled reception area they have at the Parc, and prepared to thunder out on to the pitch. But as we reached the door, an official put his hand up and told us to wait. The idea was that the teams would run out together. We stood in a fury of impatience.

Then the door to the French dressing room opened and out they came, giants in the lead. They were surprised to see us still standing there. They came to the door and then we were lined up side by side, waiting for the word. It was a charged moment. Outside, we could hear the cauldron bubbling. We started eyeballing each other, seeking out our opposite numbers for the big stare in a moody and mean silence. Once eyes locked, no-one would look away. After about forty seconds, forty seconds which seemed like an hour, full of muttering and unshaven glowering, we ran out. That charged moment sent the atmosphere of the game into orbit. As we waited for the kick-off I tried to fix Marocco, the French hooker. Some of the French were in tears when the anthem was played.

The sheer volume of row was unbelievable at the kick-off. The English contingent in the crowd was making itself heard and the French were countering. When Blanco got his first high ball in the opening stages, he was hit hard. He disappeared under bodies and was rucked out on the England side. It was the perfect New Zealand-style ruck and if you complained to a Kiwi about rucking of that sort, he would not have a clue what you were talking about. But the French were infuriated. 'England used me as a foot-mat,' Blanco wrote.

Afterwards, French people said it was a deliberate ploy to rough him up. It was not. It was a deliberate ploy to test him under the high ball. But the incident ensured that the atmosphere was now supercharged. Later, Pascal Ondarts, the French prop, gave away a penalty, and as I walked past, I called: 'Très bien, Pascal.' He chased me for a bit, then thought better of it as the ref was yards away.

It was the most ferocious, harsh, brutal match I have played in. It was a constant assault on the senses, occasionally on the body. It was also the most memorable match I have ever played in. As long as I live I will never forget the feeling. It was dangerous and heady, fast-moving and relentless, and revelling. I felt completely beyond the fear of physical harm. It was the reason I play the game. It was the ultimate feeling of being alive.

The first nickname which stuck was Cato. I was called Cato first on an England U23 tour, after the character in the Peter

Sellers films who leaps out of the fridge and attacks people. The first dog-style nickname, best spelt Rassin Frassin, was given to me by Winterbottom. It was in honour of Muttley, Dick Dastardly's angry dog in *Wacky Races*, and the hissing, muttering sound he makes when particularly furious. But Wade Dooley doled out most of the nicknames which stuck in the England squad, and it was Dooley who first called me Pit Bull, the one which has stuck to me longest and apparently, so people say, sums me up in two words. It was at a time when publicity about dangerous dogs attacking the public was at its height.

Apparently, what Wade and others had in mind was an aggression which, according to popular perception, surfaces on the rugby field during matches, in criticizing and even baiting opposition teams before and after matches in the media (as witnessed by what seemed to amount almost to a declaration of war on me by the Scottish nation after I attacked their play in the Grand Slam match at Twickenham in 1995 – their play was miserably negative, so at least I was being honest); and also in all the years of battling with the Rugby Football Union and their appalling lack of progress on the last frontier of amateurism; in the fact that I have always seemed to force myself to the forefront of any gathering or team or fuss, from school to international sport; that I went momentarily off the rails in a Nottingham pub; that I send thunderbolts at the media, then react with anger when the media send thunderbolts back at me.

These are charges both heavy and numerous, so I won't bother to answer them. I'll just plead guilty to most. It is a little tiresome when people allow the myths and legends about me to obscure the full picture of life. I don't walk away from the Pit Bull image but it is only one very small facet of my character.

People ask me if I have to work on my aggression. I assure them that I do not. Since I was born, it has come completely naturally. As for the roots of it all, you can wheel out your psychiatrist's couch if you want. I was an adopted child, so you can speculate that the rejection goaded me into anger and the need to prove myself. But it would all be theoretical since I had a thoroughly happy and secure upbringing. Put away the couch.

The Scots and the French seem to have a particular hang-up. In that 1995 Grand Slam match, Scotland's attitude was appalling. They had come to kill the game, and even though we still won, we did not have the satisfaction of running up the size of score which the gap in class between the two teams indicated. Immediately after the match, I was interviewed by BBC *Grandstand* and I attacked the whole approach of the Scottish team.

Apparently the BBC switchboard was jammed for hours. I received hordes of letters from furious Scots. It became as big an issue as the match. When they handed back to the studio after the interview as I went off for a shower, John Jeffrey, a studio guest and the former Scottish flanker, was almost apoplectic with rage – even though his quietly monotonous speech delivery made it difficult to pick up. This was surely not the same John Jeffrey who had been offside for a good deal of his international career. By his wounded tones you had also to assume that it could not have been the same John Jeffrey who, in a paper that very morning, had been quoted in a virulent article which accused English people of being not much more than Barboured yobs.

After that match, I was merely making a game-related comment about something that happened that day, nothing to do with the whole Scottish nation. Jeffrey, the man who attacked me afterwards, had made a generalized, generic and

5

inaccurate statement. And the world came down on me. It was a remarkable thin-skinned double standard. I suppose the furore could have been worse – the saving grace was that it upset them more than me.

The biggest attack on me came from John Beattie, the former Scotland No. 8 who is now a journalist. He apparently savaged me in lurid terms. Again, it did not bother me. His paper only has a small circulation in comparative terms. And people who toured with Beattie on two Lions tours are of the opinion that he was extremely lucky to be a Lion. He never played in any Tests. Journalists to whom I have spoken are of the opinion that he is not exactly a world-class journalist either. Not a man whose opinions fork much lightning.

Of course I like winding people up. Of course I do say things on occasions because I know the recipients will hate it – although I have never said anything I did not believe simply for effect. But what annoyed me about Jeffrey and Scotland's reaction was the political correctness it implicitly demanded. If a Scot had attacked the English as I had attacked the Scots, he would be acclaimed throughout his country as a nationalist, a patriot, fighting for the underdog in the face of English arrogance and political aggrandize- ment. If you are English, you are expected not to say the things you feel. It is the same with David Campese's continual sniping about the English. If it was reversed, Australia would be up in arms. The reason why I would never have made as acceptable a captain of England as Will Carling is that I would have always said exactly what I was thinking, when everyone else would have expected the PR answer.

I have made a point about commenting in the media about my friends, the French, before Five Nations matches between our two countries. It is easier to talk when you are on a victory roll, as we had been for eight years until they beat us in the dull World Cup play-off match in Pretoria. People have suggested to me that to rile the French by calling them a dirty and over-aggressive team is on the silly side of dangerous. But I am still here. And it has proved to be very successful. When I accuse them in the annual media war which rages in the days before the game, they always react in one of two ways. They either come out fighting, and they lose their discipline because we have riled them; or, as they did at Twickenham in 1995, they come out so intent not to rise to my comments, not to lose their cool, that they play passively, quietly, and lose anyway.

If I were the French I would soon shut up this Englishman. All they have to do is nothing. I would ignore it completely, never react by giving the press a reaction. I would make no comment whatsoever, I would not focus on it, not focus on me. Then I might go away!

It all surfaced in an unpleasant way when I was charged and convicted with actual bodily harm after an incident in a Nottingham pub in 1991. I was sentenced to four months in jail, suspended for four months, and heavily fined. It was an incident I now greatly regret.

It took place in a pub called the Hole in the Wall, after a match in Nottingham between my old team, Nottingham, and Harlequins, whom I had joined in 1990. It was an excellent evening, and many members of the teams were present. I had a couple of altercations with someone else who was in the pub, a man by the name of Mark Thorn. He was nothing to do with our group but had begun by saying to me that I thought that I could do what I liked as I was an international rugby player. There were two outbreaks of pushing and shoving as matters declined but I tried to detach myself from the irritant. When we clashed a third time, I lost my cool completely and hit him more than once. Witness statement said that I had tried to extricate myself from the situation on two occasions. But also that I had charged at him 'like a bull' when I finally lost control.

I was interviewed by the police back in London and the charge of actual bodily harm was laid. When the case came to court I was convicted. I did not enjoy being pursued down the street hounded by a baying pack of press photographers, and I felt aggrieved at the scale of the punishment, because if I had been advising a client in my own legal career who had committed the same offence, I would have told him to expect a small fine only, especially a man of previous good character who had done charity work. I feel that there was an element of a deterrent and an element of making an example in the case. There was also, at the time, a crackdown by the magistrates' courts in Nottingham because there had been a good deal of trouble in the city's pubs and clubs.

Statements provided to the court also pointed out that Thorn had been banned from the pub on two previous occasions, and a disposition from the landlord of the pub which was not read in open court listed the various incidents in which Thorn had been involved. Of course, well-known sportsmen do have to learn to live with being hassled. For me it has not been too bad, but the incident did remind me of the responsibility to turn around and walk away.

At that time, there was a definite suggestion that the punishment would not end there. Relations between the England team and the RFU had all but broken down at the time in the aftermath of the Welsh match at Cardiff in 1991, when we, as a gesture against RFU intransigence on the amateur issue, refused to speak to the media after the game. The case was originally to be heard immediately after that incident, when the RFU hawks were out to get me. If we had not managed to have the case adjourned to a less fraught time, I would definitely have been thrown out of the England squad.

It eventually took place later in the season and I was still summoned to Twickenham to discuss the conviction with Mike Pearey, the RFU president, and Peter Yarranton, the vice-president. On my way I stopped off at the Rosslyn Park Schools Sevens to present an award. I met Bill Beaumont. I told Bill of my suspicions that they would ask me to resign, would offer the revolver and the glass of whisky. 'Don't do that,' Bill said immediately. 'Once they get you out it won't be temporary. They'll get someone else in and get rid of you for good.'

Sure enough, Pearey and Yarranton asked me if I had considered resigning from the squad. Briefly, I did. Then I asked myself why I should throw in something I had put so much work into, tried so hard at. I decided not to bother doing the decent thing in the best traditions of the Raj. I had been punished once, fully. What had the incident got to do with rugby? Pearey recommended to the RFU executive that they should take no further action and I am extremely grateful to him.

I was able to put my character traits to far better use in being selected for England in the first place and then holding on to my position against all the legions of pretenders. My chief rival for the job as England hooker has always been Graham Dawe of Bath. We came into the squad at roughly the same time, and give or take some years when Dawe was off the scene, we have been battling ever since. It has been a fraught relationship, or non-relationship. We never spoke for seven years, even though we attended the same sessions, the same functions, the same matches. We had some major clashes in matches, clashes which usually ended in dishonourable draws. Dawesy would never say much; he would just belt you. You always had to be up for playing against him, otherwise you would go under. For years we knocked lumps out of each other, in the scrums and all over the field.

I suppose that other people vying furiously for the same place have managed to get on. Stuart Barnes and Rob Andrew never used to fight continually on the field. It was just that Dawe and I were even more than intensely competitive. We never really felt like opening peace negotiations.

When England toured South Africa in 1994, we suddenly found ourselves together in the hotel bar after other players had left. We got a drink. We sat down. We started having a very stiff and formal conversation. Then it became a bit more friendly, then it was just a normal chat between team-mates. We never even spoke about the past, about the confrontation, because that was behind us and neither of us would have changed anything that happened.

I suppose it was maturity finally overcoming bristling aggression in both of us. It was also a sign of respect. We had both been playing for so long, the end of our careers was in sight. There was this person who had always been in my way, for so long that it was a testament to him, and Graham probably felt the same about me.

As for my reaction to the media, and my reception in the press, I have to admit that the media have always come across to me as a sword with double edges. When you first speak to a press man and see yourself quoted in the paper, it is a nice feeling. Only later do you realize how careful you must be, and I suppose my attitude towards the media as a whole is one of healthy cynicism.

I was once called a 'friend of the tabloid press' in a letter to a newspaper, which is rubbish. The criticism was made after an article by me in the well-known tabloid newspaper, *The Sunday Times*! It was a nonsensical comment. But I have enjoyed some of the chases with the tabloids which happen during the course of a season. I accept that they home in on me because of my outspokenness. Once again, I should say that I never make things up for effect which I do not feel, but I have been around long enough to detect precisely what the media are after almost as soon as the interview begins.

One day before we were to play France, I realized that they had all written a mental headline: 'Moore Wants Revenge'. They were trying get me to oblige them with some suitable inflammatory quotes so that their stories could live up to the headline. I refused. They asked me the same question over and over, dressed up in different guises. They tried the trick of asking me if I agreed with a statement, but provided a statement so long and loaded that I almost forgot what they were asking me to agree to, so that the part they wanted me to agree to was well hidden. If you say 'yes' in that situation, they can then put the whole long statement which they came up with in your mouth. That didn't work either. I kept distinguishing clearly between their line and mine.

At the end, I told them that I knew exactly what they wanted but that I could not give it to them. They kept on trying. 'If you can't give it to us, then can you bloody well tell us who can,' asked John Etheridge of the *Sun*. That gave rise to laughter all around. 'Go and try Dewi Morris,' I suggested helpfully.

This incident was also the first occasion after which I had really paid attention to the general sports writers, the supposed doyens of the profession who glide around from sport to sport prognosticating on the major events. They are, of course, entitled to say whatever they like in their columns, knowing that they can write it and forget it – the next day they will be gone, onwards to their next big occasion. They can be totally wrong but there is no-one to take them to account, the subjects of their criticism will never come across them.

There was some virulent criticism of the squad and myself after the Cardiff incident. I wrote back to some of the writers, promising that one day I would meet them. After that, I paid more attention to the work of some. James Lawton of the *Express* is one writer, for example, who has angered me.

When I criticized Sean Fitzpatrick in my column in the *Sunday Times*, written in 1993, for racist abuse of Victor Ubogu during the England–New Zealand match, Lawton wrote an article saying that I was a loose cannon, I should stop crying and complaining. I wrote back pointing out that he did not, in all his article, actually address the right question. Did Fitzpatrick abuse Victor, or didn't he? And if he did (which he did), then was it not a sad illustration of a total lack of respect from one sportsman to another? I emphasized that he did, indeed, call Victor a 'black bastard' and I hadn't yet seen a writ from the All Black camp. Frankly, much of my letter was abusive. I felt that if my reply was too measured, it would slide like water off the back of a duck.

Lawton wrote back in lofty tones saying that he did not usually acknowledge abusive letters but because of his respect for me as a sportsman he was deigning to respond. I wrote back again, probably with an abuse increase, pointing out that like so many others, Lawton could dish it out but he couldn't take it. I asked him why a middle-aged fat bastard who to the best of my knowledge had no track record in playing any sport had the right to criticize a column which was entirely accurate and for which I had received a lot of support.

Another writer I am looking forward to meeting is Jeff Powell of the *Daily Mail*. I was involved in a controversial match between Harlequins and Waterloo in which a Waterloo player was injured. I was blamed for the incident even though I played no wilful part in it. It was the week in which Bobby Moore had died. For some reason, Powell decided to link up the sad death of Moore to the Waterloo incident, where I was accused of foul play. His theme was that Bobby Moore and I presented the two faces of British sport, Bobby being one of the great ambassadors for sport and/or Britain, while I was the evil, nasty face of both. His tenuous link was that we were both called Moore.

Powell never realized I had met Bobby Moore on a number of occasions. I found him a smashing man, extremely gentle and excellent company. We used to chat about rugby. He told me that he loved the way, in rugby, we could get our frustrations out. 'I love watching the physical contact,' he said. 'You lads have all done really well.' He enjoyed the physicality of rugby. I took great exception to Powell speaking for both of us, making misinterpretations as well as accusing me of violent play. It was an easy idea, a cheap shot. One day we will meet. There will be a confrontation.

There is a theory among the thousands of people attacked in the media that if you do not respond to press insults, then at least you never give them the satisfaction that they have offended you. But sometimes, you can make a point that is demonstrably true, can show that you have read the piece and that it is a complete and utter load of rubbish.

Sometimes, I can feel in the more combative press

13

conferences how Mrs Thatcher felt in her last Prime Minister's Question Time after being dumped. 'I am enjoying this,' she said. I can even sometimes understand the gross oversensationalizing of what you thought was simply an unimportant point or even a throwaway line, because you know what their sports desks and sub-editors can cook or overcook. I have also had great satisfaction from achieving one of my ambitions regarding John Reason, a rugby writer no longer number 1 on the *Sunday Telegraph*. I always told myself that I would stay as England hooker longer than he stayed as the *Telegraph*'s top writer, and I have outlasted him comfortably.

The media could retort that I like the limelight and that I am willing to co-operate with them when it suits. People who claim that they dislike the limelight, who say that they turn away from the sporting spotlight when it falls upon them, are not being honest. I enjoy being a player and a person who elicits a response. I gesticulate towards the crowd occasionally at Twickenham to try to tune them in to our fortunes and I am flattered by their response. Hopefully, they respond because they know I am wholehearted for the team. And from the time I ran scams at school, to taking the captaincy of sporting teams, to becoming the protagonist in the RFU battles, and the England pack leader, I have always enjoyed being in the thick of things.

I have also found the limits. I have not enjoyed it at all when I have ventured out of the field of sporting fame into that of a wider celebrity, someone famous for being famous. For some reason which I have never understood, I once agreed to appear on Matthew Kelly's *You Bet* show on TV. The guests were Tom O'Connor, Liz Kershaw, Cheryl Baker, formerly of Buck's Fizz, and myself. Almost as soon as we started making the programme, I started thinking: 'Why am

I here? Why am I doing this?' If I depended on profile for my living, fine. But I don't. I have never marketed myself, I am a lawyer earning a decent living.

If I moved towards TV I would want Desmond Lynam's job, when you would be working with quality people and quality sportsmen, not the ephemera of much of TV work, blankly reading autocue. I was also caught out in a big way by my colleagues at work. They caught me staring at Cheryl Baker's legs throughout the show. When I watched it again on video, it was so obvious that it was embarrassing. I no longer feel game for laughs of that sort.

The perception might be that people who are inherently combative, and who have been highly publicized for what might occasionally be perceived the wrong reasons, might have a long list of regrets, regrets over things said and done in the heat of the moment. I have none. That was all simply the way it was. Hindsight is a superb tool but I have never had much use for it. You may wish you had done some things better. It is like coming out of an exam and telling yourself that you could have done this or that bit a little better. But the truth is that you couldn't have, because if you could have, you would have. Perhaps I have sometimes balanced on a fine line, but perhaps not. I have been penalized extremely rarely for foul play on the field, have had to take more than I have dished out.

And while we all want to be loved, in the end you cannot lie awake wondering what people think of you. If you do that then you make accommodations, change your natural behaviour, twist yourself to try to meet their perceptions. In the end, you even lose track of yourself.

1

BIBLICAL PROPORTIONS

Moores, Methodism and music in adopted Yorkshire

And dark and true and tender is the North.

Tennyson

WE YORKSHIREMEN, IT GOES WITHOUT SAYING, ARE VIOLENTLY PROUD
of our heritage and our county. If you are from Yorkshire
then you understand how jealously people guard everything
that goes hand in hand with it. My friends, distinguish
some of my behaviour and traits as 'typical Yorkshire'.
Even if some of this Yorkshireness is typecasting, there
is definitely a quota of generally recognized traits, and apparently, I have them all, including a Yorkshire accent which
has lived on strongly despite having lived away from Yorkshire in either the Midlands or London for the past fifteen

years and despite my colleagues at Harlequins, who are seen as the epitome of the soft South. I like to think that I am changing Harlequins rather than Harlequins changing me. Once a Yorkshireman . . .

So it is inconvenient to admit that on 11 January, 1962 I was born in Birmingham. It may be insulting to the people of Birmingham but I have tried to keep it quiet ever since. I spent only a few months in the city, in circumstances which only became clear to me, and then rather dramatically, more than thirty years later.

A few weeks after being born, my natural mother gave me up for adoption. I went on first to a short-term foster mother, one of those incredible people who look after hordes of children in their homes as a staging post as the kids wait for a placement in a long-term foster home. Soon, through an arrangement with the Methodist Missionary Society, a couple came down to Birmingham from Yorkshire to adopt me. They signed the forms and before I was more than a few months old they took me back with them to Halifax, where they lived. After the false start, I could now get started on the business of being a Yorkshireman.

The couple were Ralph and Dorothy Moore, then in their thirties. They were each one of five children and both their families had deep roots in Methodism. My father's family can trace their roots in the Methodist movement almost as far as its foundation in the eighteenth century. They met through their devotion and were, and are, both lay preachers in the Church. Ralph Moore was a teacher of mentally and physically handicapped children. Dorothy was a school secretary.

When I arrived in the family in 1962, there were already two natural daughters, Catherine and Elizabeth. I was the second adopted member, following Ai'Lien. After me came

Paul, also adopted, and after Paul came Gwen, who was much older when she was adopted. When the numbers stopped growing I was the second youngest in the household.

It might all sound rather dramatic and upsetting. It wasn't. The Moores did not merely become a substitute Mum and Dad or a foster Mum and Dad. To me, they were, and always will be, Mum and Dad. They never hid the fact of the adoption from me. As soon as I was old enough to grasp what they were saying, they told me about it and the few details they had gleaned themselves about the circumstances. I never felt the slightest stigma.

As far as I know, my relationship with mother and father never felt the slightest bit different to that with any father and mother. I never sat down and felt cheated that I was somehow different to all my school friends. We were as close a family as any. I regarded my brothers and sisters in precisely the same way that everyone else regarded theirs. I cannot remember a single outbreak of jealousy from Catherine and Elizabeth, nor any divisions which were not under the heading of normal childish arguments. And yet it was never something that we all sat and wondered about, and celebrated, along the way. It was simply the norm, the family.

People might tend to regard my parents as saintly, taking in this enormous family, any one of whom might easily have turned out to be disturbed and uncontrollable. In that sense, to us they were just being parents. On the other hand, they have never ceased to amaze me for their compassion and also their understanding. They both had a conventional, strict and traditional Methodist upbringing. Yet they are probably more liberal-minded than the majority of people in the country. They are still strict nonconformists but they have managed to come to terms with modern-day morality, and excesses, when other people from their background might have become censorious. They certainly have seen and heard many things they did not like, but their tolerance simply evolves as they go along. I certainly surprised and disappointed them at various times in my childhood, but they still kept a perspective.

They also had the extraordinary gift of treating every member of the family as an individual depending on the requirements. When there are blood relations then there must be common traits in personalities and behaviour. In our family with four adopted children, these common traits did not exist. And they were extremely perceptive in identifying the peculiarities. I was always given fairly free rein, they perceived that this was what suited me best. Yet they kept Paul on a far tighter rein. One thing they never handed down was a love of sport, because until I brought sports home with me, we were never a sporting household. Yet they converted later, and come to Twickenham to act the proud parents to this day.

We lived in a medium-sized terraced house in Illingworth, usually two to a bedroom. Illingworth was reckoned by locals to stand somewhere between Mixenden and Saville Park in the social strata of the area. Mixenden was originally a lovely valley; then they shoved in thousands of houses and then the first tower blocks ever seen in the area were erected. It was known as the rough and tough end of the town. Saville Park was known as the top end of town.

We had a small front garden and the Yorkshire Moors were close by. I never established a Wordsworthian communion with nature by roaming the moors because I always found places like Howarth, the heart of Brontë country, bloody bleak rather than inspiring. But it was a good area for the outdoor life; and we were not exactly plagued by a wanderlust. We moved once, when I was eleven, and then only to a bigger, detached house with a garden at the rear, just around the corner from our old terrace. We used to travel around, perhaps to holidays in North and West Wales, in a rickety old dormobile van. I cannot remember it exceeding 15 mph at any time but I suspect it was secretly my father's pride and joy.

Halifax was a rather grey and depressed area when I arrived in 1962, because the mills were still closing, milling was dying in the face of foreign competition. Crossley Carpets was still a core industry in the town but the local economy was not thriving. However, since neither of my parents was tied directly into the declining industries, the depression did not impinge in a major way.

The one aspect of civic life which has most delighted me, looking back from the vantage point of time, is the sheer inertia of the Halifax town council in the late 1960s when most other towns in the area were knocking down old buildings, some of which were dilapidated and some of which were not. Huddersfield, the next town, knocked down many magnificent old structures and stuck up dreadful prefabricated replacements. Big chunks of the old town disappeared to be replaced by horrible monstrosities.

Fortunately, at that time Halifax council could never agree on anything to save their lives. The buildings remained after the ridiculous urge to demolish and renew had, thankfully, passed. Many have been restored, cleaned up, sand-blasted; they look splendid. The narrowest escape was that of Piece Hall, a massive, imposing three-tier structure in the town. Wool producers used to use the rooms, to bring in their carpets and fabrics. It was a beautiful building, a beautiful piece of architecture, and they condemned it. Yet no-one could decide what would replace it; the plans drifted along, and they never got round to knocking it down. It stands today,

21

the finest building of its type in Europe. When I go back to Halifax these days, I always admire how nice the town looks, and how, chiefly by default, the council made it so.

It may have been a childhood in a happy family but I don't think I ever allowed my parents to feel relaxed about me. I had some very, very lucky escapes. When I was four, I had a Meccano set, one of the old style with metal screwdrivers, where now they have plastic ones. I was toying with one of the screwdrivers one day when kneeling on the floor, stuck it into a power point and electrocuted myself. My father was, literally, feet away. He realized what had happened, probably when I suddenly stiffened. He kicked me away from the power point. I escaped with bad burns on my wrist and hands. If he had been in another room then it would almost certainly have been curtains, and fifty England rugby caps for Graham Dawe. It hardly bears thinking about.

Some years later, on a family visit to Aberdeen, I was waiting for a bus with my Dad and had wandered to the opposite side of a dual carriageway as we waited. When my father called out that the bus was coming, I ran out without thinking, in front of another bus, and a car which was overtaking the bus came to a stop literally an inch away from me. The driver leapt out of the car, as white as a ghost. I can remember the anger on his face to this day. He jumped out, called me a stupid boy, didn't I know I could have been killed, don't ever do that again, the whole performance. He was severely agitated and shaken. In my legal career, I have often done personal injury cases arising from road traffic accidents and going through them I have found how easy it is to get hurt on the roads. If the driver had been drinking, or had been slightly slower in reacting, I would certainly not be here today. How tragic it would have been, especially to meet your fate in Scotland.

I had another accident at the age of ten and again the full implications of my escape only struck me years afterwards. I was climbing in a tree near my home, fell backwards out of the tree and landed on my back. I was badly bruised and badly winded and suffered mild shock. In my university years, when some of the students went on a climbing trip, one of the girls fell from a rock face. She fell only around eight feet but ended paralysed from the neck downwards.

I had a rather chequered childhood although I would prefer to believe that I was peripatetic and mischievous, rather than malicious. I don't think I was quite the Rat Boy of the 1960s and 1970s but I was certainly the ringleader in many of the escapades. I used to go down the street taking people's milk bottles and pouring the milk down the drain. I and a gang of friends used to annoy the hell out of an old Irish night-watchman who used to guard a site near our home. He used to huddle next to his brazier to keep warm on the winter nights. We used to shout at him to make him chase us. I was never responsive to authority so my parents used to have the ultimate punishment for the worst offences. They used to lock me in our coalhouse, a small, hellish, pitch-dark room without windows, musty with the smell of coal. They thought it was cruel and they didn't like doing it, but it was the only way to get through to me. A photograph taken at the time shows me in a burning sulk, with a scowl on my face at some real or imagined slight. The expression has never changed to this day.

My parents have always put their faith in the Church. I used to go twice every Sunday. However, when I was fourteen I simply refused to go any more, and that was that. It has been a terrific disappointment to my parents. They had been part of the Church all their lives, to them it had so much to offer and they felt that I would miss out through life. But as usual, they adjusted, they were never intent on forcing it down my throat. I drifted quickly away from religious belief and by the time I sat an A level in Religious Education, I was put off completely. The course was two years' Bible bashing, not the more ethical course and arguments which might have proved more interesting. It was merely an exercise in history.

I quickly lost faith in the Bible. When you go through and find what it actually consists of, you find that it takes in only some of thousands of scrolls of Judaic teaching that were around at the time, and does so on a selective basis. Why are some scrolls from the period included in the Bible and some discarded? There did not seem to me to be any reason why the scrolls which were included in the Bible had more weight or validity or message than those which were left out. Moreover, some parts of the Bible have been radically revised for political reasons and propaganda, like reading Russian history that had gone through the interpretations of the Tsarist and Stalinist re-writers before you read it.

On top of this, I have never been able to square the convenient way in which the Christian and the Jewish faiths dip in and out of what is literal and what is figurative just as it suits them. If an event suits their purposes then that means it definitely happened. If not, the message is bent to fit and it strikes me that they are having it both ways. My parents and I have had many discussions. On the basis of what is presented to me from the various sources, I try to believe, but find I cannot. If others believe, fine. I wish I did, because I would find it all a lot more comforting. The fear of death might be considerably lessened.

There was another great Moore family tradition that I did not maintain. Ours was a musical household, everyone was encouraged to play an instrument. My father had a degree from the London College of Music, my mother was a church organist and played the piano. Catherine played the clarinet, Elizabeth played the violin. Paul later went to the Royal Marines and joined their band school at Deal. Although he joined to play in the band, the bandsmen had to do the same training as any other marine. He did all the training grind, all the rubbish, all the cleaning dustbins with toothbrushes and he came through. He was a very good percussionist and trumpeter and a very good rock drummer. But gradually he started to drift, being caught for minor infringements, started coming back from leave a little late. Eventually they asked him to make up his mind. Was he in or was he out? He left, which mystified me considering that he had the talent and had done the hard bits.

In the early years, with our musical leanings, we were a forerunner of the Partridge Family. Either in our family group or in a Church group, we used to go around doing concerts, especially terrorizing old people's homes. We used to do a few songs and sketches, and even though I try not to cringe when looking back, it must have been a sad sight. I seem to remember that some of the people were so senile they didn't understand a word. Lucky them.

When I was eleven, I won a regional eisteddfod competition for young singers. It was a set piece for sopranos, which all the angelic entrants from schools and churches around the country had to sing. The judges put me first. But I gave up singing shortly afterwards. Also at eleven, I refused to take any more piano lessons, shortly after reaching grade 3. I regret it. I did not regret the passing of the performing career of Halifax's answer to the Partridge Family.

My first school was Whitehill Infants. The prefabricated building was laid out in one storey in an L shape, and as you worked your way up through the school and on to the junior school, you actually progressed geographically around the building, until you ended at the extremity for your last year before you moved on to secondary school. You reached the end, literally and figuratively. The goad for good work in the infant years was the Cat in the Hat books. If you worked well and finished first, you were allowed to go outside into the library – really, a sideroom with a few books – to read the Cat books. I took that challenge very seriously indeed. It was a big source of competition to achieve that. 'Has tended to race,' said one term's report.

Competitiveness has been there ever since I can remember. And it was the same with casting for the nativity play. I was cast as one of the shepherds for one year and was furious. One of the three Kings was the best part and I wanted to play it. They kept me as a shepherd. That ensured another sulk of biblical proportions.

At the end of my fourth year in Whitehill, my report made the following conclusion: 'Brian is determined to the point of obduracy when he thinks his point of view is correct.' Several of my reports also indicated that if I was interested in a subject I would work hard at it; if I wasn't, I usually didn't bother at all.

Whitehill was not an establishment of free thinking and modern teaching techniques. We learned spelling and our times tables by rote, with endless parrot-like repeating. I am not a disciple of Gradgrind but I cannot think of a better way of drumming home the essential information. At least the elements are then in your head so that the more pleasant things can be added later.

It was certainly an old-fashioned school, and Dickensian in outlook in its attitude to eating. School dinners at Whitehill were a cruel affair because they would simply not take no for an answer when it came to your preferences. You were not allowed not to eat. However much you detested something, you had to force it down. One of the boys who detested liver used to slip it into his pocket. I always wondered what his mother thought when he got home. At the time, I was unable to eat anything creamy; rich food did not agree with me. When rice pudding was served a trial of strength always occurred between myself and the teachers. I used to force it down and hate it. One day I downed the pudding, it re-appeared immediately, came hurtling straight back up onto the plate, where it looked, perhaps not surprisingly, like rice pudding. After that, my anti-rice pudding campaign finally bore fruit. I was given a rice pudding dispensation. Victory.

People used to my assumption of authority in later years in any rugby team I played in would not be surprised to learn that I was the ringleader for most of the school scams. One brainwave was to arrange matches in various sports between our gang and other gangs or other groups. We had a scheme to charge three old pence admission to the venue, a local park. We even wrote out programmes. Then it was pointed out firmly that it was a public park and the Whitehill Games had to be abandoned. A more serious encounter came when I promoted a fight between ourselves and the boys of a Roman Catholic School called St Malachi's. They came along tooled up. They had snake belts, striped elastic belts with metal snake buckles which could be used as weapons. Drive-by shootings were still unfashionable at this time. We all congregated at the school gates for what was about a 20-a-side battle, and lurked about menacingly for a while. But teachers were tipped off, came out and broke it all up before the bell. That was the end of my empire to rival Don King.

The old unreconstructed 11-plus still existed at the time and it represented a major crossroads in more than academics. Those who failed went to a secondary modern school. If you passed there was a choice – either Highland

School, where they played soccer; or Crossley & Porter, a school with rugby traditions. I had no family background in rugby whatsoever so the rugby possibilities meant nothing, but three of my sisters had been there, and eventually all the family except Gwen attended. I was proud of the Crossley & Porter uniform – until it became a pain in the backside at around sixteen, as it does. The local education authority tried to turn the school comprehensive but a lack of will to agree the next steps led to unworkable plans being submitted to the Secretary of State for Education. Eventually, all five of us from the family got through the school before it changed.

The school buildings were old and gloomy. I suppose that the best you could say was that it had character. It had been an orphanage, and in many ways was totally unsuited to being a school. The gym facilities were appalling; the gym was the size of a basketball court. Incongruously, there were two fives courts. The science facilities were ancient, with the old gas taps to fit the piping for Bunsen burners.

Most schools have their traditions of bullying of new boys and girls on the first day. First-year pupils were called Bills and Jennies, depending on sex, and the tradition was to tie new kids to the tennis courts. I was tied on my first day but I quickly found my own protection. The official second-year bully, Garry Smith, was a friend of my brother so I operated under his protective shield until I was old enough to look after myself.

Yet I enjoyed my time there. I was still disruptive, could be obnoxious, and I would not be down in the records as a model pupil. But at the end of my time I was made a prefect so there must have been something there they found accept-able. There was an interesting mix. There were children from the rougher areas, and in my year there were three pupils who were later to be sent down for burglaries of differing severity. They were balanced by children from the more well-off areas. There was no fee-paying element and I enjoyed the social mix.

Under the buildings was a partly disused warren of rooms where the orphans had stored their belongings. The warren was meant to be blocked up and inaccessible but some of the openings had not been properly closed. With local knowledge it was possible to crawl around underneath almost the entire school. I remember crawling under the staff room and listening to them discussing us; you could crawl under rooms where lessons were progressing; you could even see people in the room above because the floors were so worn and holed. Prefects knew it was happening but we had a better knowledge of all the routes and the hiding places and you could usually give them the slip in the outer catacombs.

To see our way around in the darkness, we used to light paper torches from newspapers. One day I must have left one of the torches smouldering. I was in the dinner queue after surfacing from below the ground when suddenly smoke began to billow from under the floorboards. There was a major fire alert, the fire engines came to get the blaze under control, and it went down as a significant incident in school history. There was an investigation, they called for the culprits to own up, but the cause always remained a mystery. At least, it did until a school prize day in the 1990s when I was invited to present the prizes and say a few words. I told the story of the fire, then I came clean and owned up. The story went down a storm and a few of the teachers still there remembered it well. It was a little late for detention.

My earliest school scam was in forging dinner passes. There were two sittings and easily the most favoured was the first – things tended to run out and cool down by the second. If you did an extra-curricular activity at lunchtime you got a pass entitling you to a privileged first sitting. We used to do a roaring trade in forged passes. They were so easy to forge that it amounted to nothing more than a photocopying job. You could even take the first sitting and then reappear for the second if you were hungry enough.

Perhaps the most embarrassing episode surrounded my third form enterprise selling girlie magazines. Some of the lads used to do paper rounds and used to take the magazines down from the shelf when no-one was looking to add to our stocks. Very Kes-like. Unfortunately, the news of the scam spread like wildfire. John Vaughan, a member of staff obviously acting on a tip-off, marched down to my classroom one day, marched up to me and told me to open my desk.

I lifted the lid. There were a few schoolbooks lying on top, a book on karate just under that. 'That seems in order,' he said. Then he delved deeper and found another publication. He held it up between thumb and forefinger. He read the title: '*Big Girls*. Special bumper issue.'

'I think you had better take this to the headmaster,' he said, holding it up. I was tempted to ask him why the headmaster was so keen to see it, but kept quiet. The rest of the class was in hysterics. I claimed I had found the magazine; they knew it was nonsense, and another marketing initiative was over.

The most memorable teacher was Michael O'Donnell, who was an Irish teacher who took French. He had a wooden leg and speech impediment. Anyone who remembers from their own schooldays how cruel and cutting schoolkids' humour can be, can easily imagine the stick which he took because of his improbable set of peculiarities. At first, we were afraid of him. He commanded respect and he was extremely strict. One day his world fell apart, and from then on his working life must have been an absolute hell. One of our class, a very pleasant girl with no rebellious streak, told him that she had to go home early. He refused permission. 'You must wait, and leave later with the others,' he said. Whatever the reason for the early departure, it must have been a good one. The girl stood up. 'I'm very sorry,' she said, 'but I've got to go.' She left, and with her departed all his authority. We realized he was not everything we had cracked him up to be. He lost it from that moment on.

We used to flick our ink-pens at him when he turned his back, so that he was inked almost from head to toe. Crossley & Porter classrooms had the old-style desk units in which the seat was fixed to a frame which also held the desk itself in a single unit. As you sat, you could shuffle them back and forwards across the floor. We used to have competitions to see who get could closest to the front of the class. When he turned his back, there would be a concerted shuffling noise behind him as everyone slid forward like feverish little dodgems. He would turn back and the shuffling would stop. Eventually, the whole class used to be stuck in a wedge of desks right next to where he was standing. We used to stuff paper in the keyhole of a cupboard in his French room, so that he would never open the door to bring out his tape recorder for the lessons in French speaking. It took him ages to realize that the reason the key would neither turn nor even fit was because the hole was stuffed. Looking back, I can only feel extremely sorry for him. At the time, I was his worst nightmare.

Crossley & Porter had a well-organized system of house sport and house plays. We used to play in inter-house events in rugby, soccer, athletics and cricket, and also house plays with full make-up and costumes. There was the house music competition and all the rest. I played Cerebro in *The Hole* and Pompey in *Measure for Measure*. Teachers were not

31

allowed to intervene to help and it was all taken seriously and very well done. Then we had one teacher who steered everyone into Greek tragedy, things became more and more ambitious and we lost the plot in more ways than one. It seems improbable from this distance but I took a full part, acting, singing and even conducting the house choir. I enjoyed the culture and the variety and it was a shame that later there was so little time to develop those interests.

Eventually, I was made house captain and even made the short list for head boy. The candidates were interviewed for twenty minutes but my interview took over forty-five minutes. They asked me whether, if one of the fifth-form boys was particularly obnoxious, I could deal with it in a way which would cause no further trouble. Of course I could, I told them, but did not specify my line of action. I was passed over.

I did lead what could have been the first prefects' strike in the history of the school. When I became a prefect the school decided to do away with prefects' powers of detention. I had endured different sorts of punishment from prefects on the way up. In my first detention, they made me stand with a book on my head and a bible in each hand while they prodded me, and because the book fell off my head and I didn't catch it between the bibles, they performed a ritual which could only be described as kicking the shit out of me. Or they would give you a newspaper and tell you to fill in the zeros. Something really constructive. Then as soon as I got there, with a fourth form of little bastards to keep in check, they threatened to take away the detention weapon. I took charge from our side. 'How do you expect us to keep control, if you take away the means?' I asked. The headmaster told me that we'd just have to keep control without the punishment.

I replied that if there were no sanctions then it was a pointless job and that if there were to be no sanctions then we would refuse to do the duties. I suggested a strike to my fellow prefects and we won an overall victory. They took away the sanction to hand out lines but they kept detention.

My reports were uneven and the prevailing message from most of them was that I had ability but did not always work hard enough. 'Brian does not always work as hard as he might. He has great potential but does not always realize it. He relies a great deal on natural ability,' was one comment in a report after the second year, but a comment representative of the general tone. 'Brian tends to be a disruptive element in class,' the form master recorded one year. Another form teacher recorded: 'He is a lively member of the form, full of ideas, but he must not forget, in his enthusiasm, the consideration due to others.'

It was at around fifteen that I started to move into a world which my mother and father had nothing to do with. I had already turned my back on the piano and the Church, and I decided that it was time for the start of my drinking career. Most families probably initiated their children through the odd glass of wine, but we never had alcohol in the house so drinking became a big thing for me, a big prospect. I once procured a can of Heineken, took it home and surreptitiously started to down it. I found the taste disgusting but I told myself I was going to drink it all.

At the time everyone else was beginning to drink so it was the thing to do and to be seen doing. At least I was almost immediately cured of any potential smoking bug. Smoking got straight through to my lungs and I discovered afterwards that I have mild asthma, which explains it. I kept forcing myself to drink and hating it. The first time I came home obviously the worse for wear, my parents were completely astonished. I just about kept in their good, or goodish, books.

The one aspect of every report which was always glowing

was the comments by the masters of PE. 'Brian continues to improve as an all-round athlete.' 'Brian is a very good sportsman.' However, one PE master tempered his praise: 'His overall performances are still marred by a lack of self-control.' Me? But as I prepared, unwittingly at the time, to launch an assault on the sporting world and Halifax, perhaps a conclusion from a report in the old days at Whitehill is most appropriate, 'Treats arts and craft as a chore, music as an interest, and PE as a mania.'

2

MAKING CONTACT

Hard life in Yorkshire rugby

You are going to get into serious trouble yourself, and other
people are going to get hurt.
Mike Capelin, master, Crossley & Porter School

THE MANIA GREW FROM QUITE HUMBLE BEGINNINGS. WHEN HALIFAX
Town fell out of the Football League by virtue of finishing
last in the last division, and dropped into the GM Vauxhall
Conference, it would not be true to say that the whole town
went into mourning. Frankly, they were rubbish. My uncle,
who had once played for the Town in their, er, great days,
took me down to see them play and it was practically a first
window to the outside sporting world, because we were not
a sporting household. At the time, in my earliest teens,

Halifax Town was all I knew and I was too young to grasp how poor they were.

On the other hand, they had glorious moments. I did see them beat Manchester United in the Watney Cup, when Alex Smith, the Town goalkeeper, saved a penalty by Willie Morgan of United when the score was 1–1. I also saw them knock Manchester City out of the FA Cup. Paul Hendrie scored for Halifax to dump a club then managed by Malcolm Allison. Much was made of a sensa- tional local story – that the Town players had been hypnotized before the match by Romark, a leading local hypnotist. Romark's unsuccessful career continued when he was brought in to try to hypnotize Muhammad Ali before a fight against Richard Dunn, the British heavyweight. Dunn was despatched quickly.

Halifax's rugby league team were more successful than the soccer club but it was much later in life when I first went to see them play. The class difference struck me at the time – the secondary modern kids in my area were taught rugby league and the kids with supposedly superior intelligence at the grammar schools took rugby union. It seemed to me at the time to be a ridiculous distinction and simplification, but that was the way it was.

My sporting representative career began as an eleven-year-old striker in the Halifax Schools team. A lot of the players in the team went on to play professional soccer. I was aware at the time that I was noisier on the field than other players. I found it extremely difficult to keep quiet, not to make comments. I thought I was trying to encourage people, but perhaps from the touchline it seemed that I was just a little kid bawling at people. But if I was wholeheartedly into soccer at primary school, then I immediately became wholehearted about rugby as soon as I started at Crossley & Porter. We were an average rugby school, and we existed below the circuit of public schools like Bradford Grammar and Ample-forth, whom we used to meet only on the Sevens circuit. Since I left, first-class players like Jim Mallinder of Sale and James Naylor of Orrell have carried the school's name into senior rugby.

But I took to rugby instantaneously. Unquestionably, it was the physical contact that appealed. I had enjoyed the competitive edge in all the sports I had taken part in but rugby had this other dimension. I was hooked from the first match. Three weeks into the first term at school I was walking back from a rugby practice and I heard one of the sixth-formers talking about me. 'That lad over there is going to be a hooker,' he said. I actually favoured the backs but I started as flanker, and it was a few years later that I got my wish and departed for the pastures behind the scrum.

I was captain of the school teams in every year bar the first. I led the second-, third- and fourth-year teams as I rose through the school, and captained the first XV in season 1979–80. In fact, of all the teams I have played for, it is really only England who have yet to ask me to captain them – a shocking omission. It was not that I was the best player in the early years at school, but I think that the masters all knew I was going to do a lot of the talking anyway, so they simply made it all official.

Peter Holden, the Halifax RUFC fly-half for many years, was one of my earliest coaches. Halifax had once been one of the best clubs in the North but had fallen on hard times. They seemed to be seduced by their former glories and did not spend enough time working for future glories. They are still alive and kicking but playing way below the class of their past.

By my mid-teens I was watching the rugby internationals on the television. I treasured my Rugby Football Union schools' handbook. You could fill in your own height and weight. There was a full page for your own details and they seemed so feeble when set against those of famous players profiled, like Peter Wheeler, who was then England's hooker. The book had training hints, exercises, the rules.

I also remember one particular incident from the television when England were playing France in Paris. Imbernon, the giant French lock, was playing. He always seemed to me to be one of the most extreme players around and I remember him being caught on the floor. The whole England pack made strenuous efforts to run all over him and Wheeler took the opportunity to jump in with both feet. I remember thinking then and there that he deserved it. He had dished it out, now he had to take some back. I have never bothered too much with all the philosophical nonsense about the poor example for children, a sad day for the game. I have always been wary of the view that kids are turned off by it. When I was a kid I used to enjoy it.

My first visit to Twickenham came at sixteen, on a dark, filthy day in 1978 when Wales beat England by 9–6 in a dreadful match. I can remember Gareth Edwards running on ahead of the Welsh team because it was his fiftieth cap, Alastair Hignell missing kicks for England, and Bob Mordell, the flanker, giving away the match-losing penalty. But it was the backdrop that was more impressive than the match. I was incredibly impressed by the sheer numbers of people. Those were the days of packed standing terraces when the ground held around 70,000. I had never been to any event remotely comparable in size and the field itself seemed small, dwarfed.

We watched London Welsh play Cardiff at Old Deer Park on the morning of the match, and drank in the Triple Crown pub in Richmond, where it was so packed that you had to raise your glass through a forest of leeks. I was violently ill on the night of the game. I also remember waving a flag in the enclosure and an irate, horrible Welshman grabbing it. 'We didn't come here to watch your bloody flag,' he said. I though it was bullying and rude. I placed the rude Welshman in my memory and stored it up for later, motivational use.

There was no real depression that England had lost. England supporters didn't really feel that way at the time; they were never overburdened with expectation. Nor did I have dreams of running out on to the field in an England jersey at some time in the future. I was always dismissive about people saying I would play one day for England. I only ever looked one representative team ahead; the only time I ever dreamed about playing for England was when I was in the squad itself, and even then I think that the dream itself was delayed until the night before my first cap.

I was a terrible loser in the early sporting years and freely confess that I have been a terrible loser ever since. When Crossley & Porter were beaten in the final of the Calderdale 20-overs cricket cup, they gave us all a runners-up trophy. On the way home, I threw it over a wall. I was not quite so extreme when I was presented with my runners-up medal after the World Cup final at Twickenham in 1991. I suspect that it is still in the house somewhere but certainly I have never seen it since I first brought it home. If we had won, I would have hung the medal on the wall and polished it on a daily basis.

As my school reports suggested, I was far too angry on the field for my own good. Matters reached their first low point when we played a fourth-year match against St Michael's College, Leeds. I complained bitterly about a decision. The referee asked me to repeat what I had said and I did. He warned me to keep quiet. I summoned up the most insolent tone possible while saying 'Yes, Sir'. I was sent off. It was absolutely deserved. You cannot have fifteen-year-olds going round the field being insolent to the referee.

I was hyperactive on the field, I craved a total involvement and I never sat down to consider the consequences of my actions. I was in trouble in too many games. I did not even have the excuse that I was involved in the forward battle – for much of my younger days I played at scrum-half or centre.

After another match had ended in a major free-for-all, and after I had punched someone in a later match, I was taken aside by Mike Capelin, a member of staff whom I respected. He cornered me outside the dining room. 'You have talent,' he said. 'But you are going to get into serious trouble yourself and other people are going to get hurt.' He told me of the experiences of Steve Fenwick, the Welsh centre whom Mike knew well. He told me that Fenwick had been something of a trouble-maker in his early years in school; but now he had reformed. Capelin held him up as an example. I could not understand why Fenwick was an apposite example. He was an international and a British Lion. It was that Capelin saw the potential; although I could not grasp it at the time, he was suggesting I could have a top rugby career ahead.

Possibly partly because of my bad attitudes, I did not make smooth progress through the various levels of representative rugby. In my year as school captain, I was chosen for Yorkshire Schools 19 group for their annual fixture against Wales. We played them at Headingley early in the new year of 1980. Wales had a strong pack of forwards, five of whom were later to make their mark in senior club rugby. Stuart Barnes, still in his Welsh phase, was the opposition fly-half and we were heavily beaten.

I was dropped from the team and I felt like a scapegoat. I was devastated, especially since the next match was a traditionally tough battle between Yorkshire Schools and Yorkshire Colts. I had been desperate to play in it and I missed it. I can put hand on heart and say, quite categorically, that I have never forgiven the Yorkshire selectors and I never will.

When I reached sixteen, I was playing senior rugby in the Halifax second team. At seventeen, I was playing two games every Saturday. I used to play for the school in the centre in the morning, then rush off to play at hooker for Old Crossleyans first XV in the afternoon. It is something prohibited by authority these days. It did me good from the standpoint of experience. The only drawback was that having seen senior rugby, where people occasionally put the boot in and developed other similar habits, I was too inclined to take the adult habits back into school matches.

It was enormously draining. Some nights I got incredible cramps. It was also slightly Alf Tupperish, because in the rush to grab some lunch between the two games, the best bet was the chip shop in Harrison Road. If the weather had been bad and I had to plough through two muddy pitches every Saturday, I was almost out on my feet by Sunday, especially as I used to drink all night in trying to keep up with the older people after the match ended. The school kept a close eye on the situation, looking for signs of exhaustion on Monday mornings.

Crossleyans used to play in a tough rugby circuit, against tough, experienced teams, like Thornensians, Hymers from Hull, Doncaster, Sandal, Castleford. I was probably something of a liability for the Crossleyans as well, because I usually wanted to fight grown men. It was, in retrospect, quite remarkable that I never got filled in. I was careless where I put my feet, I would whack people even at seventeen. I think anyone who has experienced recently what you might call the youthful exuberance of Richard Cockerill, the Leicester hooker, will have an indication of what I was like.

We were even successful. We won the *Yorkshire Post* merit table in 1979–80 with a 100 per cent record, sealing it with victory over Ripon. Our captain was Brian Campsall. Years later, Campsall went over to the other side – in 1994 he was appointed to England's international refereeing panel. Campsall recalled some of the problems of having me in his team in an interview in March 1994. 'I told him when we played together that he had a great future,' he told a newspaper. 'But the most difficult job was keeping him on the field. He was a wild lad and in those days, when you played against clubs like Bramley it was like street fighting. For me, it was a case of getting in quickly and holding Brian back. He was hellishly competitive. The red mist would come down and he'd go wild. I was the scrum-half so I was round the back of him ready to dive in.'

But wild or not and tiring or not, I look back with the greatest affection on the days with Old Crossleyans. They were, and are, a great club. When I won my first cap they presented me with a lovely engraved watch. Later, I gave them a set of shirts from each major International Rugby Board nation, which I had swapped with opposite numbers after England matches. They unveiled the showcase containing the shirts at a special dinner, which was attended by eighteen former club captains from the end of the Second World War. They are beautifully presented at the club. It is a sign of the sense of belonging that the club engenders that Jim Naylor of Orrell has given them his England Students shirt and Jim Mallinder of Sale his North Division shirt.

The clubhouse itself is a big old house, wood-panelled and so different to the prefabricated clubhouses which dominate the club scene in England. The main bar features a cavernous drawing room-type space; there is also a members' bar upstairs. I have great memories of the place and its unique atmosphere. When I joined I was seventeen and was just starting my social life. I was already taking the game much more seriously, training hard and trying to improve my game. But the social pull was still strong – these were before the days when international players talked rather pompously about their training regimes which allowed no drinking, then they went off to have a drink – but that is another story.

In one sense it was a down-to-earth club. On the other hand, it was not a club where the members used to go away and smash things up. Some Old Boys clubs, especially in London, used to think it was absolutely hilarious to smash up curry houses and the like, and to cause criminal damage. It was more intelligent than that. There was also a strange sense of humour, which later I recognized as being inspired by the Peter Cooke and Dudley Moore series and by *Monty Python* derivatives. The club used to have spontaneous theme nights. On Dame Edna night, you were allowed to speak only in Dame Edna tones. On Opera Night, you had to sing everything in operatic style.

Women were not treated badly, even if full emancipation had not yet struck. If they wanted to come along and join in after the match, that was absolutely fine, as long as they did not expect accommodations to be made. The choice was to join in what was already happening, for good or bad. If they came then they went out and got pissed along with everyone else. It was the typical Yorkshire choice, take it or leave it.

There were great characters, as there are at any great club. Graham Thomas and Steve Lumb were often my props, they used to tolerate me and look after me. Hoss Horsfall and Bryan Lumb were also larger than life. Paul Jackson, another member from my early days, became a kind of father-confessor. If I want a sensible opinion on some matter, I ring him. He was a deputy head at a comprehensive school, was involved in both codes of rugby. He is not just the salt-of-the-earth type of character, he is also an intelligent bloke. If he sensed something is not quite right he would ring up and say: 'You want to sort this thing out.' He would tell me to set out my stall.

Some of the tours with Crossleyans were as memorable in their way as a Lions tour. One incident still noted in Crossleyans' history is the Grand Cream Cake fight on a tour of Watford. We stayed at the Spider's Web Motel near Watford, and on a midnight raid of the kitchens found some enormous full-cream gâteaus. A feast was planned for one of the rooms. However, it took just one person putting the cake to his face to take a bite to set off the whole thing. Someone pushed it into his face and a spectacular cake-based fight took place. Suddenly the bed, the cupboards, the whole room was plastered in cream cake.

In the morning we gathered, grim-faced, for a ritual dressing down by an enraged manager. He raged on and on. 'And who would want to stay in a room like that now?' he asked. 'Charlie Cairoli,' shouted someone at the back. Everyone collapsed. We cleaned up the rooms, put the cost of the cakes on our bills. The manager would have been mollified if, later in the tour, we had not tried to catch trout in his restaurant tank with our bare hands, and, after failing, thrown in the hotel cat to have a go. The cat was less amused than the manager, plunged to the bottom, leapt out the other side and sprinted away spluttering.

When I left school I decided to take a year out, before attending university. I thought I could take stock, and also make some money. I worked for Webster's Brewery, as a labourer, as a plumber's mate. I was now making a few waves in local rugby circles and ambition was gradually getting the better of the love of social life at homely Crossleyans. I decided to take a step up, and at eighteen I left the Old Boys to join Roundhay, who were probably the strongest club in Yorkshire at the time.

I had a vague idea that I would travel around the world as part of my year off, but everything was being overtaken. The trip suddenly seemed, on reflection, an unnecessary intrusion into a sporting career. As an eighteen-year-old hooker, promising and stroppy, my world tour ended at Roundhay. At the time, my representative career was stalled. I had played in what amounted to a semi-final trial for England Schools, but did not make the final squad. Neil Gutteridge, who went on to play in a limited role for Coventry, and Kieran Rabbitt, late of Sale, were two hookers who did make the squad. I marked those two down for some kind of revenge mission later.

What settled my mind in opting for Roundhay was a call from Richard Cardus, the powerful international centre who went on to play for Wasps. It was a big thing to have an international player request your services. Cardus was Roundhay's captain for season 1980–1. Roundhay also had three players eventually to go to league but who were distinctly useful – Andy Staniland, Andy Mason and Ian Oram. Their coach was Tony Biscombe, another to make a name later at higher levels. I missed the social life at Crossleyans but not enough to obscure my goals.

I turned up at Roundhay pre-season training, anxious to work hard, to make an impression and to find out who was in the way for a place as the first XV hooker. The answer was John Gill, the incumbent hooker. He had played for Roundhay throughout the previous season when they had won the Yorkshire Cup. I remember lapping the field in

45

pre-season training. A few of the blokes running in his company called out: 'Hey Gilly, this lad's come down to take your place.' Gill replied, loftily: 'I've seen them come and I've seen them go.'

I ran on quietly. 'Right,' I thought to myself. 'I'll get you for that.' I did. I played five games in Roundhay second XV and then the first XV had a disaster against Preston Grasshoppers. Gill was dropped and I played my first first-class game for Roundhay against Huddersfield. I stayed in the team all season. We reached the semi-finals of the Yorkshire Cup when we were knocked out by Harrogate. We drew Leicester in the John Player Cup and to play against Peter Wheeler was another formative experience. One of our props was poked in the eye by Nick Joyce, the Leicester lock, and had to leave the field. That left me with a temporary prop and against one of the most feared packs around at the time. We were under pressure throughout and lost 34–3 but I did not lose a ball on our put-in. I struck for the ball on every Leicester put-in because we were hardly in any position to disrupt them by pushing. I spoke to Wheeler afterwards.

'You should have shown a bit more respect,' he said. 'I didn't strike on any of your balls.' I told him that there was nothing else I could do. At that time, Wheeler had bigger fish to fry. Against a lesser team and an eighteen-year-old hooker he would have been content to coast through. I would do the same in the same situation. Leicester went on to win the Cup, beating Gosforth in the final.

We had some near-brutal battles as the Yorkshire rivalries began to assert themselves. Headingley were one of the deadliest enemies and they had a hooker called Tim Sinclair, who was as abrasive as I was. We had some terrible brawling battles, really punchy encounters. Peter Winterbottom played in one for Headingley, his original club. Years later, he recalled that he thought I was a complete lunatic and that I deserved to be filled in.

After another match against Headingley, and after another battle had raged, an old guy from Headingley who was also on the Yorkshire committee came up to me. I hadn't started all the trouble by any means, and the Headingley front row were never backward when it came to rough stuff. All I had done, I felt, was to stand my ground and refuse to back down. The bloke hadn't seen it that way. He came up almost puce in the face and apoplectic. 'As long as I live,' he said, 'you will never play for Yorkshire.'

I was at my most understated and witty. 'Fuck off,' I said. 'By the time I'm eligible for Yorkshire you'll be dead anyway.' We were both half right. He died soon afterwards and I never played for Yorkshire. Most of the memories of those days in the harshness of Yorkshire rugby makes me realize that, despite all the sermonizing of the modern day, rugby is nowhere remotely near as dirty as it used to be. There were no touch-judges intervening in those days, and plenty of world-class off-the-ball action.

Perhaps the worst experience of sheer scrummaging pressure came in a match against Broughton Park. Their hooker was Keith Pacey. I have always tended to be disparaging about rival hookers but he was powerful and very good. His props were Sid Harris and Keith O'Hara, great ox-like figures. We were under so much pressure from the weight coming through that I don't think I ever moved my feet. I was pinned. I had nightmares about it for months. I lost ball after ball against the head.

Pacey could put so much pressure on you, downwards and across, with his shoulders and neck that he could bend you double. On that day he bent me every which way and I had no idea how to get out. Afterwards, I asked Pacey how he did it. 'I can't tell you,' he said. 'Otherwise you'll know for the next time.' Two years later, I played against Broughton Park again, for Nottingham. Pacey was still there, still powerful and still good. By that time I was more experienced and managed to cope better. I reminded him of our previous encounter and took the improvement as a benchmark that I was making progress.

Now, with experience, I can offset the other hooker when he tries to exert pressure. I can wriggle, put my shoulder up, force my way out, try to get my shoulder above his to lean on him. These are things you can only learn the hard way, from men like Keith Pacey.

In my Roundhay season I was still eligible to play for Yorkshire Colts, and this time I was confident that I could make the England Colts team, and was incredibly determined to do so. Then they changed the age groups. Previously, the Colts team had been an U19 combination, but then they made it an U18 team. Everyone of my age throughout the country was therefore ruled out. We were a lost year. I was devastated. I believed at the time that due to a quirk in the laws dreamed up by some idiot, I had missed my last chance of wearing the England rugby jersey.

But my game developed quickly at Roundhay. Biscombe was a good coach; he was extremely encouraging. He told me one day that he had put my name forward for the England U23 squad. I was confident of my abilities but was still taken aback by this. I could not believe that he was serious. At the time, I was a mildly freakish hooker because this was before the time when it was demanded of hookers that they show up around the field and actually play a part in the game. But after spending so much of my school career in the backs I had running and handling skills.

The year with Roundhay had been excellent for a fledgling. I was still too excitable although I had calmed myself a little. By this time, I was enrolled at university in Nottingham to continue my career, and decided to join the Nottingham club. To travel back to Roundhay three times per week for training and playing was hardly practical, and in any case Nottingham were probably the kind of step-up I needed. Rugby was becoming ever more serious, ever more time-consuming. But as I prepared to leave Yorkshire rugby for the last time, I began to appreciate that some sacrifices were well worth making.

3

THE CAMPUS RIOTS

Life in the cocoon, Nottingham University 1980-3

All learned, and all drunk!

William Cowper

MY FIRST MAJOR CAREER DECISION WAS TO GO TO NOTTINGHAM University to take a degree in law. This took deeply profound thought. I decided on Nottingham because Catherine, my eldest sister, had studied there; I had never been near the city in my life. I decided on law because I used to enjoy *Crown Court*, the soapy courtroom drama which used to run on television in the afternoons. I thought that it must be nice to be a barrister, to make the jury sway this way and that with all those decisive speeches in court, and to pull off dramatic

50

victories against the odds which left the rest of the court gasping.

There was also the view of my mother, delivered in a very Alan Bennett way, that I should do a 'proper' course – in other words, a vocational degree which led directly to a career. Friends of mine who had been to university came back and told me that the law would be ideal. They said it was all about arguing. 'It will suit you down to the ground,' they said. At least I landed on both feet. Although the decisions were random, I was later to find that the faculty of law at Nottingham was one of the most distinguished around.

There was a brief earlier flirtation with Oxbridge. I actually passed entrance examinations and was intending to do a PPE course (politics, philosophy and economics). I applied to St John's College, Oxford. I turned up for the interview to be asked some searching questions. 'If God is omnipotent, can he create a stone that he cannot lift?' I told them that I wondered why God would waste time bothering with rocks because if he was so omnipotent he would surely find something more enjoyable to do. They turned me down.

People who understood the Oxford scene told me of my mistake later. St John's had absolutely no sporting tradition. In my application I proudly listed all my sporting exploits in detail and they probably left the admissions tutor completely underwhelmed. These may even have counted against me. To St John's, perhaps all rugby players were muddied oafs. I was offered postgraduate places at both universities a few years later. I stood on my pride. They hadn't wanted me, now I didn't want them.

I had never been to Nottingham University till the day I arrived to start the course. I already had my A levels before my year out after school. They accepted me unconditionally, and never asked me to attend for interview. Other students arriving to start the course had tales of testing interviews and a pre-selection test they had all sat. It was a mock law question to test powers of reasoning. I looked blankly at them. I am still surprised by the university's faith. For all they knew, I could have been an aggressive Yorkshireman who might spend most of his time playing rugby or in alcohol-fuelled riotous behaviour. Perish the thought.

I had one assignment to fulfil before I actually arrived in the city of Nottingham. I had already toured with the England U23 team in Japan and Hong Kong the year before, so had a taste of the wonderful prospects for travel which arise in the life of the better rugby players. I have gone to play rugby in almost every serious rugby country in the world and a few others besides, had adventures you could not buy and had cause to thank the game over and over again.

In the summer holidays before term, the Penguins were due to visit Brazil. The Penguins are widely known as the poor man's Barbarians, but for me they have always been preferable because they have some of the status and the glamour of the Barbarians and none of the bullshit. Their officials, led by Tony Mason, who often toured with Doris, his wife, were nothing like as pumped full of self-importance as Barbarian officials, and when they made their tours they always put together a well-balanced mixture. There would be a few caps who had not quite become fixtures in their national teams, a few experienced players nearing retirement and some promising youngsters. In Brazil, there were the likes of Stuart Evans and Geraint John, both to become leading players in Wales. Evans, then nineteen and already 19 stone, could have become a Lions prop had he not disappeared for an unsuccessful career in rugby league with St Helen's.

Derek Wyatt, the former Bath wing who was also a Penguin, was noted for ridiculously over-the-top speeches, and after the Brazil tour he made one, proclaiming that Evans and John and others would become Lions, had brilliant futures ahead of them. Actually, of the whole party I was the only one to become a Lion.

It was a tremendous tour. The captain was an astonishing Irish fly-half called Mick Quinn, a great man, great sense of humour and with massive energy. Quinn was a teetotaller which always struck me as a very good thing. He acted as if pissed most of the time so goodness knows how he would have come across had he been drunk as well. We went to Rio de Janeiro, São Paulo, and we saw the extremes of life in a wonderful country. We saw the Sugar Loaf Mountain, the Maracanã Stadium, the Christ Statue.

After one training session with a local club during the trip, we went to a bar to continue the festivities. After a time, it became obvious that the only hosts present were officials, that none of the players had arrived. We asked where they were. The answer was that they were behind the stand, smoking joints, almost to a man. They had their own way of winding down and who is to say it was a better or worse way than having a few beers. The rugby in Brazil was fun, we ran up some huge scores; it did nothing for my waistline but it was a tour to remember. I have always held a soft spot for the Penguins ever since, while the Barbarians and myself have, largely, ignored each other.

I had my own pre-university test and it prepared me perfectly for university life. Tony Biscombe, the coach at Roundhay, had already sent the message on the grapevine to Nottingham Rugby Club to herald my arrival in the university and the city. Biscombe rang Alan Davies, a Welshman who was

Nottingham's coach, to tell him I was on my way. He added a caveat. 'If you can keep him on the field you might have a good player.' I went down to Nottingham from Halifax well before the term so that I could begin the new rugby season with Nottingham, who were then a medium-sized Midlands club who were only granted fixtures against the real Midlands giants in midweek. The big surge was yet to come (so was the big dip after the big surge, but more of that later).

In order to fill in time and to fill the coffers, I started work in a steel-shearing factory, and I returned to the same job in every vacation after that. It needed some skills, or semi-skills. The company, situated in a drab factory in an industrial estate in Nottingham, used to buy huge sheets of metal in various gauges. They then cut it down to fit orders of customers, in sizes for car parts and bits of Raleigh bicycles. Some of the pieces were light and easily worked, others were huge and heavy, six-millimetre-thick chunks of the stuff which needed two men to heave around on to the shearing machine.

Every student who has ever struggled through a manual holiday job will recognize the attitude of the men in the factory – they disliked me because I was a student, because I was earning well but paying no tax. They didn't like it one bit. The philosophy of self-improvement through the pursuit of higher education, for the good of self and nation, had apparently passed them by. Essentially, it was a horrible job. It meant rising at dawn; I would get up at 5.30 and clock on at 6 and I have never been a good cold starter in the mornings. It was exhausting, it was ferociously tiring. But I was determined not to flag. The men were slightly better with me because they saw I could do the physical labour. If I had been a liability, then life would have been impossible.

In the dawn of dark Midland mornings, the benefits of this job were impossible to find. But the benefits were threefold.

First, it was all good fitness and strength training. Secondly, it gave me a motivation and an insight when I started term at Nottingham University. The factory experience made you want to succeed in studies to ensure you never had to return on a full-time basis. Thirdly, it put in the shade all the traditional student whines. Every time people came back to university after vacation, sank into a chair in the bar, looked up at the ceiling and complained that they had so much work to do, how awful it all was, how they were under such pressure, I used to think: 'Thank God I'm back here.' It was just that you didn't have to be anywhere, do anything, that you did not feel like. There was no responsibility. No-one clocked on.

I passed out after three years at Nottingham with a workmanlike 2.2 degree. The difference between a 2.2 and a 2.1 is a vast amount of work, of effort and sacrifice. On sober reflection, I am sorry I didn't work harder, but otherwise I felt that I found the balance pretty well. I didn't deserve a better degree because I was playing sport. I also did not deserve better because I was on a spectacular social bender which began in the freshers' induction period and ended when I left three years later. There was certainly not a great deal of opportunity for sober reflection. It was a bit like the Sixties. If you can remember them, then you weren't really there.

From the bits I can remember, I can only conclude that the Nottingham University years were a glorious experience, a time of abandon and of living in a cocoon, a time of freedom from responsibility – something utterly unrepeatable in the reality of the real world, which lurked around outside the cocoon, waiting for graduation day.

*   *   *

The university itself was superb. It was all set in an enormous, self-contained campus, which had a boating lake and a huge wooded and grassy expanse called The Downs. The campus gave you a nice secure feeling, it was a world away from steel shearing.

Many students believe that the burst of activity and bad behaviour which you experience on becoming a student is a question of reacting to new-found freedoms after parental oppression, real or imagined. For me it was different. I had effectively left my parents' home a year before. I had done lots of different jobs, I had lived in London for months, working in a hospital. The great thing about the whole situation was that you were surrounded by thousands of people of similar age and like mind who wanted to have a good time, whose only responsibility was to pass an exam after three years. You could tell yourself that you were going to stay in bed that day and that you might, or might not, get up in the afternoon to watch the video, and that after a few days, you might, or might not, go along to a lecture. It was the only time in your life when it happened. As soon as you lost it, you immediately became quite desperately nostalgic for it.

The riots began as early as Freshers' Week. In the grand scheme of things, the Week was followed immediately by Karnival, the equivalent of rag week. Anyone left standing after that initial fortnight then proceeded with term proper. For the first two weeks there was some function planned every night to help the process of integration. If you were accommodated in a university hall, you made new friends there too. I always felt sorry for the new students at the other seat of learning in the town, the then Trent Polytechnic. They were stuck out in bed and breakfast and bedsitter land; the only people they would normally meet were the people on their own courses, and if they didn't like them, then they were stuffed for three years.

Fortunately, I escaped one of the traditions of Sherwood Hall, my own home from home. It was to call people after their home town. Wigan was one of my closest friends. Nowadays, Wigan lives only two streets away from me in Twickenham, under the name of Andrew Holmes. There was a Crewe and a Barnsley but I had a narrow escape. An old boy of Crossley & Porter had joined Sherwood Hall in the previous academic year; he had therefore taken the name Halifax. The Hall wasn't big enough for two Halifaxes, and as no-one knew about my place of birth I avoided the name Birmingham. I was able to proceed with no nickname which stuck – until I joined the England rugby team years later and began to collect them like confetti.

The hall system was the core of Nottingham student life. Each hall had its own sports teams and interest groups. Sportsmen and sportswomen who couldn't make the university team could have a thrash around in rugby, soccer, cricket, hockey on Wednesday afternoons. Sherwood Hall dominated the five-a-side soccer event when I was there. We used to field four footballers, plus me in a role which Vinny Jones was later to make famous in the Premier League with Wimbledon.

There was even Mangold Dancing. The idea was that you dressed up in fancy dress, and stood on beer crates on one leg. On the principle of table skittles, one person had to wield a long pole and try to knock off as many people who were standing on one leg as possible. Staggeringly, it never caught on.

The opportunities for carousing were almost limitless. There were thirteen halls of residence on the university campus, each with its own bar. There was a students' union building with its own bar. That gave you fourteen ports of call without ever having to leave the campus. The bar in Sherwood Hall was especially notorious because it was the only one run by the students. Eventually, it had to be taken over because of enormous losses. The problem was not easy to miss. If you knew the bar staff then the drink was available at, well, a discount. You could go in with 10 pence in your pocket, drink 10 pints and come out completely and utterly legless, with 10 pence in your pocket.

In my first term, I drank far, far too much. The local beer was Home Ales, or Hardy Hansons. I was their best customer. I used to average nine or ten pints per night. That first term ruined my taste-buds for bitter for all time. I soon drifted on to lager and have stayed there ever since. Not a man's drink, really. On behalf of Sherwood Hall, I took a grip on the inter-hall pub games yard-of-ale contest which I never relinquished.

I also had a brave crack at the Grand Hot Curry Stakes. One night, the contenders gathered. The leading exponent was Dylan Davies, a Welsh prop whom I had met in the English Universities team. Davies was actually at Loughborough University, not at Nottingham, but he was apparently hired out to cause havoc on a freelance basis. I first came across him when we were both chosen for the Universities match against French Universities in 1982. Appropriately, somehow, it was played at Dunkirk. We had to make our own way to Dover, and book our own (godforsaken) bed and breakfast overnight in readiness for a dawn ferry to Dunkirk. Davies forgot his passport, and went through passport control on his knees amongst a group of schoolchildren. On his knees, he was the same height as the kids and the customs officers suspected nothing, even when they noticed that one of the kids had a luxuriant moustache. At least we did not return from Dunkirk in a fleet of small boats.

Davies was joined at the Hot Curry night by the other contenders – myself, Mark James, Andrew Denton and David Bradley. We went to our local takeaway and ordered them to come up with the hottest curry they had ever cooked. There was a significant interval while the chef, who obviously relished a challenge, went to work with his spices, and we took it away in its containers back to a nearby house for the battle. When we opened the containers we found the curry bubbling with evil and menace, like a malevolent volcano. It was actually crimson around the edges. It was like eating fire. The rules were that you had to take a mouthful each in turn, then take a glass of cold water; or, as the tension grew and the rounds progressed, actually to stick your head in a basin of cold water. It was a devastating experience and left my stomach in distress for days. Davies was the leading animal amongst the contenders, and to the best of my knowledge was declared the winner.

The annual dinner of the University Rugby Club followed soon afterwards. It was held at the Albany Carvery, an establishment with the proud boast that, for a flat fee, you could eat anything and everything you wanted. Dylan Davies made a statement of intent. He took a whole chicken from the buffet display and took it back to his plate. Soon, everything had disappeared, all the food, the garnishes, the lot. The serving plates were emptied. People were so stuffed, so bloated, that they could hardly talk, or drink.

However, as a second-year lawyer who thought he knew his law, this brought up for me an interesting legal point, which I took up with the manager. The advertisement said 'All you can eat', and with multi-visits allowed. Now there was nothing left. I complained bitterly (even though I felt sick) that they were in breach of contract and the argument soon escalated. There was a stand-up row. Or at least, there would have been if anyone could have stood up. No more food appeared, another victory for injustice.

Why were my guests always different to normal people? There was another night to remember when another prop to remember came to visit. Martin Whitcombe, later to play successfully for Sale, Leicester, the North and England B, had been a friend from the Yorkshire Schools team. He was stationed at the Royal Air Force base at North Luffenham. On the first night he came down, he managed to get me banned for life from my local pub and my local curry house on the same night. When our taxi reached Sherwood Hall, Whitcombe and myself and two other friends jumped out and sprinted off. For some inexplicable reason, the cabbie chased us two, and not the others, who were much smaller. I was trying to run and laugh at the same time and trying to ignore Whitcombe's great idea that we should stop and sort the cabbie out.

The cabbie was a dogged sort. He chased us into an annexe of the Hall. He chased us into one of the communal bathrooms and, while I held the door shut, Whitcombe escaped through an open window. I waited until I thought the driver had given up, released the door and began to climb through the same window. The door suddenly burst open and the cabbie came bursting in. As I tried to slip through the window, my shirt became impaled on the bobble of metal which sticks up to fasten the window. Whitcombe was pulling from the front, yanking my arms; the taxi driver was pulling my legs, back through the window.

There was a long drop on Whitcombe's side, and eventually I begged him to release me. I decided to face the music. However, Whitcombe gave an extra pull, I shot through into a thorn bush and I was sore and free. Later that same night, he sprayed my room with a fire extinguisher. He ruined every lecture note I had made in the whole term, which admittedly was not many, and I had to spend days at the photocopier to replace them. I really looked forward to Whitcombe's next visit.

Looking back at my younger days, it does seem that some vestige of responsibility occasionally emerged. I eventually became president of the Junior Common Room at Sherwood. The holder of that sort of office was usually a complete and utter prat but I was actually quite proud of the Hall and I thought I could do something to represent our interest. I used to sit in meetings of the University Council, which comprised all the presidents of all the halls of residence plus representatives of all the various societies. Chiefly, they comprised union hacks, activists and dull fanatics from the ends of the political spectrum. The idea was supposed to be that we would deal with matters which affected student life and the lot of our colleagues on campus. What actually happened was that we used to spend time endlessly debating vast world issues on behalf of students who cared only where their next drink was coming from. We used to have a pompous publication called the Nottingham University Policy Book, which used to list our official line on such issues as the Middle East and vivisection. Most of the policies were left-wing because most of the people who attended were left-wingers.

I used to listen and fume quietly for so long, as the left and right bickered incessantly, posturing on issues over which they had no control whatsoever. Then I used to crack. I used to become so angry that I couldn't hold it in for any longer. I used to have strong views on many of the external issues. But at one meeting, I declared that we should move some motions which affected students on campus directly and that all the posturing rubbish like Israel's occupation of the West Bank and vivisection could come later. I said that I didn't see what a bunch of twenty-year-old quasi-political hacks could achieve by ranting on at bi-monthly meetings. I was loudly shouted down by the left and the right.

At the end of my second year I and a girlfriend went to Edmonton, Canada, for a few months, to stay with relatives of hers. I joined a small club called St Albert in Edmonton, and found more than enough people to give me employment even though I had no work permit. St Albert were a small and friendly club and like all the other teams in the area their home ground had always been Ellerslie Park, which was shared by around ten rugby teams. But if they lacked basic resources they did not lack commercial cunning. Like the Aborigines in Australia, the Indian community in Edmonton were compulsive gamblers. St Albert used to run a big monthly draw, with large cash prizes. Inside two years, they made enough money to buy their own headquarters, one of very few teams in the whole of North America to own their own facilities.

Without a work permit, I scraped around for work. One of my jobs was in a drive-in movie. I worked in the refreshment stand, did repair work on their speakers, and worked in the toll booth at the point of entry. It suited me because I needed the money and had no work permit; it suited the drive-in owners because as it was all unofficial they could pay me below the normal rates. Their big night used to be called the Longest Night, when they would screen four feature films back to back. I was in the toll booth taking the money. So that no big-value notes were lying around for too long the manager would pop up occasionally and clean out the till. On the Longest Night, he had just left with the big notes when a guy wearing a stocking mask on his head jumped around the corner. He had a green wet-weather poncho draped around him, he had a bag, which he threw through the window of the booth at me. And he had a gun, which he pointed at me.

He started shouting; 'Throw the fucking money in the bag, throw the money in the bag.' Even though it all took microseconds it all seemed to unravel quite slowly in my mind. I laughed. 'You're joking,' I said. Then almost instantaneously I realized that he wasn't, and in the next portion of a second tried to work out if I could reach through and grab his gun.

Realization then piled in. It wasn't my money. I stuck some notes in his bag and was still feeling faintly blithe about the whole thing. Then he shouted: 'Kneel down in the corner with your back to me!' I thought then that he might well shoot me, but I heard his footsteps moving away. 'Stay there for five minutes,' he shouted as he made his escape.

I ran down to the concessions hut, shouting with added histrionics, 'We've been robbed, we've been robbed.' A grand total of $200 had been taken. It was only a week later that the narrowness of my escape hit me. I read that a similar incident had occurred locally in a 7–11 store and that someone had been shot dead for $50. That brought it home. I was glad I didn't keep up the smiling idea that it was all a joke.

There was no joke in the police reaction. They clearly thought I had something to do with the whole thing. They soon found I had no work permit and was low on funds. They demanded to know how much money I had come into the country with; they knew I had just been on a trip around the country so might be a little strapped. Then they told me that there were no witnesses whatsoever to the robbery – there could hardly have been, because the toll booth was right at the back of the drive-in complex and every single customer was facing the other way, looking at the screen. It quickly became clear they thought I had a part in the whole thing, perhaps even had simply pocketed the loot myself.

'Hold on a moment,' I said. 'I had nothing to do with this. I know I haven't got a work permit but I am not putting my hands up to armed robbery.' I told them I knew they could fine me for working without a permit, that they could even deduct the fine from my grant in England if they wanted to pursue it that far. But that was as far I was going.

Gradually they were convinced. There was a sergeant in the department who played for St Albert, and he vouched for me. I was released and told not to work again without a permit. Then we fell out with my girlfriend's relatives. It was a serious fall-out, mostly their fault, and it made it uncomfortable to stay. We moved out. Then rugby took a hand again. One of the coaches at St Albert, Roger Scott, told us that he was off to Seattle for a month. He gave us his house, his car, told us to make ourselves at home until he got back.

I have always found that kind of generosity in rugby. If people know you are involved in the game then they tend to assume you are a certain type of person, one to be trusted and helped. It may sound a little far-fetched but it is true. It is one of the best things about being involved in the sport. Canada was and is a great country, the rugby was not too testing because this was before the time when Canada rose to what could be called the top of Division 2 of world rugby. It was a superb intermission in university life.

At the end of the three years, I got a degree in what amounted to photocopying. Andrew Denton and I copied reams and reams of notes from missed lectures, armed with a treasury full of 5 pence pieces, which the photocopier feasted upon; crammed like fury at the end of the course as exams approached, staying up staring at books until three in the morning; and regurgitated stuff from short-term memory. I had already found, however, that law was principally common sense. Perhaps I was not an academic of professorial standards; but I did have common sense. I got my 2.2.

There were some appropriate functions to mark the end of the university years. Every hall had a massive end-of-year party, with a decent budget to launch it. We once had Culture Club to play, just before they became infamous; another hall had Madness, and there was also Wishbone Ash, Black Lace and Gary Glitter. Every president of a hall would stage a president's reception before the full piss-up got under way and would invite all the presidents of the other halls. I was invited to Lincoln Hall's President's Party. Earlier that day, I had played for Nottingham in a momentous victory over London Scottish in the John Player Cup. I was already flying high when I arrived.

I was able to piece together what had happened at Lincoln Hall with the help of friends. Another tradition of the hall parties was that the president's function would be graced by a lethal punch. The Lincoln concoction was lethal to the point of devilish. I got stuck into it. I remember nothing after that, but I understand that during the meal I suddenly got up and announced that I was going to the toilet. They came to find me when I never returned. I walked out of the loo with my jacket, shirt and tie on, but with my trousers and underpants over my shoulder, like a waiter. I said, with staggering insight: 'I'm too pissed. I'm leaving.'

I walked down the middle of the president's reception towards what I thought was the way out. I got to a blank wall at the end of the room. I said: 'This is not the way out.' I turned, walked back through the distinguished and incredulous ranks of the great and good, and went outside. I fell over a privet bush and couldn't get up. Assistance was summoned, I was found, and carried home.

It was the sort of situation where, later, you ask yourself: 'Did I *really* do that?' It was a fair question to pose at the end of my life as a student.

4

DEMISE OF THE DEAD ANTS
The ladder to England

LUCKILY, WE HAD STILL NOT REACHED THE ERA WHEN RUGBY AND alcohol were regarded as mutually exclusive to a top rugby career. Indeed, we were still in the era when many people regarded the two as inseparable. I managed to emerge occasionally from the hazes to maintain my playing progress. Some players have had their careers held back considerably by leaving their normal environment for three years in university rugby, and at first, I did turn out for the university team, on Wednesdays. The Nottingham club intervened and told me that I was doing my own game little good, and that I was simply coasting in midweek, trying to get through the university games to be fit for the club games on Saturdays.

The university team did have some success. In 1984, we fought our way through to the final of the UAU Championship, and I played at Twickenham for the first time. When we beat Swansea University in the semi-final at Stroud, the thrill of realization that we were going to run out on to Twickenham was incredible, and statistically it was unlikely that any of us would ever play there again. That is why the Pilkington Junior Cup is such a worthwhile competition. People play at Twickenham who would never normally get within miles of the field.

We met Loughborough, then the overwhelming force in student rugby, in the final, and as ever they were strong. They had in their pack John Morrison and Dave Egerton, who were both to become leading forwards in the first-class game with Egerton making the England team, and also Steve Burnhill, a centre who showed up well in a few student games at the time, and out of nowhere was chosen for the England tour of South Africa in 1984. It was his performance in the UAU final against Nottingham which did more than anything to clinch his selection. It all but finished his rugby career too, because the step up was too soon and too great. England fielded a weak and unfit bunch and were annihilated, and Burnhill's meteoric career never recovered.

My first impressions of playing at Twickenham were mixed. On that March day it was not the teeming, packed ground of popular conception. It was simply a giant, echoing green cavern with gaunt stands. There were only around 5,000 fans there, all in one side of the ground; Loughborough won 23–10, Burnhill scored a cracking try, and although we fought back later in the match we were never real contenders.

I was desperately upset at the end. But at least it had been a tremendous day out, for the team and for all the people who came down for the day from the university. There was also crowd trouble. There was a good deal of beer throwing and fighting and general irresponsibility, all happening under the noses of the RFU committee, looking on from the committee box in the West Stand. It is the proudest boast of some of my friends that they showed their backsides to the committee box.

Perhaps the most memorable game I played in the university team was a quarter-final of the Notts Cup, against Mellish. In most games between student and club teams, the club team, as a matter of course, try to beat the students up. But in the university team at the time we had some good forwards who could look after themselves – we had two good locks and John Ward, the prop who went on to play for England U23. We pushed Mellish all over the field, we gave them some stick at the bottom of the rucks and we rather gathered from their reaction that they were not used to being kicked around by students. It developed into an appalling running battle, and for some unbelievable reason the ref sent nobody off.

I also have a scar to this day from when I was kicked playing for the university against Leeds University. I felt a terrific blow in the head as I lay on the floor at the edge of a ruck and when I looked up, trying to collect my senses, I saw the culprit sneaking away. It was certainly the worst foul I ever suffered in rugby. This was about the stage when the Nottingham club began to make noises and I phased out the student games for good, while I still had a head attached to my shoulders.

It was now 1980 and, under the prevailing circumstances, a good time to throw in your lot with Nottingham. I played my first game for them in 1980 and I was to spend a decade there, before leaving for London and Harlequins in 1990. At the start of the Eighties, we were an amiable club bumbling along, having fun and not dwelling too long if we lost. But gradually we began to lift our performances and our horizons. We established a settled and competent team and the surge was on. We had as core players men like Gary Rees, such an effective flanker who would have won many more than his 23 caps if not for the incredibly tough competition from David Cooke, Andy Robinson and Peter Winterbottom; Peter Cook, the flanker; Gary Hartley, one of the best uncapped centres around, Steve Holdstock, the wing; Neil Mantell and, later, Chris Gray of Scotland in the second row, and John Ward, from Nottingham University. It was a joint effort between us to lift the whole status and outlook of the club.

We also produced, or at least helped to develop, a vast amount of talent which was then stolen away by other clubs – Rob Andrew played for us; Richard Moon came for a period; we also produced or developed Chris Oti, Neil Back, Stuart Potter, Wayne Kilford, Harvey Thorneycroft. Who knows, had we all stayed Nottingham could have done a Bath. We also, at one time, had that dangerous unit, a thinking front row. The *Daily Telegraph*'s Rugby People feature, written by Michael Austin, revealed in 1986 that our front row of Mick Grindle, myself and John Ward had thirty O levels, eleven A levels and three degrees between us. In that same article, I took the chance to lay down my defence of the smaller hookers in case I needed it in future. I did.

In the early years, we took some fearsome beatings from the likes of Coventry, Moseley and Leicester, the old giants who came along to patronize us. But we were avidly storing away the experiences. It made the feeling even richer when we came back in later seasons to haunt them.

We were still lacking the extra edge of conviction, the talent for going out on to the field expecting to win, when help came from an unlikely event – the County Championship, that correctly maligned competition which is apparently designed simply to give the RFU committee a reason to exist (and which has failed to give them that reason). In the 1984–5 season we committed ourselves to the event as a club, and as Notts, Lincs and Derbyshire, what was essentially the Nottingham club team in disguise, and coached by Alan Davies, fought our way through to the final, and I was back at Twickenham. We lost in the final to a very strong Middlesex team, which featured John Olver, the Harlequins hooker, and Andy Ripley. But the boost which the run gave our confidence and our club was palpable; especially since in the semi-final we had gone to the Memorial Ground, Bristol and beaten Gloucestershire, one of the counties where the County Championship still meant something. They had Stuart Barnes and Mike Teague, they had all the usual noisy fans, and we outplayed them.

From round the mid-1980s, we began the breakthrough to the top echelon. In the first year of league action in 1987 we were competitive in Division 1, and in the season afterwards, for a few heady weeks, we led the table. Simon Hodgkinson, at fly-half, was a superb controller and goal-kicker and at the time we would give a game to any team in the country, especially at our ground at Ireland Avenue, tucked away among the residential streets of Beeston. We reached the quarter-final of the Cup on several occasions, drew at home to Wasps in that round in 1986 and went out on the away team rule. We beat Bath at home in the league, an extremely rare defeat for them, and a day for vast celebration, if not dancing in the streets of Beeston. We also appeared in two Middlesex Sevens finals.

Ultimately, we never quite made the next breakthrough into the top four and to the summit itself. The agonizing lack of the final touch was best illustrated in a Cup match in 1985, one of the least memorable games I played in my career. We drew London Welsh at home in the fourth round and we had been playing well beforehand. We duly dominated most of the match. They hardly even got past the half-way line, and with all that pressure they were bound to concede penalties. They did, persistently. Rob Andrew missed nine kicks at goal, which for a kicker of Rob's ability was a quite astonishing feat. We lost 12–11, having thrown away around 30 points. Some of Rob's attempts were from such short range that I could have kicked them with my left foot.

Neil Mantell was the captain and he had Hodgkinson, a superb back-up kicker, at full-back, just waiting for the emergency call. For some reason, Mantell kept on calling up Rob. Rob would miss. We would have another kick. Rob would miss. Mantell said afterwards that some of the kicks seemed so easy that he decided to let Rob carry on trying, thinking that he was bound to slot one sooner or later and would therefore receive a massive injection of confidence. So much for that theory.

Whenever Rob was going through his preparations, the London Welsh centre, Robert Ackerman, who also played for Wales and the Lions and never came near to making my Christmas list, kept on shouting across at us, gloating. When the final whistle blew I was on the point of exploding completely. Accounts of the match revealed that I ignored every attempt by London Welsh players to shake my hand as we walked off.

We may not have won anything silver but the Nottingham years were memorable years. It was a club with few natural resources and no depth in the pocket, but the supporters we had were very loyal, and in the team and the club, the social life and the friendships were strong. The players operated one of the most savage circles of satirical humour in the history of the game, and unless you stood up to it and gave some back, you were likely to sink without trace. Harvey Thorneycroft, when he arrived fresh-faced from Trent Poly-technic, was mercilessly savaged by the verbals, so much so that Harvey, normally gregarious, was forced to shut up completely in case he gave us free ammunition. The great ringleaders, Rees, Hodgkinson and Hartley, were merciless. When people talk about team spirit, they would be amazed in what forms that spirit can sometimes come.

Alan Davies was quite obviously a vast influence on my career. He was coach of the club when I joined and he was still coach when I left in 1990, although he was just about to go on to greater things because, after Wales had endured a shambolic tour to Australia in 1991, he was summoned to the land of his fathers and took over as the Welsh team coach. I was lucky to have spent my formative years with him. These are years when you are very open to suggestion and when a bad coach at your club could set you back so far that you might never recover – and there are plenty of bad coaches around. Davies was excellent. He was also superb at setting goals, not only for the long term but for the next match. In this game it was important to get round the front of the line-out and pressurize the scrum-half. In that game it was important to scrummage well, or outplay your opposite number across the field, or concentrate on the throwing. He was very methodical, he had lots of ideas of his own. He would focus me so well that a good deal of the unchannelled elements, the headless parts, were gradually diminished.

Davies also helped me simply by calming me down a little, and there were never quite the same outbursts at Nottingham as there had been back up in Yorkshire. He also had the ability to coach international players. The problem once you have made the national team is that so many coaches stop coaching you; perhaps they do not trust their own knowledge, perhaps they feel that you no longer want to listen to them, you've made it, you know all there is to know. That is all nonsense. You just need a different type of coaching, someone to observe quietly and then come up with suggested refinements and reassessments. A year after I left Nottingham for London, Davies left Nottingham for Wales, to take on the national squad duties. The fact that Davies departed never affected the warm relationship I had with him and his family, although due to the distances involved we have not had contact anything like as regularly as before. But it is easy to fall back into the relationship.

Davies, of course, could have stayed far closer to me because at one time he was heir apparent as England coach. He was officially designated the England coach on the 1988 tour of Australia, with Dave Robinson from Cumbria as assistant. However, at that time Geoff Cooke, the manager, still wanted his fingers in the coaching pie and maintained a major technical input. It made Alan's job difficult because he was never in complete control. After the tour, which was unsuccessful, he was edged out. There was no way that Cooke and Davies would get on, on a long-term basis. Davies was very much a players' man. When his coaching work was over, when the match was over, he would become just one of the lads. Like the rest of us he would relax with a few beers, and like the rest of us, with a few more beers. Cooke was never that kind of animal. There was always a huge separation between Cooke on the one hand, and the rest of the management team and players on the other.

Davies took some fierce stick in Wales in the season before the 1995 World Cup. Wales subsided to the wooden spoon position, he was sacked while preparing to name his squad for South Africa, and apparently hordes of Welshmen disappointed by their team's results suggested that he couldn't coach. They were very wrong. I would place him among the top three coaches with whom I have been involved, along with Jack Rowell and Ian McGeechan. Wales failed to qualify for the quarter-finals in any case.

I earned my first England cap the hard way. Some people have one showy season with their club and are drafted in straightaway. I had to take it all step by laborious step right up through the heart of the England representative programme, from the English Universities to the English Students to England B to the full cap. All the way up, I kept suspicious eyes on other hookers, read their press, tried to outdo them on the training field and, if we met, during the matches. It was out of the question, still, to dream about becoming a full English international player; there was always the next hurdle, there was always the next step to think and worry about first, the next contending hooker to knock off. If only I had found a fast-track promotion and cut out all the rungs, it would have saved me no end of trouble!

And it would have been easier if all the various age-group squads were as well organized as they are now. Unfortunately, they were still often shambolic, badly managed and backed up, badly selected, badly run. A state lottery. And even though a national representative tour is a major event, we were still not out of the era when all tours, however exalted, were seen as a glorious chance for a massive piss-up, as well as a chance to further your playing career wearing some England jersey or another.

I had two feet on the ladder of representative rugby in my time at Nottingham University, in 1982 with the trip to Dunkirk to play for England Students against France, in the dangerous company of Dylan Davies. I stayed in the team for the next match, when we beat Wales by 50–7 on a windy day in Birmingham. The *Daily Telegraph* reported that I had 'taken countless strikes against the head'. I celebrated by moving into the back row when we lost a player, and scored the last try.

That performance was much-needed. The England Students, an amalgam of all the students' sectors, were to tour the Far East at the end of season 1981–2. I focused in on that tour and on doing my best to be selected. There was also a demonstration that, when the selectors are making up their minds, it is often the matches you miss which do you most good. Julian Johnson, the Cambridge University hooker, was picked for the Students XV for a match against Wales at Gloucester. England were thrashed, Johnson was never sighted at representative level again. That gift of mine for missing all the right matches was to help me at full England level in the years ahead.

One afternoon in late season 1982, in Sherwood Hall, the news came that I had been chosen for the tour. Paul Sidi, another Yorkshireman later to play for Harlequins, was the other hooker. Mark Bailey, Andy Dun, Simon Halliday, Barry Evans, Chris Martin, Steve Bates, Simon Smith and myself, all chosen for the trip, were to go on to be capped for England, which just showed how wrong were the RFU's priorities. All the funding went to the Colts set-up; they got far better treatment and yet produced far fewer England players.

The centrepiece of the trip was a tripartite event between New Zealand Universities, Japan and ourselves. We warmed up by beating Japan B by 99–0, inspired by Mike Perry, the fly-half who was at the time the latest great white England hope at fly-half (and later went the same way as the previous twenty). The match against New Zealand was obviously the first I had ever played against Kiwis and I was desperately anxious to play well against them, to prick the bubble of all they stood for. At the time, New Zealand teams could win matches on their aura alone.

The build-up was an odd experience. We were staying in the same hotel, lurking in the same foyer, we trained at the same pitches. We spent several days fixing each other across the foyer with the evil eye, without speaking or without any social contact. I beat off the challenge of Paul Sidi to play against them in what was obviously the 'test' of the tour. It poured with rain throughout the match, but we outplayed them up front, we outrucked them. We beat them. It was a great feeling, especially to beat them at their traditional game. It meant that I disposed of most of the invincible aura early in my career. New Zealand did come back to haunt me, especially in the heavy defeat in the 1995 World Cup semi-final, but I did manage to play in enough winning teams against them not to let the aura envelop me.

The off-field humour in Japan, as you would expect from a bunch of precocious students, was rather more highbrow than I had been used to back in Yorkshire rugby. There was a tour court every single day, in which I filled the role of prosecutor. There was also a chance to put one over on the refined Halliday. At one meal, with the team split on different tables, we told Halliday that the drink of the evening was sake. Every now and again, our table would raise their glasses, call a toast and drink the contents of our glasses – cold water. Only Halliday was actually following the rule and drinking sake, only Halliday did not realize we were all downing water. Half-way through the dinner, in the middle of the speeches, Halliday, one of the aristocrats of the game, had to be carried out of the room, gibbering loudly. Not Hallers' style at all.

The next step was the England U23 tour to Romania and

it was here that I first experienced the coaching of Dick Greenwood, the northerner who was later to become full England coach. Romania was an experience then, it is still an experience now, and not one to treasure. We flew over on their national airline, TAROM (wind it up and throw more wood on), and we found out about their safety record only after we landed, which was a good job because otherwise we would never have taken off. In Romania, there was very little to eat, very little to drink, so the staple was chips and coke. There was also one of the most memorable cultural evenings I have ever been on in any tour. We went out to a large theatre at the invitation of our hosts to see a leading Romanian comedienne. The theatre was absolutely full – of Romanians, laughing at Romanian jokes. There were no subtitles. The thirty-man England squad sat near the back, incredulous and uncomprehending, while the audience laughed their socks off.

We filled in the time on that tour by training like maniacs. Greenwood, to me, was a significant figure in English rugby because he realized that international players in England were nothing like fit enough, that we were only really playing with the new fitness techniques, and that the old philosophy in English rugby, that real hard work had to be frowned upon as being somehow not cricket, had to be overcome. Greenwood must be given a lot of credit for changing those attitudes, for dragging the leading players and England, often kicking and screaming and wheezing, into a new era of fitness, and a new era of 'attitude'. He prepared the way for the people who were effectively professors of conditioning and training to come in with their hi-tech stuff in later years.

Greenwood's defect was that while he knew the effect that we should all be striving for, he did not know how best to translate theory into fitness; the other problem was that he thought he did. At training sessions at Marlow, he would put us through ferocious training, then prescribe a four-mile warmdown run around Marlow before we could finish. Hiding in bushes near the complex was the best way.

In Romania, he flogged us to death. One day, with the temperature over 100 degrees, we trained in a vast concrete bowl of a stadium. It was bare, baked and airless. He put us through timed 400-metre runs. On the next day, with the same temperature, he consoled us by saying that we could play five-a-side football. 'Thank Christ for that,' we all said. What happened was that Greenwood had us jogging the width of the pitch, sprinting the diagonal to the far corner, repeated for over twenty minutes in the burning sun. When he had finished, with everyone half dead, he threw in a soccer ball. 'There,' he said, 'everyone who wants to play five-a-side can carry on.'

If you turn up short of fitness for a ten-day tour, which is how long the Romania trip lasted, you simply cannot improve the situation while you are there. When games approach you need to stay off your feet, to conserve energy. Massive bulk training, that should have been done months before, simply makes people tired and heavy in the legs for the actual matches. It is better to tell everyone that if they don't get fit for the next time then they won't be chosen; or, as happens now, to test for fitness way before. Dick Greenwood prepared some of the ground for later English attitudes. He knew that, come hell or high water, England had to get fitter. But in terms of the technical knowledge required, he was little more than a flogger.

But I was receptive to his aims. For me, it was a way in, a way to attack other hookers contending for the various positions who were bigger than me. I could see why it was relevant for others too.

The next major step was a tour to Spain with England U23, and I continued my efforts to drag myself above any other hooker they brought along. Alan Black of Wasps, who is now the RFU's National Promotions Officer, was the coach, and Mike Weston, an anxious-looking former England fly-half, was the manager. They were an ill-assorted pair. Weston had a serious defect as manager. Managers are there to take all the hassle and to sort it, to keep it all away from the team; they are not there to say, as Weston did in Spain: 'God. If you think you are having a hard tour, what about me?' I wasn't bothered about his admin problems; that was why he was there. Stop whining and get on with it.

He had some major run-ins with the players because he was over the top. John Goodwin, the Moseley wing, wound him up terribly badly. This was at the time when the full England team were preparing to tour South Africa. Goodwin was from another planet in any case, so they were always going to clash. He would lie under people's beds in hotels for hour after hour, then jump out when they came back to their room. He was yet another example of the hundreds of talented England players of the last twenty years who simply drifted away; he was never given the environment to make the best of his talents. 'If they call me from South Africa and ask if you are capable of joining them as a replacement,' said Weston to Goodwin, 'I would have to say no.'

Alan Black was a good character. He started half the best off-field celebrations, then had the art of walking away when it all went horribly wrong. It was difficult for him to keep control because he was laughing so much. It had the feeling of a club tour, not some serious exercise in preparing us for later full England duty. On tour were players like Alex Woodhouse, the Harlequins scrum-half, who were essentially out for a good time, rather than for a headlong and selfless pursuit of higher honours.

At one venue in Spain I was sharing a hotel room with Kevin Simms, the fresh-faced, serious young Cambridge University centre. I remember coming in one night after a full-scale celebration with John Ward, my old colleague at Nottingham University, lying down in bed feeling dreadful, with the room spinning, realizing I was going to be sick, and, despite my state, becoming desperately anxious not to be sick over my innocent room-mate, or his daily prayer guide which he devotedly kept near the bed. I loyally managed to stagger into the bathroom where I threw up all over the floor. That was true team spirit.

It gives some indication of the relative lack of seriousness with which these tours were undertaken that we were still doing the Dead Ants call, that wonderfully childish relic of every club tour in the history of the sport. There can be few people in the game who have not heard the call, but the upshot is that suddenly the whole party falls to the ground, lies on their backs and waves their legs and arms in the air. The tour rule was that if there was a quorum of eight at any time, senior members of the party could call a Dead Ants. There was one occasion when a lift reached the ground floor of the hotel and the doors opened to reveal all the passengers flat on their backs, but the prize call came at breakfast in a hotel in San Sebastian, in the Basque country.

Peter Buckton, the flanker from the North of England, called Dead Ants in the breakfast room. The whole party dived straight to the floor, tables and cutlery flew everywhere. The commitment of the team to hitting the deck was outstanding. However, no-one reacted quicker than the locals. They were absolutely convinced that the Basque separatist movement, ETA, were attacking. Some of them hit the floor

81

along with the rest, others sprinted out of the breakfast room and never came back, their breakfasts uneaten and congealing on their plates.

Weston finally snapped after a midweek match against some up-country opposition. We won by 50 points, and as captain for the day I lined the lads up to clap off the opposition. As they were walking through our ranks I made the Dead Ants call, and the whole team hit the deck. Weston left his seat in the stand in a fury. 'If you ever do that again,' he said, 'you will never pull on an England representative jersey again.' He was lucky. I had planned to call it after one of the conversions had been taken. The Dead Ants call has recently fallen into disuse.

Possibly the highlight of Weston's management came on a free day. We were staying near Seville and heard that the England U21 soccer team were playing their Spanish counterparts in Seville. Weston thought it would be an excellent idea to watch the match. He also thought it would be an excellent idea if we showed the flag by wearing our number ones, full blazer, badge and flannels. We got to the stadium, filed off the coach in our blazers and were given a few suspicious looks from the locals. As yet, they had no idea who we were. We took our seats. After ten minutes England had the temerity to score and we all leapt up as one, greeting the goal. The stadium was dead silent except for this little pocket of Englishmen in their blazers. The mood in the stadium changed dramatically. People rushed from all parts of the ground and stood menacingly around the portion of the stand where we were sitting. They muttered and growled, waved Spanish flags in front of our faces, threw lighted matches, gave us black looks and nudged each other menacingly.

With ten minutes of the match remaining, we decided to

beat a retreat back to the coach. We stood up, bottles and cans started raining down on us. People walked after us as we walked, and as we tried desperately not to break into an all-out sprint. We got to the coach with half of Seville on our heels, only to find that the driver had locked it and gone off for his break. In the best traditions of the Wild West, we formed a defensive circle facing outwards. Eventually, the bus driver arrived, we jumped into the bus and drove off. It was a great decision by Weston to travel in our formal gear. We could not have been more conspicuous if we had all gone with signs stuck to our heads: 'English.'

I kept on the ladder. I kept trying to stalk the other hookers who were struggling up the rungs. Andy Simpson, the Sale hooker whom no-one in the squad seemed to particularly like, came back down to the B squad after being on the fringes of the full team and I was on the bench to him for the Test match on a B tour of Italy in 1986; I tried to ensure that it never happened again and that the roles were thereafter reversed.

Years later, after I had been capped, I played against Sale and Simpson for Nottingham. In one scrum, Simpson took the ball against the head. 'That was a good one, that was a good one,' he kept rabbiting. 'It's one more than the number of caps you've won, too,' I pointed out helpfully. He was to sit on the bench about twenty-eight times for England and never got on. People said that I would have stayed on the field with a broken leg rather than give up a cap to him, and to others who were waiting for me to come off injured. They are right. I have never left the field in a full England Test match.

Perhaps the only hooker I really respected, of all those bubbling around with me on the fringes of the undercard of England teams, was a fellow northerner, Mike Dixon of Fylde.

He was a fine player and a big man. I was keenly aware of his progress because he would dynamite the big hooker/ small hooker controversy. He did not represent a choice between big and good. He was big and he was good, which is the final answer to the debate. He was chosen for some of the U23 games, he was well written up in the papers, he played in some of the great Lancashire teams when they dominated the County Championship, alongside giants like Bill Beaumont and Fran Cotton. He is the only hooker around in my time in or around the England squad who I felt might have edged me out of the junior England teams.

He wasn't. Dixon carried on playing for Fylde for many seasons, but he seemed to fade from the national scene. I often wonder why. Perhaps he simply did not want it badly enough; perhaps rugby was never a huge part of his life and ambitions. Perhaps the increasing severity of preparation did not appeal to him. I turned from Dixon and began to pay attention to two new rising names. They were John Olver, not yet a major contender but carving out a niche at Harlequins. And I also began hearing about a Cornishman who had joined Bath, a player called Graham Dawe. I stored away the names.

I took the penultimate step on the ladder in 1985 when I was asked to captain the England B team at Twickenham, in a match against Italy. I was then twenty-three, and was surprised to be asked. We fielded a monster pack, with Bob Kimmins and Brian Kidner, both 6'8" plus, in the second row, with the mountainous Peter Stiff of Bristol at prop, and Graham Robbins of Coventry at No. 8. We started well but we wilted in the heat of a warm Twickenham afternoon, and although we still won comfortably, it was something of a typical England performance in that our basics were better than our finishing. This was all going extremely well – if

I was captain of England B at twenty-three, then perhaps I could even look forward to a long tenure in later life as England captain. At the time, no-one had ever heard of Will Carling. So much for that theory.

One weekend in 1986, Nottingham were playing in London and I was called up to train with the England squad. Steve Brain, then the England hooker, had gone down with an injury and I came in as stand-by. I took part in a training session, and threw the ball in to Maurice Colclough, then the England lock, in practice. Colclough belied what other players said about him by coming up to me afterwards and telling me that I had thrown in very well. It was appreciated.

When I came into the England squad in my own right later in that year, there was a profoundly different atmosphere to that prevailing today. We had only just started summer sessions and what might be called more scientific training methods. Tom McNab, a distinguished athletics coach, author, a nice man and a prize-winning bullshitter of the first order, was brought in by the RFU to supervise. McNab had trained Daley Thompson and a host of other great athletes, as he recalled frequently before being asked to. He had the bullshit but he also had credibility: you knew that if you listened to what he said and followed his advice, it would have the effect that he said it would.

He also had a cultural problem. It was now only one season from the first World Cup but it was still almost frowned upon to take rugby too seriously, even in the national squad. Chris Butcher and Peter Winterbottom had toured with England in South Africa in 1984, and from their account I gathered that England had been on the beer for four weeks. They said that the tour was a complete joke, that people went missing, missed flights, that Ron Jacobs and Derek Morgan of the

RFU ran it all badly. These days, you would be shot for that kind of behaviour. Then, it did not seem to stand out.

Nowadays people like John Goodwin and Alex Woodhouse would never survive five minutes in any England squad. Nor would the attitudes we played with in my early representative years. We would be slapped down. 'Do it our way, or you are out.' These days, in rugby squads at or near the top level, you have to be serious, full of intent. You can have fun but only in a certain, limited way, in the interaction of personalities in the squad rather than in overt behaviour. But already characters are diminished, the great stories and the great escapades are being quickly phased out. You are forced to hold back a lot, unless it is the night after the match and you can let a few strands of your hair down. And be sure to get up for training next morning, or the axe falls again.

Perhaps it is perceived that the severity of the era suits me. Perhaps it does. I have always found an avenue into teams through sheer hard work and dedication. And it may seem strange that someone like me, as bound up as anyone in the drive to make England better, took a full part in all the levity, even diving for the Dead Ants wearing various England jerseys. Certainly you cannot help being carried along with the attitudes of the time, of your peers. But after all, I had the old colts rugby upbringing, with the rugby songs, the pranks, the Ralgex rubbed into the testicles, and all those other quasi-gay things that we all used to do. The levity, the fun element, the whole tenor of the life of a rugby player at the top level, has changed dramatically. The Dead Ants have died for the last time. Hardly anyone knows a rugby song any more. Or rubs on the Ralgex. I applaud the passing of those more innocent days, when England usually lost. I also miss them terribly.

Back in 1987, I was one of the first people to enter a new

world of rugby, of scientific preparation where no stone was left unturned, where the business of a rugby player became a business, and no longer revolved around the whole experience but around the narrow experience of actually playing the game. I had fought my way laboriously up to the fringes of the England team, through the tours, the rivals, the Ants, the pranks, and the first stirrings of the New Severity. This was all, as it turned out, a picnic.

5

DOOM OF GRAND DESIGNS

The sawn-off revival of English rugby, 1987–90

I have been trying all my life to like Scotchmen, and am
obliged to desist from the experiment in despair.

Charles Lamb

SUDDENLY, THERE WAS EFFECTIVELY ONLY ONE HOOKER LEFT IN MY way. I was in the A team, I had my taste of the England squad. Technically, after all the battles for all the hooking positions in all the teams on all the fields, there was only one man in England above me. Steve Brain had come into the England team on their disastrous tour of South Africa in 1984 when apparently the drinking had been world-class and the play abject.

He had stayed in for the next two seasons and it pained

me at the time to say it, but Brain was a very good hooker. He was very strong, he was highly aggressive, he could throw in well. He was no giant but he was bigger than me. He really should have been able to look forward to another two or three seasons in the team.

But Brain had one drawback. He was not a Renaissance man. He did not like the new era one bit. He did not like listening to Tom McNab and all his theories of conditioning. He used to say aloud that fitness could tell you nothing about what sort of player he was. It was a mood which hung on in the squad. Players used to ask what the ability to do a vast number of push-ups or a fast 400-metre time had to do with international rugby. This was the crossover period and Brain, and others, were not crossing over. They were just cross.

I felt that they were missing the point. Of course it didn't actually make you a better player technically, but you are better if you are fitter, you last longer, your techniques can be maintained for longer. If Brain had just made a gesture, if he had simply pretended to adopt the new fitness techniques and then cut all the corners, he might indeed have stayed in the team. If only he had shown willing. But his hostility was obvious. They would have carried on with him, he might easily have played in the 1987 World Cup. But he kept his stance. He may have been a fine player and he was more experienced than me by far. But what I had on him was attitude. I lapped up McNab and all the new training theories. It was my point of entry, the place where I could score.

You could hardly blame Brain for under-achievement because he was a child of his time. What was wrong with English rugby in the post-war period, when we had far more resources and players than any other country in the Five Nations and far, far less success – humiliatingly little, in fact

– was also running through society at large. There was a trait of English reserve, of people who could turn their hands to anything, civil service-style, but who never spent enough time being any good at anything, let alone outstanding. It was the same thing as ministers having no experience in the field of their ministry; it was also the cult of the amateur. It ran through the English psyche that chaps like us could get along without needing to sweat too much.

It was rampant in rugby. When some of us did extra training when the sessions proper had ended in my first years in the squad, there were still fellow players who would say: 'Look at that prat,' and nudge each other and laugh at us. It was not that people played with anything other than pride in the English jersey. It was just that people were ignorant of the fact that we were all seriously under-achieving.

At the start of season 1986–7, Brain had already started to fade and Graham Dawe, the Bath hooker, and I were vying for the job in the 1987 Five Nations tournament. I did not know Dawe well at all – and that situation did not change for a long, long time. We were deadly rivals from the start, we were to have some climactic, over-the-top battles when-ever we met on the field. And it was to be all of seven years before we ever sat down and had a decent conversation. There was a time when we did not even nod to each other. I think the ice was broken in around 1993, and by the time of the World Cup we were friends, respecting what each other had achieved.

It is so easy to trace the roots of the antipathy. Dawe, from the start, carried around the same attitudes. He coveted the same jersey. He also grasped the new training, saw that with the natural fitness of a farmer, he could push his case too. People like Dawe, Jon Hall, the young Bath flanker, and myself embraced it all wholeheartedly.

Rugby historians specializing in the 1980s now say that it was the approaching World Cup which caused England, followed later by the other home countries, to dynamite the old under-achievement and happy-go-lucky approach and actually do something about getting fit and properly prepared. Possibly, but to me it was just a new mood in the game, it was the prodding of people like Dick Greenwood. By the 1987 World Cup, when the fitness pennies were dropping, we thought we had taken fitness to a new level – and then we found that after all the effort put in by all the players, there was only one really fit team out there. New Zealand were still far fitter than the rest and they won the event. That was a lesson that the redoubled efforts had to be redoubled, and we were off on the treadmill, were in the shock of the new preparation culture. We gradually became the un-English English.

I had another lesson reinforced in the Five Nations of 1987. Some games can profoundly help your career providing you miss them. Dawe was chosen for the first match, and for his first cap, against Ireland in Dublin. He could then reasonably have expected a decent run in the side. But they were thrashed in Ireland, 17–0, on a horrendous dark day when everything went wrong; then he played for England in defeat against the French at Twickenham when England lost 19–15; again, there was bad, squally weather, desperate conditions for a hooker and his throwing-in. Then he was part of the England term which went to Cardiff to try to save their season. Instead, England lost to Wales in a luridly publicized brawl, Phil Davies had his jaw broken with a punch from Wade Dooley, and there were massive headlines afterwards about thuggery.

After the match, the RFU threw out four England players – Richard Hill, Gareth Chilcott, Wade Dooley and Dawe – on disciplinary grounds. Hill must take some of the blame because his team talk before the match is legendary. I listened to the first instalment as a replacement, but the real highlights from the rant came along afterwards. Apparently it was a steam of violent anti-Welsh invective. I would guess that it was only what was being said in the other dressing room, with the names changed, but that sort of bawling no longer works and it shouldn't be done.

This was around the time when England packs decided that they were going to take it no longer; England were always intimidated when they went to Wales and France and a change of attitude was creeping in. Players like Dooley were not inclined to be intimidated. But to suggest that England caused all the trouble was patently ridiculous, and yet no Welsh player was disciplined by the Welsh Rugby Union. The RFU seemed to feel that, instead of trying to back their players, they had to be seen to be taking some pompous action. The Welsh stood back and said: 'We've been bullied.' The English copped all the blame, all the punishment, and the boys were bewildered. What is the point, they were asking. We go out there, they punch us. Do they expect us to stand there and take it? The answer, apparently, was yes.

Dawe's treatment was ridiculous. At least Wade had hit someone. Dawe had done nothing. He seemed to be guilty by association. I thought I was a better player than him, I was desperate to play for England. But I felt very sorry for Dawesy. He never deserved to lose a Test jersey on those grounds. I would have commiserated with him at the time. Unfortunately, we were not talking.

In the local paper just before the news came of my call-up to the England team, my mother expressed my anxiety that it was all passing me by. 'Brian is worried that he is nearly twenty-five and time might be running out for him to break into the international arena,' she was quoted as saying. I think the panic has since been proved to be a little premature.

I took the fateful call in my office in Nottingham, where I was still an articled clerk. Mike Weston was by now chairman of selectors. It took a few seconds to sink in. The euphoria piled in immediately afterwards. There is always the fear that having fought your way up, you will not actually make it, will stall a few yards from the summit. I had finally fought my way past the lot of them. I was the leading hooker in England.

We were playing Scotland at Twickenham, and in the wreckage of our season we had to win to avoid a whitewash. They came bragging and were out for the Triple Crown. In fact, the atmosphere in the squad had improved. Mike Harrison, the Wakefield and Yorkshire wing, came in as captain and he defused some of the resentment, got things back on an even keel. It was less intense under Mike, and in the right sort of way. England played very well; Peter Williams, a vastly underrated fly-half who really should have gone on to win many more caps, was outstanding and we won 21–12. Like so many others in a long line of wasted talent, he was treated appallingly by England and was driven away to rugby league, a tremendous player lost, or more precisely, thrown away.

To play the first match against Scotland was a significant event in the light of what was to come, because throughout my England career the Scots were deadly rivals and the relationship between the teams was never warm. As for my relationship with the Scottish nation, that remained trapped in a refrigerator. I was to play eleven times against Scotland and I am delighted that we lost only once. But that one defeat did have a profound effect on me, and on the course of England rugby.

*   *   *

Colin Deans was the Scottish hooker at Twickenham that day in 1987. He was an icon and he was playing his last Five Nations match. At about the third scrum, I struck for the ball, hooked it back, and then it hit Jon Hall on the knee and bounced back to Scotland. Colin Deans said: 'You've got a lot to learn, laddie.' I wanted to say: 'We'll see, you Scottish twat.' But I didn't say it. I only thought it.

When we were 21–12 up, the people in the old North Stand started singing 'Jerusalem' while someone was being treated. The old stand, for those who know only the new high-tech, low-atmosphere Twickenham, was a kind of popular end, with standing terraces in front. The sound came rolling off. We knew we were going to win, the atmosphere was joyous. I thought as it was happening, as the singing grew, that there could not be a better feeling in life than this. I remember willing myself to remember it, to experience it, to savour it, in case it never happened again. That night Alan Grimsdell, president of the RFU, presented me with my cap. I also got the official tie. On the bus until then, when everyone had been wearing the England tie, red with silver roses, I had a blue tour tie. Now, I had the cachet, the tie, the cap.

Even under Harrison's calm guidance, the atmosphere in the squad was insecure when I joined. There was tremendous resentment at the RFU for their heavy-handed action, their unilateral action, after the Welsh match. Apparently it was not the first time the squad felt let down by the RFU committee. Now, after eight seasons of playing for England and more than sixty caps, I can testify that it was very far from the last time we felt like that!

At that time, the committee felt quite free to come into the dressing room when we were trying to prepare, to give us advice, to tell us how to play. Past presidents who had no idea of the modern game used to wander along, people who had not played for twenty years and more. They would even make comments in training, harangue you in bars, and enter the dressing room when you were trying to build up.

Presumably they simply wanted to go back to their mates upstairs in the committee room and say: 'I've just had a word with the lads, they are all in good form.' 'I've just given Wade a couple of tips.' People like John Burgess and Mickey Steele-Bodger used to come in all the time. They stopped round 1990, when we started being downright rude to them. 'What's that wanker doing here?' we used to ask in stage-whispers. 'We don't want that lot here, why don't they go back to their gin and tonics?' The RFU view has always been that we were merely temporary actors on their stage, that we were only a tiny part of their framework. The attitude was that if we didn't like it and didn't conform, they could always get in another fifteen to take our places.

I admit that they all riled me from the start, these people Will Carling was, perfectly correctly, to call 'fifty-seven old farts' in the notorious Carling Affair of 1995, when the mis-management and cravenness of the RFU was seen in its worst light. It always seemed to me that we were the people at the sharp end and that we were never treated as such. Mike Burton's corporate hospitality activities at Twickenham have long drawn expressions of disapproval from the rugby purists. Players often used to wonder how Burton was given such latitude. Quite simply, he stated to me, over a drink in a bar, that there were few committee men who at one time or another had not sold tickets. This would provide an explanation as to why the RFU seem powerless to support the cause for Burton's head.

Things are better now. People do realize that the whole thing, the new stand, the whole framework, stands or falls on what happens on the field. The old grandees thought that they could run things and could do so without ever bothering what the players felt. We had to be seen, but not heard. They used to say to me, at the start: 'Of course, we didn't do things like that in my day.' I used to shoot straight back at them: 'Exactly. Your day was thirty years ago. They had leather studs in your day. We don't have them any more either.'

Dawe and myself were the hookers in the England squad for the World Cup in Australia and New Zealand. I have never admitted before how very close I came to missing the whole thing. When I was out training for the Calcutta Cup I felt something go in my foot when I was running. I slowed down and carried on. Next day I could hardly walk.

As the Scotland match approached the problem was still there. I had an X-ray which showed nothing. Briefly, I thought I would have to withdraw from my first cap, which was the worst feeling in the world. I formulated a plan of campaign with Kevin Murphy, the England physio. He built me a little makeshift arch to slip into my boot to ease the pain. It helped a little but in the days before the match I was in absolute agony. When we walked out to inspect the field on the day, I went across to the sidelines to chat to some Old Crossleyans who had arrived early. I could not stop myself limping. But I was so hyped for the game and so full of painkillers that I got through.

After a few weeks' rest we met for the World Cup. Dawe, desperate to get back the place he had lost, approached me as soon as we met. 'Let battle commence,' he said. On the plane, where your feet sometimes swell anyway, my foot felt like it was on fire. It felt like it was twice the normal size. On one of the early training runs, at Rushcutters Bay, Sydney, I had to stop and drop out of the run, in a black fit of despair.

Kevin Murphy did his best. He packed the foot in ice, tried some more wedges under the foot arch. I remember Dooley and Paul Rendall, with typical sympathy, jogging around the field singing: 'Underneath the Arches'. Pictures of the squad at leisure in the World Cup always show me with socks and training shoes, even in the hottest sunbathing weather, so that I could hide the masses of strapping on the foot. At one stage I didn't think I could take any more, although the subterfuge worked because no news of the injury ever appeared in the press.

It came down to a final fitness test. I had to complete a session, otherwise they were talking about sending for a replacement. I told myself that I was not going home. I didn't care how much it hurt but I had to get through that session. I managed it, managed to limp through the tournament, unsuspected.

All those helped by the science of orthotics will recognize the next moves. I saw an orthotics expert in London called Barry Francis. He took plaster casts of my feet, found that one leg was shorter than the other, and so to correct the imbalance had customized orthotics made, to slip into my shoes and rugby boots. Apparently, a ligament under the foot arch was swelling and pushing together two bones in the foot. The orthotics made me plant my foot correctly. In many ways it was a miracle cure, because the pain quickly disappeared.

Just after I was proved fit came a significant episode in the rivalry with Dawe. We were training inside a gym at a Sydney school. People were lapping the gym to warm up and as the pace started to increase a little, I found myself running alongside the dreaded Dawe. He sensed me there and started to go a little quicker. I accelerated because there was no way he was going to outpace me. We started accelerating rapidly until we were both sprinting flat out around the gym. I got in front. He got in front. We were hurtling round and round.

Gradually, the other runners stopped and stood aside, nudging each other. 'Look at those two.' Everyone started cheering as we careered around. In the end Martin Green, the coach, stopped it; he stood in our way with his arms out. Some of the boys were rolling around laughing, others were completely bewildered.

The build-up to that first tournament was almost quaint by comparison with the build-up for 1995, even though at the time it felt reasonably high-tech. Essentially, we were still playing with it all. We had no clear definitions as to our goals and playing policy. We were still in the English mood of let's do our best. I don't think anyone in the team seriously felt that we could win the World Cup in any case. On the flight over, Dean Richards and I wore Gorbachev and Reagan masks, a kind of levity which would never happen these days.

We still looked at the World Cup even as some sort of jolly, a festival, not the end of the world. England had even been against the concept entirely and only jumped on board when the RFU realized that the rest of the world was going ahead without them. People even said it would be the first and last World Cup. There were also fewer real contenders – the Wallabies were not as huge in Australia 87 as they are now; South Africa did not compete; and the smaller nations were still disorganized.

We began the tournament in defeat against Australia, the favourites. Keith Lawrence, the referee, gave David Campese a try which he actually bounced over the line from a height of about 4 feet. The headlines all said that we had been magnificent in defeat but it was getting to the stage where I and some of the others didn't want to be magnificent in defeat. If it came down to it, we would rather be awful in victory.

The seminal match for us, and for England rugby history, was the quarter-final against Wales at Ballymore. Wales came with severe injury problems; we were favourites having played reasonably well against Australia and then also beaten the USA and Japan in our group. But it was a horrible match on a horrible day and a truly awful England performance. Wales had Bob Norster operating on one leg in the line-out and they had to bring in a new cap in the front row in David Young, who was only nineteen; but they played with more determination. Ludicrously, before the match the RFU hierarchy demanded that we should not have Wade Dooley marking Norster, because of the bad blood from the previous Welsh match in Cardiff, and in case it all blew up again. This pathetic and craven decision meant that we had to have Nigel Redman marking Norster. Martin Green said he didn't want the confrontation to develop, forgetting that Test rugby is essentially confrontation. We lost the confrontation and we were out.

The immediate fall-out saw every Englishman on or off the field trying desperately to pass the buck. If we had passed the ball with the dexterity with which they passed the buck, we would have won the whole World Cup. This was a stage when no-one in English rugby would take responsibility for anything. There was unseemly buck-passing as we packed to go home. Chalky White, a paid coaching administrator, fingered everyone in his report; Don Rutherford was critical of various aspects even though he had been in power as technical administrator for twenty years and any coaching failures should have been laid at his door, for him to do something about. Wales went on to beat Australia in the third-place play-off, a not inconsiderable performance. We went home with loads to think about, and after the optimism of the win over Scotland in my first match, the revival completely stalled.

It became apparent to me and to others in 1987 that we did not want to be in a team that always lost. It was nothing so formal as the players sitting down and making a pact, but young players with commitment were now appearing in and around the squad, and it became a priority within the RFU and the squad to turn the whole thing around, to turn the shambles of Brisbane into something better. This was the start of my role as a senior player. I wanted a say, a voice in the preparations of the team.

Weston and Green, the latter a thoughtful man who agonized over the coaching and who knew a lot about the game, disappeared, and in their place came a new team manager, a man with no track record anywhere in the game to speak of, a man the players hardly knew. We were very dubious. Old Crossleyans even had a story that Geoff Cooke had joined but had to move on again because he had been unable to get out of the third team. Dubious, dubious.

But as soon as Cooke came in, things immediately felt better. He had no caps but he had charisma and organization. He remained as team manager from the autumn of 1987 to the end of the Five Nations in 1994. During that time England won two Grand Slams, could easily have won two more, regained the respect that had almost completely evaporated round the world, and helped galvanize the whole profile and standing of English rugby. To call this all the Cooke era would be ridiculous because so many people were so heavily involved, but Cooke gave the team a level of organization that it never had before. He also handled the press well.

I told him more recently that I would be happy to negotiate the rights to his book because he has so many inside stories to tell. He became unpopular with the blimps on the RFU, who told him he was becoming too close to the players, but the blimps never explained how he was supposed to be England team manager without getting close to the team. They saw him as their spy in the camp, a role he refused to fill.

Strangely, although I played in England teams throughout his years as team manager, I never really came to know him, and he never confided in me. He had an edge to him and perhaps felt he needed to keep a distance; only Will Carling seemed to be taken into his confidence, a fact that did not always go down well in the squad. In seven years I probably spoke no more than five sentences to him in any one conversation. Now and again, though not nearly as often as I expected, he asked my opinion on technical things. But I never had a long conversation with him. He was not unfriendly, but exceedingly difficult to get to know well.

To jump a couple of years, there was a watershed in Argentina, where England toured in 1990, when he and I lost the plot. I had been pack leader for a season or two. I thought at the time that Cooke felt I had something to offer, especially in terms of organization on the field. But we had just lost the Grand Slam match in Scotland, where some questions had been raised about Will Carling's captaincy and where we had been criticized because, so newspapers alleged, I was running the whole show on the field and Will could not get a look in.

I was not playing well. I was mentally and physically exhausted and I never should have made the Argentina tour. The tour selection got my back up from the start because they chose three loose heads, Mark Linnett, Jason Leonard and Victor Ubogu (who had not yet converted to tight-head), and only Jeff Probyn as a tight head. Since I was involved in the midweek team I was always playing with an unbalanced front row, with someone out of position.

My attitude was probably a little confrontational. I brought up the problem of the unbalanced front row with Will; he told me I had to stop complaining and get on with it. In selection meetings I expressed disagreement with certain things, but only, I felt, in a constructive way for the benefit of the tour. I said my piece as I had always done and continue to do. I think that, perhaps subconsciously and perhaps not, Cooke and Carling may have realized that I was more trouble than I was worth, that I made their lives difficult for them and for smooth running between the two of them.

They basically formed an inner circle of two which kept together for much of that tour, and the next four years till Cooke departed. From that tour onwards, my leadership of the England pack was alternately taken away then returned, Dean Richards and Peter Winterbottom, at different times, taking over, and I never quite became the figure of influence in the England camp which all my publicity often seems to suggest. Cooke still consulted me occasionally on specific areas, especially my views on props. But I suppose we were always slightly ambivalent towards each other, and looking back it was a little disappointing. I would like to sit down with Geoff now and look back. I never found out if he liked me or not. He once said in the press that Dean Richards was one of his favourite players (even though he dropped him for the later stages of the 1991 World Cup). Not too remarkable a statement, you might suppose, except that it was the first and last time I ever heard him say anything in the press about a player.

However, the epitaph on Cooke's career as England manager must be that he took a team and a sport which was the laughing stock of everyone around Britain and the world, and helped to make it the team sport of the era where people expected England to win. He was a good manager, and brave to resist the influence of those who wanted him to be the

RFU spy, people who had appointed him but who were then dismayed that they could not control him. They could never quite get their knives back into him because he had such good results, and was therefore protected by public opinion. When he resigned in 1994, just before the England tour to South Africa, he said he needed a change and a break. I am far more inclined to believe it was because he survived a vote of confidence on the RFU, the body for whom he had done so much, only narrowly, perhaps only by one vote. He delivered two Grand Slams and a World Cup final, and understandably could take the backbiting no longer, could not abide the treachery. I am sure he was tired, because he had put in all that work with the only reward a few deals here and there, amounting to not very much.

But he was part of a great experience. Maybe one day we will sit down together. Good luck to Geoff Cooke, whoever he is!

When Cooke started, England were mentally in a mess, a tribute to the years of shocking selection, lack of confidence and failure. Our first match in the 1988 Five Nations was in France, which was in a way a godsend. It was a match we were not expected to win, a far better proposition that a home match when the pressure of expectation would probably have killed us.

We actually dominated most of the match in Paris, but when Mike Harrison, towards the end, tried to pick up a ball he should have fallen on, Laurent Rodriguez of France hacked it on and scored and we lost 7–6. On the way off, television picked me up angrily kicking over the trainer's bucket. We failed to take our chances, notably when Kevin Simms failed to attack the line with a try there for the taking. Les Cusworth, in the team after a long media campaign led by John Reason of the *Sunday Telegraph*, missed with three dropped goals, and also missed a crucial tackle. Les was a great player and entertainer, but definitely, he was not able to exist at international level. The Reason campaign soon petered out after that.

But it was encouraging and it was one of my best performances for England. We won most of the line-outs and I took three balls against the head in the scrum. Daniel Dubroca, the French hooker, was not amused. At one stage we tried to wheel them into touch near their own line but we didn't wheel it properly. They drove straight through us, the second rows went under us, and we in the front row went over backwards. I could see Dubroca's boot coming a mile away. He kicked me on the head and I had eight stitches later. At the time, not wanting him to know he had hurt me, I carried on playing and had some attention later, hoping he would think it was for another injury!

But it was hardly the start of anything massive. We scraped past Scotland by 9–6. It was a terrible game, with full-scale killing of the ball. We had to win to establish some credibility, but we were deservedly slagged off for being negative. Derrick Grant, the Scottish coach, was so angry that he came into our dressing room later. 'What sort of game was that?' he complained. 'You killed the game.' That was difficult to take from a Scot, but there was the realization that our new era was in trouble if we did not win. We lost down in Cardiff yet again, however, and only saved the season with an exciting, slightly bizarre win over Ireland when Chris Oti scored four tries. It showed that we could play some rugby when we relaxed.

However, the pressure and tension quickly returned. We made a disastrous two-Test tour of Australia. The captaincy was a shambles. In Oti's match, the joy at a major win had been severely tempered by an injury to the then captain, Nigel Melville, who suffered a horrendous leg injury. John Orwin, a lock who was only ever a mediocre force at international level, took over the captaincy during the match. Just because the match ended in a feel-good result, Orwin, with no real qualifications to captain any team, let alone England, was made tour captain. He was so unfit, so unattuned to the task, that he hardly completed a single training session on tour, was short-tempered with any criticism, played badly. But on the last count he was in good company.

The tour also saw the final departure of Alan Davies, who had risen through the ranks and was appointed as a sort of tour coach under the overall technical control of Cooke, and with Dave Robinson, the loud Cumbrian, as assistant coach. The lines of communication were hopelessly tangled. Davies is a strong-willed person and he obviously wished to have full control. Cooke, who to my mind was always better handling the administration, organization and dissemination of information, wanted to keep the coaching reins. On the tour and afterwards, Davies fell out badly with Cooke and Don Rutherford, and afterwards, seeing the paths blocked, quietly dropped out of the national structure, to resurface some time later as coach of Wales.

Orwin became a sad figure. It is so difficult to establish momentum on a tour when everyone realizes that the captain is wrong. On a visit to Expo in Brisbane, he and Jeff Probyn had an altercation at which Orwin even suggested that he wanted Probes sent home. He limped out of yet another training session before the Test against Fiji on the way home, and we played better for him missing the Test itself. Looking back, we had felt that we were making some progress from the years of humiliation but the results provided precious little evidence of it.

The team spirit was also lacking. We played New South Wales and it was another poor performance. At the inquest after, Rory Underwood stood up and complained that all he had to do all day was to chase high balls. I said afterwards to Andy Robinson, who like me had given everything he had in a difficult match: 'I can't believe people are allowed to say these things. We get our heads kicked in down on the floor, we get tramped on trying to win the ball. Why don't we tell Rory to come and get the ball, instead of standing out on his wing all day complaining?'

At least the immediate post-match period was lively. One of the New South Wales props was a character with a reputation as a hard man, called Peter Kay. In the press prior to the match, he had been on about how hard he was. When it came to it, he wasn't good enough and the scrum kept on dropping on his side. We were so tired of that that Gareth Chilcott and I formulated a plan. If he dropped it again, we would keep on walking and if he was hanging round on the floor then hard luck. He did, we did and he was, hard luck.

When the final whistle blew, Chilcott extended his hand in common courtesy and practice. Kay attacked him, and to subdue him Cooch had to throw him over and jump on him. A very attractive sight for all the hordes who had come on. We lost both Test matches, in Brisbane and Sydney, and we played badly. Australia were no world-beaters. They did not have to be.

The post-shambles history of English rugby really began in earnest before a relatively sparse crowd at Twickenham later that same year, 1988, when a rather humble-looking and, by today's standards, under-prepared London Division team came out to play Australia, who were making a reciprocal tour. The coach of the London team was Dick Best, the former Harlequins flanker, who had never aspired to the very top class but who had already impressed people with what they saw as his forceful and knowledgeable coaching style. These were the years before Best joined the England set-up and before he had to compromise his attacking philosophy for the wet-blanket demands of international rugby.

London went out and attacked the Australians from all parts of the field, led by some brilliant running from Andrew Harriman on the right wing. London won, and their performance won many column inches because it was a flash of colour in a dull landscape. That victory started something of a forest fire. The Australians were attacked and beaten by both the South-West and the North; I played against them for the Midlands, and if that was the only divisional match they won then at least I had the excuse that by this stage they had flown over the outstanding Michael Lynagh to reinforce the struggling team. But Best and London had kick-started something, you could almost feel long-lost confidence oozing back. Englishmen playing with a swagger? It was unheard of.

Geoff Cooke was keen to keep that confidence surging and also to establish some continuity in the England team, whereas before, players and captains were shunted in and out like unwanted railway carriages. At a meeting during preparations for the Test match against Australia at Twickenham he dropped what amounted to a full-scale bombshell, both to the England team and to the public at large and the media. He said that Will Carling would be his captain, not just for the forthcoming match or even the season, but until the end of the 1991 World Cup.

I was staggered. Deep down, I probably felt at the time that it should have been me. Carling had won eight caps, had made only part of the tour of Australia because of exams. He was one of the youngest players in the team. It took me a long time to see the point of Cooke's choice; perhaps in some ways I was never 100 per cent convinced. But under Carling, whether or not he was largely responsible, and whose reign was to last through two World Cups, England at last began to achieve the results that everyone, players and followers, had been crying out for for so long, crying out in a wilderness of spectacular under-achievement.

Of course, not even Will would claim that the subsequent triumphs were all down to him, because England could have achieved the same results if any one of four or five of the other senior players had been leading the side. I do not believe that captains can win Grand Slams that would otherwise not have been won. I do not believe that they can make that sort of difference on the field. They can make a slight difference, they can galvanize individuals, they can make occasional blunders or inspired decisions. But sometimes, an atmosphere creeps into a game that you cannot change, never mind if you shout until you are blue in the face.

Will Carling, like all other Test captains, has taken far too much stick when England lost and been given far too much praise when they won. Off the field, captains can have a massive impact. The RFU mutter to themselves about alleged self-interest on the part of Will, how much money he makes from his association with the game. This is a culpable blindness. They should have always celebrated what Carling has given to them. They are so lucky to have someone who has managed to command such vast media attention without rancour and, until the altercation with the committee arising from his remark that they were 'fifty-seven old farts', without sensationalism. He has been scandal free in an era when leading sportsmen in other sports have been exposed in various scandals involving drugs, violence, plain greed and corruption. His agent, Jon Holmes, has done an extremely good job with his image.

Many people ask me if I have regrets that I never captained England. Of course I do. But in the cold light of day, while I believe that our results would have been the same under a Moore regime, I cannot believe I would have carried it all off with the image and the patience of Will. The RFU, as they well know, would have got all sorts of baggage from me. I would have said all the things that Will, diplomatically, has left unsaid. I have never bothered with the language of diplomacy, could never have stood for the things the RFU have inflicted on the players without going public in a big way.

I would certainly have been in favour of a players' strike when some of the main battles were raging, even of getting changed and sitting in the dressing room until some of the more cowardly and obstructive RFU slights on the players were thrashed out. Not even outstanding results would have saved me, if it had been me, and not Will, who was invested with the leadership all those matches ago. At least I have been spared an appearance in the Quorn advertisement.

The Test at Twickenham, back in 1988, under this captain who was clearly still trying to find his feet, was thrillingly infectious. A large policeman called Paul Ackford played and won his first cap, and made a massive difference from the Orwin era. Ackford had always impressed me. He always had good hands, always won loads of line-out balls; he really put himself around in that first match, and was still putting himself around when he retired, perhaps prematurely, in 1991. We won 28–19, beating an Australia team which went on to hammer Scotland and which was to become a truly great side. Unlike the Oti match, which was a one-off, this was a massive encouraging sign of better days.

We could only draw, 12–12, with Scotland, a traditional match at the time because we missed all our kicks and John Jeffrey, the Scottish flanker, was offside for most of the match. Nothing new there. It was a messy game. But we won in Dublin where the pack rolled over for two tries. After one of the drives, Dewi Morris and I fell over the line together with the ball. I had never scored a try for England. I outmanoeuvred Dewi with complete ease afterwards. When the match ended, I made for the nearest TV camera, and loudly claimed the try as quickly as I could. I announced the clarification that I had indeed scored to every passing press-man. Dewi's campaign to claim it never got off the ground. He claimed he was being magnanimous in conceding the try to me. In fact, he was bullied out of it. But as the forwards had done all the hard work, I didn't feel guilty. It was 16–3 at the end.

When France came to Twickenham a fortnight later, we had not beaten them for seven years. But they were not to meet the usual fallible, nervy England. By now, the likes of Dooley and Ackford, Probyn and Richards and Robinson, were the nucleus of a pack which did not cave in. To me, that day against France, when we won 11–0, was another of the little watersheds. We stuffed them up front, we shut them out, we never gave Blanco and their backs a chance. We scored a forwards' try when a steaming run from Dean Richards put Andy Robinson over.

In the euphoria of that victory, however, there is not one single Englishman alive who would have dreamed what would happen in the immediate aftermath of the fixture – that, in fact, we would reel off seven successive resounding victories against France, that they only ended the run in the World

Cup play-off match in Pretoria in 1995, have still not ended the run in Paris or Twickenham, and that it has never mattered to us whether we were playing at Twickenham or their lair, the Parc des Princes. We have beaten them everywhere and that is something of which I am extremely proud. This success has also given me *carte blanche* to wind up the French at every opportunity before every match.

The extra edge of conviction, however, was still absent as we approached the last 1989 Five Nations game. We may have ended the French bogey but the Welsh wall still loomed. We had not won there since 1953 and we did not win in 1989. Robert Jones, well served by Bob Norster in the line-out, pinned us down with some superb kicking, we took some wrong options. Mike Hall was awarded a try which seemed doubtful and Wales just got better and better, with Jones ruling. At the time it was very hard to take, because it was so long since England had won the Championship.

Yet later that season we thrashed Romania on a boiling hot day in Bucharest, when Jeremy Guscott played brilliantly in his first international. Looking back, despite the heat we played as if fit and athletic and confident. People said that Romania were poor but it was roughly the same Romania team which had beaten Wales in Cardiff earlier in the season. Then came the 1989 Lions tour, when we won the series with a major contingent of Englishmen, especially in the forwards. Mike Teague was voted man of the series and Richards, Ackford, Dooley and myself played a highly significant part in the three-match series. That gave a terrific fillip to the conscious and the unconscious, it was all part of the surging confidence, the growing air of authority in English rugby.

By this time, the new era that Steve Brain had disliked so much was in full operation. Proper and rigorous fitness testing had come in, we had a camp around the New Year in Lanzarote, everything was becoming more and more high-tech, the media were following the squad ever more avidly. To do extra work on the training field was no longer a joke. It did not mean you were ridiculed, it meant that you were admired for your professionalism.

We were almost runaway favourites to win the Five Nations in 1990, even though we had to go to Paris and Murrayfield. And it turned into a remarkable season, in some ways the defining season for the next five years of English rugby, because we played so well in the first three games that we convinced everyone in Britain, it seemed, that we would finally win something, one of the mythical but crucial trophies, the Triple Crown or the Grand Slam.

We beat Ireland by tying them down in a dull first half, then we broke out in the second with some superb rugby. Guscott showed that he had an extra gear, a searing burst of pace, and that he could reproduce his skills in the international arena. We proved to a home audience that we could play the kind of rugby we had produced in Romania.

Then came the trip to Paris, a massive match and ordeal in any season, but this time with the extra bite that we knew we could win. Paris was as intimidating as ever, and the recipe was also the same. The plan to shut down France is almost the same as the plan to shut down New Zealand. You have to hit them hard and early on their side of the gain line. And the row from the crowd was as hostile as ever. Even the weather was fiery. The wind seemed to blow from four different directions at once; it had demolished some tennis courts on an outdoor complex next to the Parc in the morning, and it blew a gale even in the bowl of the stadium itself. But we coped brilliantly with whatever the elements or the French could throw at us.

Simon Hodgkinson, the full-back whose contribution to

England in that era has always been underrated, kicked us 9–0 ahead with three penalties, which in the impossible conditions was a remarkable performance. We scored a try on half-time when Rob Andrew chipped for Rory Underwood, and Guscott and Carling both scored in the second half as, basically, we took France apart. There was the sweet sound of the Parisian crowd turning on their own team, giving them stick. There was this wonderful atmosphere of elation during and after the match. After a gap of perhaps twenty years, there was a genuine relish and anticipation about being an English player.

People said that the victory over France was one of the best English performances in history, and we managed then to do what so few England teams have ever done – maintain the standard and the concentration for the next match. We thrashed Wales at Twickenham. We found it so comfortable in the tight that Paul Rendall and myself managed to get around the field. Unfortunately I had a bang on the head courtesy of Mike Griffiths and was in something of a daze for parts of the match. Andrew was particularly upset to find me wandering around at fly-half at one stage.

There was a massive confidence boost in a first-half scrum, where we dipped, won the ball against the head and drove for the pushover. We went on and on, and since we were heading for the eleventh row of the stand I assumed that, behind us, the back row had scored a comfortable try. Unfortunately, Teague had jumped the gun, as many No. 8s do. He had made his pick-up and lunge for the line too early and had knocked on. That was one of very few disappointments. Again, we played fluid and concerted rugby; again, Hodgkinson kicked his goals.

While this run was taking place, Scotland were staggering through the season. They had a scruffy win in Ireland, they beat Wales and France but without half the style we had shown. But they came to Murrayfield for what was a Grand Slam shoot-out, and the match was steadily hyped so that it became probably the biggest Five Nations match ever played to that date. The one drawback for England was that we had a month between the Welsh victory and the Grand Slam match and, considering we had built up such a head of steam, that did us no good at all. But we had obviously been the better team throughout the season, and Cooke and Roger Uttley, still the coach, clearly believed that the biggest danger to our aspirations of winning a Grand Slam at last was overconfidence. Scotland were bystanders in most of the build-up, in which England were eulogized in the media.

But the Scots used this as a powerful motivating factor. And they also seized, in the team, the country and the media, on the Scottish nationalism and also the rampant anti-Thatcherism that was rolling around the whole country. It was a time when the Tories were securely in power but had little support in Scotland – and the small-nation mentality was working hard on the dislike and the jealousy. It did seem strange to me since Scottish rugby is so upper-middle class and all the garbage about Thatcher and jobs and Scottish nationalism probably meant little to them. They simply used it all as a way to hate the English rugby team and to become working-class Scottish nationalists for eighty minutes on Saturday. But whatever the reason, the anti-Englishness was rampaging around Edinburgh from the time we arrived to the time we departed.

And to all intents, in rugby at least, it is still rampaging around Scotland to this day. Over that weekend and on many weekends since, my popularity in Scotland seems to have sunk without trace, a situation over which I have lost not one second of sleep.

Were England overconfident and seduced by their own publicity in 1990? Probably so. We appreciated the dangers and Carling and I worked hard in the days before the game to dampen down the euphoria and to hammer home to the boys the fact that Scotland would come at us as if the countries were at war. But perhaps, ultimately, we believed that if we played as well as we could, we would win. That is a bad state of mind because the edge given by fear of failure is a vital part of any sporting make-up. Another factor that did not help at all was that on the Friday before the match we had the best training session I have ever been involved in with England. It was as smooth as silk, not one single ball was dropped, it zipped along at huge pace. Bill McLaren said to me afterwards: 'That was very impressive.' We also seemed to lose the plot a little in the mental state. On Friday afternoon and even on Saturday morning, people were signing things, people from outside the team were even heard discussing where the champagne should be delivered. If it was a sea change that the England rugby team were suddenly in a situation where everything was going too well, then it did not bode well for the Saturday. I believe that you have to have doubts.

We lost 13–7, and it was the worst I have ever felt after a rugby match. The affair started with a much-vaunted Scotland gesture when the team apparently showed their intent by walking on to the field instead of galloping. People made much of this gesture and the blow to our morale, not realizing that it had no effect whatsoever on anything. For all we cared, the Scots could have come on in taxis.

We did seem to settle with a superb try in the first half, scored by Guscott after a back movement. But they scored a try, replayed in Scotland daily for the past five years, when Gavin Hastings kicked ahead and Tony Stanger followed up to score. After that, we were always trying in vain to catch up and the Scottish commitment and noise reached a crescendo.

The match was a watershed in so many ways. It all meant that, for all our improvement and blistering form in the season to date, we had still won nothing. It also altered my relationship with Will Carling. At the time, I felt that I had the confidence of the forwards as the pack leader, and we also felt that we were good enough in the scrums to do some damage, perhaps even to push the Scots over if we were given a scrum close to their line. At one stage of the match, when Dave Bishop, the referee, gave us a penalty, I said 'We'll have a scrum' before Will could come up and make his decision. As we went down for the scrum I told myself that I should have waited for Will, but we had discussed going for the scrum in that situation before the match.

This all set in motion a chain of events. After the match, the story broke that I had been taking all the decisions on the field, that Will had been unable to get a look in, that we had run kickable penalties because of a breakdown in communications between us. In fact, after that first scrum I did not call any other moves or make any other major decisions, far less overrule him as some people suggested. Also, we were given no penalty try when Scotland dropped retreating scrums; all the scores we gave away were what you might call self-inflicted; silly mistakes and infringements. The Stanger try came about when Mike Teague, trying to launch a back-row move from a scrum on halfway, knocked the ball on. It was in the opening stages of the second half and we should have been looking to kick downwind and make 40 yards; instead we gave up the ball and a try from the next scrum.

After that match, Will felt compelled to take a more forceful position out on the field and I realized that you cannot have two people calling the shots. I also feel that the affair rankled with Will, and that it was the root of the fact that on the Argentinian tour later in the year the pack leadership was taken from me with what amounted to a pincer movement between Geoff Cooke and Carling. They may have thought I had reached above my station.

I felt that at Murrayfield we still played a good deal of good rugby, even though their back row of Calder, White and Jeffrey disrupted us. But at the end we were devastated, totally devastated. It was very difficult for me to take. It was impossible for Roger Uttley, who had been keenly looking for revenge after the slights he had suffered at the hands of the Scots in the previous year's Lions tour. We had played easily the best rugby over the season, Scotland had won a Grand Slam with turgid rugby, but they had won a Grand Slam.

On the Sunday, I had to go to a function full of celebrating Scots. I had promised Chris Gray, the Scotland lock who played for Nottingham, that I would attend a lunch at Myreside. There were 200 of them present, all cock-a-hoop. I even had to make a short speech congratulating the Scots. All I could do was to take it on the chin.

So, despite our revival we had still won nothing. We had tried to win a Grand Slam by playing expansive and exciting rugby. After the horrors of Murrayfield 1990, we determined that we would have to try to win the next Grand Slam by whatever means it took, and if everyone called us boring then it was tough. They could go to hell. We were not going to go through that type of experience again, an experience which was scarring for us all. If you have nothing to show for a revival bar badly bruised hearts and minds, then there is effectively no revival anyway.

6

VICTORY IN EUROPE, KNIFE IN BACK

The twin Grand Slams, the 1991 World Cup, and Twickenham's betrayal

There's always something fishy about the French!

Noel Coward

THE SPORTING GRIEF OF THE GRAND SLAM THAT NEVER HAPPENED did not dissipate for long months. Looking back, I cannot fathom why I did not withdraw from the tour of Argentina that summer. I had been playing almost continuously for four years, I had gone through a Lions tour, my body had practically come to the end, and was complaining loudly. As I have said, not only was the selection for the tour extremely poor, with three loose heads to unbalance the front row, not only did I find Carling and Cooke unsympathetic, but the

Bath time for baby Brian.

Doing duty as page-boy at the wedding of Auntie Lyn and Uncle Alan. Front row, from left: Michael, Katherine, myself. Middle row, from left: Rosalind, Ai-Lien, Wendy. And Gran at the back.

Wild celebrations after Illingworth Moor Boys Brigade storm to the soccer five-a-side Cup.

On the track to victory in the 110m hurdles, Crossley & Porter school sports.

Old Crossleyans first XV, skipper Brian Campsall with ball. Sadly, Campsall was later to leap the fence and become an international referee. *John Philburn*

An Old Crossleyans dinner, sharing rugby league's Challenge Cup with Chris Anderson, Halifax RLFC player-coach, after their win in 1987. Wigan have won it ever since.

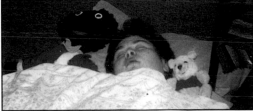

The Curry-Eating Stakes reach the final furlong with Dylan Davies, the eventual winner, on the right.

Peaceful scenes as the golliwog, the teddy bear and myself sleep it off after my twentieth-birthday celebrations.

Mum and Dad.

A picture exclusive. The Calcutta Cup is already
taking on a bent and battered air in the charge of
Dean Richards, assisted by Raymond Horsfall of
the Old Crossleyans, and John Jeffrey of Scotland.
It later became flat enough to be called a plate,
and both players were suspended.

New cap. Old enemy. Gary Pearce, myself and
Paul Rendall prepare to engage Colin Deans and
the Scots during my first appearance for
England, 1987. *Colorsport*

That most dangerous unit, the intelligent front row, prepares to do battle for Notts, Lincs and Derbys. One newspaper column calculated that John Ward, myself and Mick Grindle had thirty O levels, eleven A levels and three degrees between us. *Times Newspapers*

With Dean Richards on the England tour of Australia, 1988. The hotels were a sight better than the results.

In full lawyers' regalia outside Nottingham Crown Court. *Mike Hewitt*

Being crowned a well-deserved winner of the Beauty Contest, post-tournament dinner, Hong Kong Sevens, 1990. Other contenders come to terms with their disappointment.
Allsport/Russell Cheyne

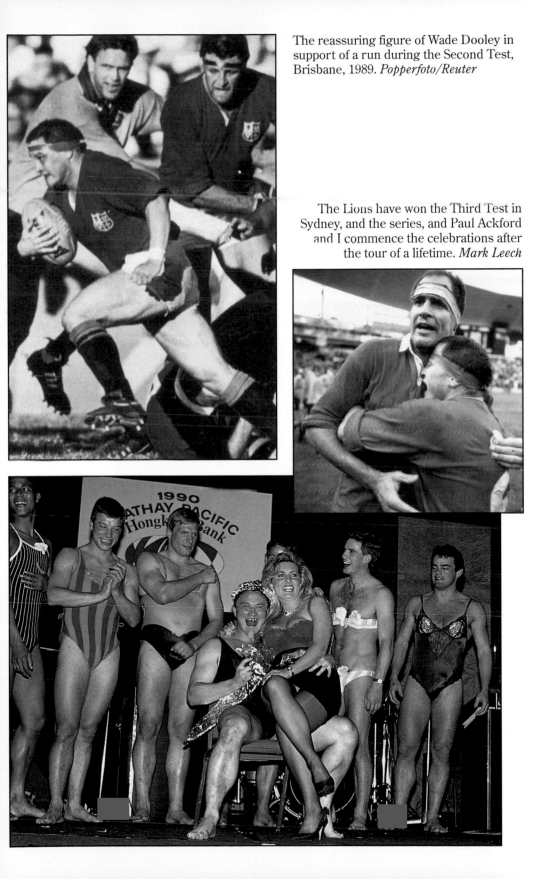

The reassuring figure of Wade Dooley in support of a run during the Second Test, Brisbane, 1989. *Popperfoto/Reuter*

The Lions have won the Third Test in Sydney, and the series, and Paul Ackford and I commence the celebrations after the tour of a lifetime. *Mark Leech*

I commiserate with Andy Allen of Wales after a try by Will Carling puts us ahead at Twickenham in 1990. The shot was to become an advertisement for Cellnet.
Colorsport

Herbie Hancock, the Nottingham scrum-half, initiates a tap penalty move with myself, Lee Johnson and Glyn Mosses preparing to deceive.
Colorsport

A blow for the glamorous backs as a mere hooker carries off the 1990 Whitbread-Rugby World Player of the Year
Colorsport

process which surreptitiously began at Murrayfield, when I was probably seen as another and unwanted source of authority on the field, clearly got their backs ups. The whole mini-era marked the end of my prospects as a contender for Cooke's cabinet. During the tour, they told me that they were taking the pack leadership away from me and giving it to Peter Winterbottom, telling me that they wanted me to concentrate on my game. I was not happy at all. Winters stood up at the first forwards' meeting after I had been ejected from office, and told the lads that he still wanted me to be the effective pack leader.

It was also a building tour, which was fine for long-term prospects but some of us were still hungry for something tangible to show for our achievements and, probably, impatient at the problems of those who were making their way. Perhaps I was not in the best mood to become a rugby teacher and welfare counsellor to budding starlets.

Yet Argentina had its compensations. Off the field, it was a great tour. We were still, just, in the age where we had time for richer experiences on tour than merely training, playing and flying on, which is what later tours have become. The food, unless you were a vegetarian, was wonderful; the restaurants bulged with the produce of the Pampas. In one restaurant they brought along, instead of a menu, a huge silver platter with cuts of meat. They were about 2 inches thick and weighed, it seemed, about 2 pounds. They were not exactly presented with the subtlety of a French chef – all that happened was that they cooked the cut to your liking, bunged on a ton of chips and served it up. But the meat was of outstanding quality. They had their own wine but there was also Chilean wine, very good and very cheap. Very nice.

And because of the massive cattle industry, the leather goods were cheap and excellent. The Argentinians had a

119

tremendous sense of style and dress sense, a kind of Latin/Continental combination and if you could afford to buy, then the designer labels peeped out all over the place. The well-heeled in the country were extremely rich and well protected, with their own social settings and circles. Some of the private sporting clubs were luxurious. There were also, of course, poor areas, huge and depressing estates and ramshackle squatter camps, and even if the extremes were not as marked as in, say, Brazil, then they were still marked. Even some of the elegance was a little faded.

The middle-class young had a very Continental view of socializing. They would not think of going out before 10; they might then meet their friends for dinner, hit the night clubs at around one or two in the morning. This played havoc with our socializing body clocks. The matches on that tour would finish at around 4.30, we would begin celebrations at around 5.30, would be feeling the first signs of dizziness about 10.00, and by the time Argentina was coming alive we would all be completely gone. We did our best to keep up.

It is not cool, however, to drink vast amounts in Argentina. (And therefore we were some of the least cool visitors the country had seen.) One evening, we were taken by bus to a club in Buenos Aires called New York New York. We had been, as Mike Teague used to say, 'on it large'. When we arrived at the club, a line of elegant and pristine Argentinians were waiting to enter. We piled off the bus; John Buckton, our centre, was first off, staggered towards them, fell over in the gutter and was sick. A great day for reputation and diplomacy.

At the back of our minds, there did lurk the possibility of some kind of demonstration because we were the first English national team in any sport to visit since the Falklands War. However, we did not encounter much ill-will. Some people said that, although they were in favour of the Malvinas being returned to Argentina, they did not favour armed conflict at the expense of negotiation, and that the military dictatorship tended to railroad everyone towards the idea of war. There was some ill-feeling in the raucous, splendidly hostile crowd at Tucuman, where the locals burned a Union flag. And in one of the games, a pair of scissors were thrown at me. I was quite prepared to believe that this was not a political gesture. It was not anti-Falklands, it was just anti-me.

However, there had to be caution. We all remembered the story of Willie Anderson, who had toured with the Penguins, was caught trying to steal an Argentinian flag from a flagpole, and was stuck under a long house arrest and even in one of the jails for a spell. We had all seen *Midnight Express*.

Buckton was not the only liability. One evening Chris Oti and Victor Ubogu, the two black boys about town, came back to the hotel wildly enthusing about this bar they had found, full of gorgeous women. 'They were really friendly,' said Chris and Victor. 'We have all got to go there tomorrow night.' A squad outing was arranged, and next evening, we all arrived *en bloc*. There were one or two men hanging around and about twenty women, and well before we ordered our first drink and stood around the side of the bar, it was blindingly obvious to everyone in the squad except Chris and Vic that it was a brothel. They were right, the girls were gorgeous. But it was still a brothel.

Mick Skinner, the flanker from Harlequins by way of Blackheath, was gradually establishing himself in the squad at the time. One match day on the tour, Roger Uttley held a session for dirt-trackers. Six of the lads, including Skinner, had been out on the beer the night before, and as a twist in training's tail, Uttley ordered that they run back to the hotel from training, a comfortable distance of around 2 miles. The six set off while the rest of us climbed aboard our bus. After a few minutes' driving, we started passing the runners. Then we passed Skinner. His timing was dreadful because he had managed to hail a taxi and was climbing in at the exact moment that we drove by.

We got back and assembled outside the hotel, with Uttley waiting to count in all those he had counted out at training. Presently a taxi came gliding up, ostensibly with no-one in the back. It inched forward, mysteriously stopped near us, then glided on around the side of the hotel. Skinner was lying on the floor of the cab directing operations. He was able to get out unseen. Then he found he had no money and had to ask Uttley for a sub.

By this time, of course, Wade Dooley was a senior player, vastly popular and respected. And it did him no good whatsoever. He got a level of stick entirely at odds with a figure of his standing. His tragic error was to try to tell a humorous story. He battled through it but it was desperately unfunny. He got the name Boring Bob, the man who could send anyone to sleep. When he boarded the coach in Argentina, there would be a Johnny Carson-like call of 'Heeerrrrre's Bobby!' Then everyone would slump asleep. In the back of the bus was a compartment where the kit was supposed to go. It became the Dooley Booth. John Olver would sit in it like a contestant sitting before the conveyor belt in a mock Generation Game, calling out the objects that he saw before him, all related to Dooley and sleep. 'A pair of comfy slippers, a toothbrush, a duvet.' Normally that sort of thing lasts about two days before we all pick on someone else. This one lasted until the end of Big Wade's career.

The rugby we played on the tour was lacking. We lost three of the first four matches. We lost to Banco Nacion, for whom Hugo Porta, the great fly-half, turned out and kicked 21 points. We also lost to a Buenos Aires selection and, even though we won the First Test by 25–12, we lost the Second Test and had to leave with mixed playing memories and a drawn series. Some of the refereeing was extremely poor, partly because local officials are under such pressure from Argentinian crowds. In Cordoba, John Olver led the team and at one stage, with violence building and the referee taking no action, he threatened to take the team off the field. The match at Tucuman, surely the most hostile place to play in the world, was a real test for the younger players. It was patently obvious in that match that Jason Leonard, new to the squad at loose head, was going to be an outstanding player. He stood his ground. If the tour produced little of merit for English rugby then at least it produced Jason.

My own form was poor. I did make the Test teams above John Olver, but that was chiefly for experience in a tour that was off the rails. I was annoyed because my influence was clearly waning and I was being slowly excluded from the inner circle of two, Cooke and Carling. I probably should have been encouraging young players more, but some of them had extremely poor tours. Matt Poole in the second row was out of his depth; John Liley at full-back once missed a high ball by 6 yards; and neither of the two younger centres they took, Graham Childs and Gavin Thompson, made any impression.

At least the atmosphere in the Test matches appealed. The Velez Sarsfield Stadium in Buenos Aires is a real bear pit. You come up a tunnel into the arena, which has a sunken pitch and the rows of seats banked up high all around. Very intimidating. Few touring teams have enjoyed an easy passage past the Pumas at home.

The action in the First Test was briefly interrupted by a kicking incident, when Dooley was vigorously rucking out a prone body. 'Hey, Wade,' said a pained voice at the bottom of the ruck. 'It's me.' It was Dean Ryan. Then a medium-strength fight started at a scrum when one of their props kicked Jeff Probyn. Brian Kinsey, the referee from Australia, told us that he had seen it and that everyone should calm down. At the next scrum, Probyn kicked his man back. 'I knew you were going to get him back,' said the referee. 'But I didn't think it was going to be that quick.' Three points to Argentina.

We lost Wade in the Second Test and we lost our way. They got five kicks, we scored two tries to nil, but it was a suitably low note on which to end what was for me, in playing terms, a low tour. The Argentinians celebrated as if they had won the World Cup itself.

When Argentina made their reciprocal tour a few months later, I was dropped from the team and John Olver won a cap at hooker. Cooke told me that he felt I was not playing well, that I needed a rest, that I needed to rediscover my appetite. There was also the possibility of a political factor in the decision because I had already clashed with the RFU on several occasions. Perhaps my suspicions were slightly aroused when I first ran into Will Carling after the decision to leave me out had been made known. 'It wasn't political,' he blurted out, perhaps a little too readily. Or perhaps I was a little too suspicious. I could not disagree with Cooke's assessment of my playing form.

We avenged the indignities of our tour by thrashing them 51–0, and during and after the match Paul Ackford discovered that being one of the key and most respected men in the team meant nothing in the team affairs. He was poleaxed by a brilliant punch from behind from Federico Mendez, then still a schoolboy but extraordinarily strong in the front row. Ackford was briefly known as Bambi on Ice, because his legs splayed out like the cartoon character as he staggered around on his way off the field. That evening at the dinner, as he sat groggily, we were walking past his table, throwing in white napkins and shouting: 'Bring him out, bring him out, my boy's had enough.'

That was the end of the levity for the season. Once again we were favourites to win the Grand Slam, and in a team that was now highly experienced, there was an almost fanatical determination not to let it slip again. If ever that determination did wander, all we had to do was raise the ghosts of Murrayfield 1990, and we all got back to the tasks in hand.

The first match was in Cardiff, and if we have dealt comfortably with Wales in general over the past five years, it must be remembered that even a poor Welsh side still constituted a major hurdle in 1991, because we had still not won there for nearly thirty years. However, we had become hard-headed through experience, and we approached the Cardiff Experience in a much more practical manner. We trained at Gloucester, one of my favourite locations. There was even a good crowd for the training. Geoff Cooke had organized the playing of the Welsh National Anthem over the loudspeaker system at Kingsholm, to try to desensitize us to the moment when it rang out around Cardiff Arms Park. It was still playing on the coach as we drove to Cardiff from Gloucester.

Usually, we had stayed for the Welsh match at the St Pierre Golf and Country Club, out near the Severn Bridge. It was a luxurious and peaceful location but it meant that we did not get to Cardiff itself until the morning of the match. It was a huge culture shock, to be so suddenly immersed in the tension and bustle and aggression of Cardiff on match day. Cooke decided we would break tradition and would go down two days before the match and head straight for the

Crest Hotel in the city centre. We would face the experience head on.

It was good thinking. By the time we had been assailed by Welsh supporters saying, 'Why are you bothering, you haven't won here for years?' on the way to buy a paper, we were all in the correct frame of mind. We even walked the 150 yards or so from the hotel to the ground for the match itself. By the time we reached the dressing rooms, the process of desensitization was complete, the bogey had ceased to register, it was just another international rugby match, one in which we had the better team.

In the end, the bastion fell easily. We won 25–6, grinding it out against Wales and scoring just one try, a forward drive led by Mike Teague. Simon Hodgkinson kicked seven penalties. It was not pretty but in the squad there was not a shred of regret on that count. That season we were interested in our results, and only results. The resolve was massive. By the end, Cardiff Arms Park was as quiet as I can ever remember. At least ten minutes from the final whistle we could sense people leaving in droves. I could make the line-out calls from the touchline, and needed to call only once. Usually at Cardiff you have to scream at your scrum-half, who then walks up and down the line trying to scream the signal against the noise. We had control of the ball, we had control of the match, and England had won at Cardiff for the first time since 1963. It exorcized a demon in English rugby culture.

And so it may be strange to say that the prevailing emotion inside me, and others, at the end of the match was anger. Because there was a sub-plot to the whole Cardiff weekend which almost relegated the match, huge though it was, into second place. I had become bitterly frustrated since arriving in the England team over the appalling hidebound attitudes of the RFU, and, more recently, about their obstructive attitude to players earning anything from ancillary activities.

In November 1990, the International Rugby Board had lifted the ban on certain forms of commercial activity. It was a highly significant move if, at the time, a limited move, couched in impossibly imprecise wordage, and it allowed, disastrously, for different interpretations. It did not take Nostradamus to work out that the RFU would interpret every clause in such a way as to deny as many rightful aspirations of the players as humanly possible, and that the Southern Hemisphere unions would see the change to give the players some of their just deserts. The gap in interpretations duly became cavernous.

Whenever we made even the most tentative moves to cash in in a minor way we found obstructions round every corner from the RFU diehards, led by Dudley Wood, the secretary, and some of the (faceless) old guard. Before the Welsh match, we had engaged the services of a company run by Bob Willis, the former England fast bowler, to market us within the limitations imposed by the IRB. We had by then set up our own company, Playervision, along with Will Carling and others. I had done hours and hours of background legal work in setting up the company and, although the whole Playervision controversy is explained in a later chapter, for now suffice to say that I put hundreds of hours into it.

We had been assured by various individuals on the RFU committee that we were now allowed to accept money from certain media sources in return for interviews and other co-operation with the media. Since the BBC made quite substantial demands on us during any international season, Bob Willis approached them near the start of the Five Nations to ask for a sum to be given to Playervision in exchange for the full co-operation of the squad during the forthcoming internationals.

The BBC checked with Dudley Wood at Twickenham, and they were spun an official line which said that we were not allowed to accept any money; and they went back to Willis and turned down our request. The players were livid. We felt that we had been lied to by the RFU. The mood became militant. It was, I suppose, encapsulated in the following philosophy: Fuck the RFU. Fuck the BBC.

We called a meeting at the Crest Hotel in the days before the match. We thrashed out a policy that we would not speak to the BBC. That was widened on the prompting of several people, including Geoff Cooke, to cover the whole media, broadcast or written. That latter move gained substantial support too, because in the period we had all been inundated with calls from the media, even at ridiculous hours. One journalist called me eight times in one day. Cooke also revealed that he had been snowed under with calls. We regarded ourselves as a media-friendly team, we have made ourselves available for all sorts of things. Now, our expectation of some limited reward had been raised, then knocked down by an impossibly narrow interpretation of new by-laws; an interpretation which was nothing less than dogmatic obstruction by frightened men.

So we formulated the policy that after the match we would attend no press conferences, give no interviews. It was a blanket ban. I insisted that we kept a party line and Will went among the troops to emphasize the main points. Some of the younger players may not have realized how enormous the fuss would be. I knew full well that it would blow up into a major storm. I did not give a damn. That was the depth of my anger. And although all the publicity at the time portrayed me as the ringleader, the shop steward, there was so much anger in the team that no-one needed to encourage them.

Since so many journalists these days seem to cover the press conferences and the quotes instead of the match, there were obviously hordes of extremely disturbed and anxious hacks storming around after the game. The squad solidarity had been excellent; the kind of feeling we had generated was one of the reasons why we had won the match. But back at the hotel, I encountered some of the bereft hacks in a lift. 'This will go down very badly,' one said. The lift stopped at one of the floors and a member of the public got out. 'I don't know why you talk to that lot in the first place,' he said to me as he left. I got out a floor above, shrugged at the pressmen. 'There you are,' I said.

Much of the press reaction was completely at odds with public perception and public opinion, as it so often is. Our armed forces were in the Gulf at the time and Ian Robertson, of BBC Radio, told me he had been rung by a soldier who said he felt that the players should talk. Robertson said that if he had put out that particular reaction on the air, it would have been bad for me and for the image of the players. I was forced to point out forcibly to Robertson that if all the troops in the Gulf knew the full story, if I could explain the background to them, they would have agreed completely with our point of view and that they, above all people, would have understood the concept of loyalty to the team. I never detected in the country a groundswell of opinion that was anti-player. The only people who criticized us were the RFU and the media. The rest of the English rugby public were loudly celebrating a big win in Cardiff, in any case.

Perhaps the one regret I had was on behalf of Simon Hodgkinson. His part in the strength of England rugby at the time has always been considerably undervalued for all sorts of reasons. He was very special to that England side. He was no great shakes as an attacking force but he was a superb footballer and a brilliant goalkicker.

His efforts in the hurricane in Paris the previous season had been astonishing, and to kick seven penalties, then a record, at Cardiff was another remarkable feat. Obviously, since he maintained solidarity when scores of pressmen wanted to interview him about the performance, he missed out on some excellent publicity, well-deserved publicity. But if we had not stayed united there would have been scapegoating, and the RFU could have picked off stragglers still keeping the line while others caved in.

In the aftermath, there was even talk that Geoff Cooke would be sacked, since he had clearly lined up on the team side, and he was given a rough ride for his pains. He was given a rap on the knuckles by the RFU, and it is said that people like Jeff Addison, representative from the Midlands, never forgave him, that a vociferous minority sniped at him thereafter – the fact that he was the most successful post-war England manager, of course, never seemed to enter their calculations.

If there was one aspect calculated to stir the pot further it was that the next opposition were Scotland. This was probably the most emotional time of my career in an England jersey because, as well as the focus we were trying to maintain, in order to break our trophy duck, there was the revenge for Murrayfield to deal with – and there was the fact that in all the pressure of the season, the RFU at Twickenham and the England rugby team were now in two different camps, as antagonistic towards each other as the England and Scotland teams.

Among the back-stabbers, it was difficult to work out who the real enemy was as we built up for the Scots. The press line that we were playing boring rugby was only a minor irritant in the mix.

The commercial fuss rumbled on unabated. We had a deal with Timberland to advertise their products and we did a picture which was intended to go into the match programme for the Calcutta Cup. One of the tortuous new by-laws said that players could not benefit from advertisements if they were rugby-related or if the players were wearing England rugby kit. In the Timberland advert we were all wearing Timberland gear. It was an advert unrelated to rugby, it never mentioned rugby. It met every criteria under the new by-laws.

Then the RFU pulled the plug again. They said that as the ad was appearing in a programme, then it was rugby-related. This was a patent nonsense. This was twisting the rules for their own ends, it was putting a slant on the laws which they were never intended to have. It was a disgrace, it was moving the goalposts.

To their credit, the Scottish Rugby Union allowed precisely the same sort of advertisement in their programme for a later match. And scandalously, the RFU printed an advertisement for their sponsors in the programme they had denied to us, and without permission used pictures of the players. They really did want it all ways. It was clear in my mind that the result of the forthcoming match meant less to them than the process of pushing the players closer to the edge.

There was an added pressure for me. At the time, the court case against me for actual bodily harm was looming. It was due to be heard in the middle of the Five Nations, just when the RFU and I were daggers drawn. There is no doubt in my mind that if we had not been able to gain an adjournment, I would have been thrown out of the England squad when the conviction was announced. We won an adjournment on the grounds that we were still deciding on the mode for trial, and it took place in a quieter time when I managed to escape a double punishment. By the time the case was heard we had won the Grand Slam, so I was sheltered from their ire by public opinion too.

In all this time, only one man on the RFU made a serious attempt to leap the chasm. Mike Pearey was then the RFU president. He is one of the few men on the RFU with whom I have established a rapport in the last decade. He was fair, he listened to our case. I asked him why he bothered, considering the criticism he must have had to take from the die-hards, in public and private. We understood that there was even the possibility of a motion of no confidence in him from the committee, for the heinous crime of trying to be fair to both sides.

There was even talk that we would refuse to play, even sit in the dressing room and refuse to take the field. It was idle talk rather than serious planning, but players like Mike Teague and others were of the opinion that, drastic though it was, it was the only way we would get our position across and get the RFU to listen. If it was never a serious suggestion then it was indicative of the mood, because to play for England was an enormous privilege for us all, and we would not have taken that privilege lightly in any way.

In the team meetings, there was heavy concern expressed that we might get side-tracked. Paul Ackford gave a wise contribution. His line was that we had to beat the Scots or it was all over for the team. 'If we don't win we've got nowhere else to go. It will be the end. The team will have failed twice, and we cannot allow that to happen.' Eventually, the twenty-one in the squad pulled together in a powerful way. There are twenty-one players here, and this is it. It was us against the world; and if we lost, then the danger that the RFU would try to get rid of us increased. Scotland had to pay a price for many things.

The focus when we lined up for the anthems was incredible. Not one England player smiled or moved. The Scots were lined up alongside; John Jeffrey was smiling and pointing. You won't be laughing for much longer, mate, I thought as I watched him. It was the only game I have ever gone into with a entirely cynical attitude with obstruction, tripping, deliberate offside all featuring. I did not care what I had to do, I was not going to lose that game.

We won 21–12, and if we would have liked to rub it in a little more we were well worth the win. There was only one try, when a back movement after some forward driving put Nigel Heslop over on the right wing. After the match, Will Carling was effectively in tears. It was an indication of relief, but a reflection more of the pressure he had been under as captain, as the man who had to bear the brunt, as the man in the middle whom the RFU did not lift a finger to help. We were two legs along the road, and with the French game coming last we had a shot at the Triple Crown in Dublin.

And in Dublin we finally won something. The Triple Crown may be a mythical trophy, but it still means a lot to players. Rob Saunders, the captain of Ireland, helped us along beautifully. He said in the press before the game that if Ireland did not concede penalties, then we did not have much left to offer to beat them. It was the perfect goad; England players were discussing his article, pointing out that he had one cap, that he could start shouting the odds when he had achieved something.

It was a tight contest for a long time. It was a wet day and a major battle to subdue the Irish. Indeed, it was still in the balance towards the end. But by this stage in the development of the team we had learned not to flap and panic, but to keep our shape and composure. Eventually Rory Underwood threaded his way through for a superb try when Dean Richards won a ball in the middle of the field. And then Richard Hill worked Mike Teague over for a try right at the end. In the television replays, as Teague scores you can see Hill and Saunders having a pint-sized dust-up in the corner of the screen. Even though Hodgkinson had a rare off day, we won 16–7, for our first Triple Crown since 1980.

And it was typical of that team that in the aftermath we felt no real sense of achievement. We wanted the lot, and we had to beat France at Twickenham to win the lot. That match against France was one of the most hyped internationals there has ever been in Britain. It was also one of the last occasions to take place in front of the old stands. I enjoyed the atmosphere of the ground as it was then, and the atmosphere in the new high-tech monster stadium is not nearly as good.

The policy against the French has never changed in all the years I have played them. You must stop them on the advantage line or they will skin you. You must tackle your man and go through with the hit so that he cannot immediately get up and move in support. And at the time, you had to nail Blanco, the great full-back.

So much for theory. In the early stages, inspired by Blanco and Berbizier, France broke out from behind their own line and scored a brilliant try, one of the best I have seen. It was finished when Saint-André came down the middle and took a cross-kick to score. I managed to tackle Mesnel in the movement, which gave me the chance to annoy everyone later by claiming I had done my bit. But it was one of those tries when you walk back for the conversion, shrug your shoulders and tell yourself that it was pure genius.

However, our forwards soon took control. They had no answer to us in the line-out and Teague, Dean Richards and

Peter Winterbottom were outstanding in the back row. Hill and Rob Andrew controlled the match at half-back, and Hodgy harvested another 14 points. Rory scored a try with a tremendous finishing burst, and even though we conceded three tries to France we even managed to satisfy our critics with the width of our play. We won 21–19.

It was a great match, an atmospheric day. The crowd came on in their thousands at the end, chairing Will and others from the field to acclaim the Grand Slam, so near one year, no mistake the next. The occasion lightened the mood of the season, even though we kept ourselves pretty much to ourselves that night. The feeling of relief was extraordinary, the praise from the press and the country was welcome. As we walked off the field the RFU, in the cause of anti-commercialism which they obviously espoused, flashed up a message on the giant screens: 'Get your England Grand Slam merchandise.' The message 'Congratulations England' flashed up afterwards.

The pulse of rugby was already quickening in anticipation of the second World Cup, which was shared between the four home nations and France and was to take place in our autumn of 1991. It had meant that we had been virtually full-time players for two years and there was no summer respite in 1991 – Geoff Cooke had decided that we needed exposure to the top Southern Hemisphere nations to assess properly where our game was, so we made a seven-match tour of Australia and Fiji, with a Test in each country. We found that while we may have been European Champions, our hegemony did not extend too far outside for the moment. We lost four times, and although we won the Test against Fiji we were heavily beaten by Australia in a burningly fast game at the Sydney Football Stadium. Salutary.

At least there were some compensations, not least the Fijian leg of the tour. Fiji is rugby mad and there was the added bonus that we were installed in a magnificent hotel on the seafront in Nadi. The standard of surroundings and of cuisine was marvellous. I also ensured that my tour quarters were up to the standard to which I had always hoped to become accustomed. Dudley Wood had intended to travel as part of the party but for some reason he could not make the trip and had to change plans. Early in the tour, I saw that his name was still on the register.

'Your name, sir?' they asked at the check-in at reception. 'Dudley Wood,' I said. They gave me the keys to a huge suite, while all the players shared in twin rooms. I presented myself as Dudley Wood at reception desks for the rest of the tour, lived in palatial style and no-one, not the players nor the management nor Dudley Wood, ever found out.

We were in Fiji when the team to play the test against Australia was announced, and as is traditional, those who didn't make it went off to drown their sorrows. I left our hotel to have dinner with Colin Herridge, then secretary of Harlequins, in a nearby hotel where all the media were staying. As I left, the lads were just getting into their stride. When I got back, much later, they were still going strong. I went to bed, but even later, four or five of them decided on an impromptu concert, and commandeered some instruments belonging to a Fijian band (who played superb ethnic songs like 'Y Viva España') who were taking a break. John Olver took the lead role by the microphone and the others prepared to play various instruments.

The hotel manager had seen and heard enough. He went to rouse Geoff Cooke, who had gone to bed hours before, and he complained about the drunken new rock stars. Olver bawled 'Hello Wembley' in his best rock star voice, and then he noticed Cooke striding purposefully across the lawns towards him. 'Fair play to you, Geoff,' shouted Nigel Redman. 'Still up with the boys at this time of night.' He was too far gone to notice the grim expression on Cooke's face, or to notice that the remainder of his troupe, on seeing Cooke's approach, had dived off into the bushes. Cooke issued a family-sized bollocking, one of his best 'go to bed and grow up' speeches.

Earlier, we had a major stroke of luck for the Fijian Test, which was played across the Islands in Suva. On the day before the game the temperature at match time had been around 100 degrees, with high humidity. Yet overnight there was a major storm, it cleared away the humidity, took the hardness out of the playing surface and lowered the temperature to that of a decent English spring day.

Fijian rugby can be extremely hard going – in the match against Fiji B in Lautoka a few days before the Test, those of us not playing had offered up a prayer of thanks when some early hits from the Fijians were reverberating around the stadium. But although we had some initial problems in the Test, we eventually won 28–12 with three tries. There was a collector's item in that Rob Andrew scored his first try for England. Say what you like about Rob, no-one could ever accuse him of being a heavy try-scorer. The same went for Jeff Probyn, who also scored, and Rory Underwood, who was a little more familiar with the sensation, also touched down. We were helped by a good display in the middle of the line-out from Martin Bayfield, the giant winning his first cap because Wade was injured.

But we had not taken Australia by storm in the early part of the tour. We had already lost to New South Wales and to Queensland, and although our second string won a superb victory over Australia Emerging Players at Gosford, it was still a major challenge to take on Australia, especially without Dooley. It must have been a great match for the neutral to watch, but it was a painful experience for an Englishman to play in. We lost 40–15, conceding five tries. Perhaps the only good news was that our backs played some good rugby, with Jeremy Guscott highly effective. But it was a telling experience in the light of the forthcoming World Cup to see Tim Gavin and Willie Ofahengaue play so brilliantly in the Australian back row, to see John Eales dominate the line-out, and to see the Australian backs look so sharp.

Inevitably, the forwards got the blame for the heavy defeat. The implication was that, with our backs on such form, we could have been in the game if only the forwards had won enough ball. At least that would have been a pleasant change, because there had been times when we felt as a pack we had dominated games but then the backs had missed chances that other teams never seemed to miss. Even as recently as the 1995 Grand Slam match against Scotland at Twickenham, we still felt that our backs had passed up three gilt-edged chances of a try. That made me dislike backs in general even more than I did already.

And I felt that the blame in Sydney in 1991 was misplaced. The backs did play with skill and pace, but too often they either went too far and were trapped or they failed to recycle the ball. It was an extremely fast match played on a fast pitch, and the backing up was slightly off the pace until we assimilated the conditions. I felt that the backs tended to take the ball too far, even to die with it by going blindly on when detached from the rest of the team, looking back as if to say 'Where were you?' to the others.

It was also significant in the annals of that England team that Australia scored two tries from attacking scrums. Dean Richards was given stick about his apparent lack of pace and generally blamed by the hierarchy for the concession of the two tries. It was certainly the root cause of the fact that he was eventually dropped from the team for the later stages of the World Cup itself. The whole affair suggested to me that coaches and selectors are as guilty an anyone of simplistic assessments, because the Australian attacks were devastating, and in that situation teams now put an extra defender over to cover the gap. I have never found the stereotypical thinking about Dean to have been borne out in any way. However, he had two black marks against his name as we flew home to complete our preparations for the big one.

It was amazing to think, as the full blast of publicity rose around the 1991 World Cup, that at the inaugural event in 1987 people expressed strong doubts if the concept of a rugby World Cup would catch on. By 1991 the event had become very powerful, commanded vast interest from the media and commercial concerns, and was demanding an even more disproportionate amount of time from the players. The battle with the RFU was, in effect, in abeyance. We were so committed to the campaign, we believed we had a chance of winning the title, and we did not want to let anything get in the way. People were still bitter in the squad, we were still finding the RFU committee appallingly niggardly, but personal pride came through strongly.

I felt we had a reasonable, though perhaps not a glittering chance. Whereas New Zealand were runaway victors in 1987, I felt that there were at least four teams who could win in 1991 and who would be reasonably closely matched. I had a personal goal to take on New Zealand, because England had not met them in a Test since 1985, far, far too long to remain unexposed to the All Black commitment and excellence.

The tournament was also a watershed for the profile of the game. Areas of the media and entertainment industry which had never bothered with the sport became heavily involved. It was also the advent of something approaching the celebrity syndrome for some of the top England players. Now and again before the World Cup we might be recognized in the street. After the World Cup, it was never the same again. People would recognize you all over the place, speak in stage-whispers about you as you went by. It was something to get used to, and at least I have the consolation when taking the tube to work in the mornings that everyone is so miserable on the Underground that they all keep themselves to themselves.

The opening match of the whole thing was our pool game against New Zealand. At the time, it was of critical importance. Whichever team finished second in the pool faced a quarter-final against France in Paris. The tournament was the swansong for Serge Blanco and it was easy to imagine the kind of devil and passion the French would summon up in the quarter-final, to avoid letting down their own people and Blanco, their own rugby god.

Yet after the intensity of the build-up, we almost seemed to freeze at the magnitude of our task against New Zealand. They controlled the match, we never really played our game. They were also such an unknown quantity for us. These days, you see all their players in the Super-10, you see them shorn of the black jersey, and you see them with the aura missing. Then, despite what we tried to tell ourselves, that aura was probably still there.

In the first half especially, we rushed things. Richard Hill sprayed passes around, people shipped on ball they should have held on to, and only towards the end did we remember ourselves and the strengths which had made us champions of Europe. But then it was too late, Michael Jones had scored from a set move from a scrum and we lost 18–12.

We cruised through the other two pool matches, against the USA and Italy, in front of enormous crowds at Twickenham, while elsewhere the tournament was becoming increasingly high-profile and exciting. At least the defeat against New Zealand enabled us to focus. We knew from an early stage that we had to go to Paris, that to come through we would have to ride an incredible storm and give our greatest collective performance since the team had come together.

We did. I explained earlier the intensity of the occasion, the build-up, the glowering, the danger, the feeling of being almost beyond pain. And we began to make our scores. In a move we had practised time and again, Jerry Guscott made a run and set up a try for Rory Underwood. Once we had the lead, our resistance, our defiance, our defence was brilliant. France tried to come back at us, to upset us. Lafond scored a try for France in their best spell but we even had the last word. Will Carling grabbed the ball in heavy traffic in the French in-goal area and dived to score in the closing stages and we won 19–10. There is no point even trying to describe the feeling when we walked off at the end.

It was only later that we learned that Daniel Dubroca, the French coach, had manhandled Dave Bishop, the New Zealand referee, in the tunnel after the match. I thought that Bishop had done the best he could in difficult circumstances, and as he was a Kiwi, at least the French could not raise their normal cry of Anglo-Saxon stitch-up.

We had a break which was not only fiercely welcome but well deserved. The RFU, bless them, paid for a weekend in Jersey with wives and girlfriends. Peter Winterbottom, who had been unusually moved by the French match for such an undemonstrative man, went out of character even further by getting completely plastered in the hotel, telling all and sundry how much he loved them, and revealing loudly his plans to move to South Africa and have five children. It was even better because the whole tottering, gibbering episode was captured on video. Next morning, Winterbottom never surfaced. Perhaps he had revealed more of himself than he really wanted to, and as the strong, silent type decided to keep a low profile. Or more likely by far, he knew precisely the kind of concerted piss-taking which was lying in wait for him whenever he reappeared.

Paris was history, but since we now faced Scotland in the semi-final at Murrayfield, another arena where it was not actually deemed stylish to be English (even if it was infinitely more genteel that the Parc des Princes), then I suppose you could say that there was no shortage of motivation, especially since it was our first visit since the tribulations of 1990.

The relationship between the two countries at rugby was still extremely poor, both at union and player level. The anti-England bandwagon was set rolling all week before the match. I suppose it reached the depths of disgust for us after we had disposed of the Scots. They turned up to watch the final wearing Australia scarves and other regalia. No doubt they thought it was a great joke. We thought they were pathetic. Other people can perform those nasty, narrow nationalistic rituals while if the England team start dealing out the same sort of stick and insults, we are castigated for our superiority complex.

That was one of the reasons I went public and attacked the appalling Scotland approach to the 1995 Grand Slam match at Twickenham. I was not prepared any longer to live by the kind of politically correct rules which only apply to England.

We controlled our semi-final from start to finish in the

forwards. We only won when Rob Andrew broke the deadlock at 6–6 with a late dropped goal for a 9–6 win and Gavin Hastings had missed an easy penalty at 6–6, kicking wide from almost point-blank range. But not at any point did I feel that we would not win; it was never so emotional because it was always in our control. Wade Dooley had a major match, and won some notoriety by elbowing Doddie Weir in the head. He could not exactly claim that he was playing the ball because the ball was 60 metres away.

We moved on to Twickenham and the final. The day after we had disposed of Scotland, we watched on television as Australia despatched New Zealand with something approaching ease, with a try each from David Campese and Tim Horan.

The week of the World Cup final was remarkable. Rugby was on the back page, the front page, on pages and places where it had never been before. It was plastered across the consciousness of the whole nation. The week also featured a debate in the England camp, a debate which I deeply regret not taking a fuller part in, regret which still lingers on strongly. In the tournament so far we had relied on the power of our forwards and on kicking. We had controlled the games so there was hardly any need to expand our game if we were so successful with the style we were using. We were criticized, but so what? We were in the final.

But when Geoff Cooke, Roger Uttley and Will Carling drew up the game plan, they decided to assume that we would not achieve anything like the same measure of control against the highly rated Australia pack, and that we should plan a wider game in case we were shaded for possession. They felt that we could not beat Australia up front. I said that the game needed to be only slightly expanded because we simply had not practised a wide game. The Australians were cunning because they kept hammering on in the media, criticizing us for not running the ball. I had very little support in the small consultative group, who stuck to their plans for a deficit of ball. We went out on to the field with me hoping that we would play a restricted game, and suddenly I found myself in a running free-for-all. It was a bizarre and bewildering experience.

The irony was heavy. Dooley dominated Eales and Australia in the line-out, our scrummaging was tight and low, we won plenty of loose ball. We won a percentage of possession in the forwards which our hierarchy could never bring themselves to believe we would win. Yet we were running ball after ball, getting carried away, and frankly, making very little real headway against a well-organized Australia defence. I could not understand why we were not kicking more. We put one ball above Marty Roebuck, the Australian full-back, and he promptly dropped it. We had found that Campese was weak under the high ball when we toured with the Lions in 1989 and we never box-kicked him all day, and after the initial testing of Roebuck we let him escape.

Then we went back to the running free-for-all. Tony Daly scored a try for Australia from a line-out, and we subsided 12–6 on a day when we really should have become World Champions. Cooke told me later that he felt the forwards should have tucked the ball up their jumpers. He seemed to have changed his tune a fair bit. I also felt that it was up to the half-backs to make the tactical changes: if the scrum-half calls for the ball, we let him have it.

I was not so much devastated afterwards as angry, pissed off. We had played the wrong game. I looked at people like Dooley, Ackford and Teague, who had given it a tremendous shot, and I felt for them. We had won enough ball to win the match, I had failed to keep insisting during the week that our game plan was drifting off course, and we had meandered through a major match losing focus, trying to play a style of game we had never really practised. We had a tactical disaster.

There was a great deal of gushing praise for our gallant failure. Teague was more realistic. 'We lost. We lost,' he kept on repeating. The only good thing about reaching the final is that it gives you the chance to win the whole thing. The sense of occasion and the achievements of battling through to the final were satisfying, but would never outweigh for me the sense that we had blown the opportunity of a lifetime. I was never happy with the gallant loser tag, I mentally tore it up, threw my runners-up medal in the loft when I got home, and I have never seen it again.

To go back to work on the Monday, on a rush-hour tube, was horrendous. It was a shock return to real life. It was like coming off a drug. I felt numb for about three weeks, went out on what amounted to a three-week drinking spree.

There was further celebration of second place later in the year, when we were given the BBC Team of the Year Award. For some grossly insensitive reason the BBC had dragged David Campese over to present the award – the man who had slagged us off throughout the tournament. He can say whatever he likes, and most of it is complete nonsense. But he does take advantage of the loophole in public perception which allows other nationalities to say whatever they like about the England team, only to get incensed when the England team return the verbal pasting.

Even Campese wasn't the worst thing that happened. I found it embarrassing to receive the award. As we walked up, I looked across to where our men's 4 x 400-metre relay team were sitting, winners like Black, Akabusi and Redmond. They were champions. In fact, as a carve-up and a sop they made it a joint award, so the athletes came up for a presentation too.

I could imagine Campo returning home to Australia and telling his mates all about it. Some TV station paid for me to go over and present an award to the Poms, the lot we had beaten. Typical English. I would have to agree with him.

The benefit of the knowledge that we could have won the World Cup was reaped in the next Five Nations season, because we played with tremendous confidence and we won a second Grand Slam. It was crushing. We were hardly in trouble for five minutes of any of the four games. It was our first back-to-back Grand Slam for nearly seventy years.

Paul Ackford had decided to retire and had been replaced by Martin Bayfield. I admired Ackford's expertise at getting out at the top, but in my book he still left too early, with two seasons of dominating play still left in him. Roger Uttley had also gone, to be replaced by the man who had been heir apparent for a long time, Dick Best. I always felt that Best was a good sessions man. There was no massive strategic change between him and Roger Uttley. I never felt that the strengths of either Best or Uttley were in the analytical field, the field where Jack Rowell was to prove so strong.

But Best had a rapport with the players and with Cooke. Compared to the previous Grand Slam, the arrival at full-back of Jon Webb had given us an attacking dimension that Simon Hodgkinson could never quite provide. Apart from that, it was all a question of application and confidence.

We opened against Scotland in Edinburgh, but a Scotland now without their famous and aggravating flankers, Jeffrey and Calder. I was absolutely furious with a Scotland try. We had a put-in near our own line; I had been injured immediately prior to the scrum, and when we got down we were a little uncoordinated and the Scots were ready. They packed down, got the weight on and took us by surprise. They drove us back over our line and White touched down at No. 8. I was still absolutely fuming well into the evening although some-one tried to cheer me up with some other news – we had won the game easily, 25–7.

We scored a try through Rory Underwood after a brilliant diagonal run from Simon Halliday, who was press-ganged into service on the wing that season. Dewi Morris, who had not played a single match in the World Cup campaign but was now back in the team after three years, also scored. We had been in a little bother in the second half, but when Tim Rodber, winning his first cap, had to leave the field he was replaced by Dean Richards, who had spent some of the World Cup out in the cold, but who came on, controlled the ball and the rest of the match, and made something of a nonsense of his non-selection.

We were now good enough to blow poor teams away. We thrashed Ireland by 38–9 at Twickenham, scoring through Webb in the first passages of play, and scoring six tries in all, every one by the backs. It was seen as one of the most complete England performances, even though we could easily have scored more. Jeremy Guscott had a superb match, making you realize again that his pace and skills were something special.

I was able to make a stab at least at emulating him, because, after an outrageous dummy and some inter-passing I put Dewi Morris over for a try down the left. I don't know if Jerry felt threatened by my performance or not.

It set us up perfectly for another outing to the Parc, and whereas the World Cup quarter-final had always threatened to explode but didn't quite, this one always threatened to explode – and did completely. One of the French problems in recent seasons was that, for all their macho image as a nation of hard forwards, we had turned them over in the pack time after time. They always played into our hands as well because they invariably chose a lame donkey lock to ruin their front five – one year it might be Cadieu, one year it might be Mougeot, and in 1992 when they duly chose Mougeot, they did not even put a proper jumper in alongside him. They chucked Cecillon in from the back row.

I also had a few words for the French in the press in the week before the match: that their rugby was dirty because their club rugby was dirty. People said, 'You're only trying to wind them up,' which was undeniably true. But what I said about them was also true.

The French were probably further wound up by the fact that they suddenly appeared to be playing away. I have no idea where they got their tickets or how they managed to do it, but our supporters made an unbelievable noise; you could hear them from all parts of the ground, and in a place like the Parc des Princes that is an absolutely immeasurable boost.

The first scrum set the tone. The push came on, the front rows went up in the air and Gimbert, the tight-head from Bègles, gouged me in the eye. It was quite plain on the video afterwards. I spoke to Steve Hilditch, the referee: 'I know you can't see everything, but can't you do something about this?'

However, we soon established ourselves, and of all our wins in Paris, this was the most clear-cut. We dominated them in the line-out and we scored four tries, from Webb, Underwood, Morris and a penalty try. We were pretty well in control of the whole match, and the French supporters had gone even more quiet.

In the final quarter, when we thought the initial ill-feeling had died down, the match suddenly burned up. The touch judge saw Lascube, the prop, raking back at Bayfield, who was on the floor. Opinions vary as to whether he deserved to go but Hilditch sent him off. That sent the French wild. They lost all reason and all sanity. Philippe Sella, the captain, was off the field and the one man who might have kept them cool was gone.

After Lascube departed the French wanted blood. Jeff Tordo, highly excitable, came up from flanker to hook and Moscato, my opposite number, went to prop against Jeff Probyn. Moscato was a good player, he was big and powerful and had been playing well. But by the time he was forming for his first scrum on the loose-head, he had gone. He was crying tears of rage. Hilditch could see what was about to happen. He spoke to him in French. 'Do not butt in the next scrum,' he said, time and again. Probyn, who was listening to all this, gave it a Probyn smile, which inflamed the situation further. He knew what was coming. When Probyn went down for the scrum, he bent his head to protect himself as Moscato duly came in with the head butt. Moscato had to go. Moscato went.

The rest of the match was a giant free-for-all. I went into a ruck shortly afterwards and met Tordo's fist coming the other way. I was very close to being concussed by the blow and was very disorientated on the field. I remember thinking to myself: 'Fucking hell. That hurt.' For the rest of the match players went around knee-dropping each other. Others could have gone to join Lascube and Moscato.

The RFU committee actually backed us up. John Burgess came over and told me that I had done well. 'With your temperament, you came through well,' he said. The Anglo-Saxon conspiracy theory was raised again the length and breadth of France, small-town mayors threatened to have Hilditch banned from the town boundaries. At the dinner there was not so much a frosty atmosphere between the teams as no atmosphere at all. Some of the French players never turned up and their table was situated way across the floor from ours anyway. It might help relationships between the two countries if we ever actually sat down together, but that night things were simply too far gone. We extended our record against France, and despite all the conspiracy theories we had given them another hiding, they reacted appallingly badly, and they left the referee no option. The mayors should have faced facts.

The Grand Slam finale, a 24–0 win over Wales at Twickenham, did not have the thunderous qualities of the occasion of the win over France which had brought the first Grand Slam a year earlier. Wales came to defend; they were not really good enough to trouble us as we scored through Carling and Skinner and even, towards the end, Dooley, who extended his frame over the line. We tried to cut loose but never quite managed it. It seemed almost flat; or perhaps if you have achieved something once, it never feels quite the same when you achieve it again.

That summer of 1992 was a summer off; there was no tour. It was my first full break and first full summer at home for eleven years. What do you do in the summer when you don't tour, people often asked me. 'I don't know,' I reply. 'I've only ever had one.' That summer, Penny and I were married and the honeymoon we took constituted one of only two holidays together we ever managed to fit in. England had taken over European rugby, rugby had long ago taken over me.

7

FIFTY UP, AND FALLING

The decline and the fallow years of England, 1992–4

If ever a nation can be kicked in the crotch, the last swing of
Jon Callard's boot had that effect at Murrayfield.

Hugh McIlvanney

IN LIFE'S JUGGLING ACT, I FINALLY DROPPED THE BALLS. THE LONGER
my sporting and legal career have progressed, the more
difficult it has been to do justice to both and they impinged
on each other in a big way in and around 1992. I had begun
work on what was at first a smallish case in 1991, a small
project on a point of law. The case mushroomed until it
involved hundreds and hundreds of cases, reached the Court
of Appeal and the House of Lords, and the build-up and
outcome are explained in a later chapter.

Ultimately, it came to a head and a draining torrent of work in 1992 and the judgement was not given until the middle of 1993. So if I was feeling refreshed after my summer away from the game in 1992 then it all quickly caught up with me again. There is no doubt that my form at the time, and especially during the 1993 Five Nations, was my poorest since I came into the England squad; the case dominated weekdays, dominated evenings, and eventually dominated weekends as well.

There were compensations during the season but it was a time of playing decline for the England team. New playing laws had been introduced by the International Rugby Board's laws committee, traditionally one of the least successful bodies in the sport, which took the emphasis away from tight forward play and made the game ostensibly quicker but less attractive to watch and more defensively orientated.

Those law changes affected England more than any other nation – indeed, that was precisely the idea behind them, as the Southern Hemisphere tried to check England's progress. The England team, although it was difficult to assess at the time or to accept, lost some of its hunger, began to struggle against poor opposition as well as against the new laws. And the process in which I had felt increasingly undervalued and underused by the England hierarchy of Cooke and Carling continued.

The compensation did not outweigh the difficulties of the team, but during the season I became the most capped English hooker of all time, and in the next season, 1994, I joined the select 50 Club, those people who have won fifty caps for their country.

The new laws gave possession at scrums to the team which had not taken the ball into indeterminate rucks and mauls, and they changed rugby for the worse. They were inspired by the Southern Hemisphere to stop England playing the way they were, and also, so the new laws' sponsors said, to try to speed up the game and make it more attractive. They had all the wrong results. They meant that you had to give the ball back to a team that was not as good as you, which was good only in a negative way – they were able to kill the ball in the mauls and rucks. Previously, if they were never good enough to win the ball then they never won it, which is just how it should be. Of all the major rugby-playing nations, it was probably England that had most difficulty in coming to terms with the new-style game.

England began the season with a laborious win over Canada at Wembley stadium. I was injured and John Olver wore the hooking jersey. But it is probable that Olver would have played anyway. I was not playing well, Olver was quicker off the blocks for the new season. The match was significant because it was played at Wembley, while Twickenham was being rebuilt. It was significant because we introduced new players, such as Tony Underwood and Ian Hunter on the wings – Rory Underwood was in one of his retirement periods. He came back later.

But the most significant newcomer for me was Victor Ubogu on the tight-head and I watched him closely from the stands. The selectors had deduced that the new laws put a premium on forwards who would run with the ball, and so Victor was introduced to bring his speed and skills to the front row. However, he hardly put in one decent run against Canada. That suggested to me that if a forward had to work so hard in the scrum to shore up his own weakness, then he would have nothing left for other stuff anyway. England beat Canada by 26–13, more through some good finishing by

Jeremy Guscott and Hunter than any running from Victor. Jeff Probyn, easily the best tight-head I had ever played with, was still fit and available but did not, it seemed, fit into the vision of Cooke, Dick Best and Carling as to what was needed in new rugby.

I did have to fight my way back into the England team. South Africa were making their first tour of Europe since the years of isolation had ended. They struggled in France, and while they improved by the time they got to England to play the divisional teams, it was obvious that for all their satisfaction that they were back, they were still playing a style of game which belonged to the Seventies. Perhaps they should have come out and played in flared trousers. It was apparent that, if you could deal with the strength of their forwards, then they could be beaten, and that it would take them two or three years to get back into the swing of Test rugby in the great wide world outside.

I was perhaps a little long in the tooth to have to prove myself again, but I did play for England B against them a week before the South Africa Test as a kind of live trial, and won my place back for Twickenham. It was obviously an emotional occasion because South Africa had not been around for so long. It gave me the chance to complete the set of international jerseys, and it was a great game in which to play. It was a foul day, dark and wet and dripping. But in the end it was a very good and relatively comfortable victory for England.

It was my first Test alongside Victor Ubogu and it would be an exaggeration to say that I enjoyed all of the scrummages with Victor under my right arm. South Africa were still based on forward power and scrummaging and they shunted us around the field almost at will in the first half. Victor did pull it all together a little in the second half, where our scrummaging was much better. So while we were 16–8 down at one stage, we recovered. Tony Underwood scored a try in the first half and South Africa began to crack under pressure in the second, especially under some deadly high kicks from Rob Andrew. Guscott, Carling and Morris also scored tries and we came through 33–16. It was extremely satisfying.

The only outstanding problem I had after the match was with Willie Hills, the South African hooker. I had played against him on successive Saturdays, for the B team and the full England side; and he persisted in smiling at me throughout both games. I was extremely concerned about this sharp practice. I have still not worked out what he was smiling at, but there is not exactly an epidemic of it in international rugby these days. Hills soon lost his place in the Springbok team. That served him right!

After the match, I realized how vulnerable I felt without the reassuring Probyn alongside me. He was always a superb scrummager, an incredible player. Victor had talents but as a scrummager he did not measure up to Jeff, and to be fair to Victor, no-one else did either. There was a concerted effort to put over the views of the senior forwards to Cooke and the powers that be, that we wanted Probyn back. Yet my views were quickly dismissed as those of someone trying to defend his friend, which I found insulting. Will came to me to discuss the situation. I told him my view that, as yet, Victor was not up to the job in the front row at the top level. Will's response was extremely disappointing. He effectively told me that I would just have to work harder. That response made me particularly angry.

For a start, I believed that my views on an experienced front-row player were as relevant, or perhaps even more so, than those of anyone else in the team. On the one hand, Jeff was a mate. On the other, Victor was severely outgunned, so much so that he could not show his excellence as a running forward. Every now and again he lost concentration – he still does, to this day. Probyn concentrated in every scrum. It was not my views, however, but those of Dooley and others which dragged Jeff back into the team for the Five Nations. Big Wade simply waded in. He told the selectors that Probyn had to come back in.

And he did. But it was another indication to me that I was held in something which might even be called suspicion by the hierarchy. I probably did not feel that I had the respect I deserved.

Later that season, I heard second-hand about a serious move that Victor should be converted to hooker. All my career, before that season and since, I have had to contend with the widespread view throughout the game that only giant hookers could possibly be any good. They still whispered that I was too small, long after I had won fifty caps for my country and long after I had been in England teams which had beaten all the other major rugby nations. Still they whisper.

The news about the possible switch came from Jason Leonard, who had overheard a conversation on the way from a training session for the 1993 Five Nations Championship. 'I'm telling you this because you are a mate,' said Jason. 'They're thinking of asking Victor to switch to become a hooker.' Jason had been asked for his view on the possibilities of Victor metamorphosing.

'Who asked you?' I said. 'Will,' said Jason. I felt completely insulted, not trusted and cheesed off by the whole thing. No-one had even mentioned it to me, of course. Perhaps they knew what my reaction would be. It was, and is, blindingly obvious to me that if hookers were to be large then they had to be large hookers, not converted props. Converts will always find hooking life a struggle because, without a long apprenticeship, they will lack the skills of born-and-bred operators. To learn all the skills and tricks of hooking, in the scrummaging and in the line-out throwing and the loose play, is a long haul. I have played against a number of French front rows which contained converted props in the hooking positions, and I and any other opposing hookers would testify that to play against a real hooker like Philippe Dintrans was always far more of a challenge than playing against some former prop who was tough but clueless.

More recently John Elliott, the former assistant team manager, has tried to create an élite squad of players culled from various positions who wanted to try to make the switch; or at least, who could see no prospect of advancing up the England ladder in their normal positions and fancied a shot at another. Elliott's plan, therefore, would give England the large hooker for whom parts of the game are, apparently, craving.

It seems to me a non-starter. Which clubs are going to throw in some experimental hooker, instead of their specialist, to give him experience, with so much kudos and so much money available for clubs successful in the competitions? It is wishful thinking that, for a serious match, any team is going to throw a tyro into the most important ball-winning position. And yet without experience of serious matches, how can the switch be made to work? I suppose that the most successful switch has been that of Gareth Adams, the former Bath flanker who switched to hooker, played in some of the league matches in season 1994-5 and, because Graham Dawe was coming back from a long period of absence injured, also played in the Pilkington Cup Final in May 1995. However, if he is the best conversion then it did not seem to me that he was any great shakes, and ironically, he is certainly no bigger than the rest of us supposed midgets. It is interesting that, until he was sent off in the pool match against Canada, the South African World Cup hooker was James Dalton, who is smaller than me. Perhaps Dawe, Dalton and I should start a Real Hookers club, like they have Real Ale societies.

I also feel that the experiment would never have been mooted, that non-specialists would never have existed, if referees had not abrogated their responsibilities to have the ball put in straight in the scrums. People might feel that leading hookers would like the unspoken, unwritten but universal dispensation for scrum-halves to be able to put the ball in under the feet of their own front row. But the converse is true. Once you allow a crooked feed, you allow the inferior hooker to thrive, to sew up his own ball, and you rule out some of the skills of the hooking position. It does not matter how good you are and how superior you are compared to the other guy, if his scrum-half is allowed to feed it straight to him.

I would be delighted beyond expression if one season referees were ordered to see fair play and a dead-straight feed to every scrum. Then they would see who the real hookers were, then we would see the best strikers, the best men for the job. I don't feel that many of John Elliott's conversion jobs would be seen again.

Jeff Probyn was back for the opening match of the Five Nations season, against France at Twickenham. The scrum-maging improved. It was just the rest of our performance that was dreadful! The 1993 series was easily the worst Five Nations campaign we had been involved with, even including some of the bad old days. If the hunger was not so intense, if the laws were plain silly, then the focus was poor too.

People had at least one eye on the forthcoming Lions tour of New Zealand, to take place at the end of the season. We had by now two Grand Slams, and so the entire psychology of the season was different. But these mental deficiencies can often be detected only with the benefit of hindsight. At the time, we all surmised that we were as 'up' for the season as we had been for the previous seasons.

We were extremely lucky to beat France, squeezing in by 16–15 only after Jean-Baptiste Lafond had seen a drop kick, which might have won the match, cannon back into play from the crossbar. It was a tale of two crossbars, in effect. We had scored our only try of the match in the first half when a penalty attempt from Jon Webb had bounced back off the bar and Ian Hunter, following up well, picked up the bounce and scored. We could hardly claim that we had been working on that one in training. It was freakish. But we defended badly, conceding two tries to Philippe Saint-André, the French left wing, due to sloppy defending under the high ball, especially by Webb at full-back.

Down at Cardiff for the next match, the whole Grand Slam train came hurtling off the tracks. All talk of a three-peat, an unprecedented third Grand Slam, died in depressing circumstances. We had most of the match, had a try disallowed in mysterious circumstances, we did nothing with a fair percentage of possession, we gave Wales a try for nothing, and we lost 10–9. All in all, it must have recalled in the minds of our supporters some of the Cardiffian horrors of our past history.

But the match did mark my forty-third cap, which made me the most-capped England hooker of all time. John Pullin, the previous holder on forty-two, was therefore erased from the record books. The papers made a big deal of it. It was not so much the statistics which appealed to me, but the realization that I was now mentioned in the same breath as players like Pullin and Peter Wheeler, whom I had always held in the highest esteem from the time when I first followed rugby as a schoolboy. It was difficult to believe that the statistics bracketed me in that company.

And suddenly, after focusing my energies and attack on all the hookers in all the teams, I had beaten them all. It was not a case of lifting two fingers, figuratively, to the lot of them, shouting that I was now history's number one. But there was a quiet, sneaking satisfaction that despite all my real or imagined weaknesses, I had played through the most successful period in English rugby history; I had overcome the inconvenient fact that I did not weigh 20 stone, and therefore overcome the prejudices of those who really felt that, to be a Test hooker, that was indeed how much I had to weigh.

The Welsh match was one of the best Dewi Morris has played for England. He made some brilliant runs, and forced his way over the line after one burst. It seemed a perfectly fair try in the eyes of everyone but the referee. The Welsh try was not the greatest moment in the defensive career of Rory Underwood. Wales attacked to the right and, as I closed down on Emyr Lewis, the Welsh flanker, he hoofed the ball hopefully down the field. It was bouncing behind Rory, but since there was no following Welshman even on the horizon, Rory had hours, it seemed, to react, to pick the ball up and kick it or simply shepherd it into touch. But as if almost thunderstruck, he moved with desperate and mystifying slowness. Suddenly, Ieuan Evans was on him, kicked the ball on as Rory belatedly realized the danger, chased it and dived on it. There was no point in remonstrating with Rory afterwards. It had been a totally inexplicable lapse and a try which amazed Wales as much as it amazed us.

We had conclusively the better of the Welsh front row as well, but it was not enough. The Welsh hooker, Nigel Meek, was winning his first cap, so obviously did not wish to give up his first Welsh jersey by swapping it in the traditional manner. After the match, I went into the Welsh dressing room and gave him my jersey anyway, with a show of magnanimity which I probably did not feel.

There was a huge clamour after the Welsh game. We had played badly, we had essentially not existed as an attacking force. But before this one defeat, we had enjoyed a long run of success, then lost one game unluckily, by one point. Suddenly, everyone wanted to replace half the team and began to raise the theory that the England team was a comfort zone in which, because we were mostly assured of our places, we did not actually bother to try too hard. That was rubbish, of course. But it was a fact that we had not developed our game in any way in the season to date.

There were no mass executions after all, but for the next match, against Scotland at Twickenham, Rob Andrew was finally jettisoned. He and Stuart Barnes had been vying for the fly-half position for years, and although Andrew had always won the vote, that actually fuelled the debate rather than killed it, especially since Barnes had always been a key figure in the long and successful march of Bath.

For me, the Andrew–Barnes debate was never an issue. I once discussed the choice with Finlay Calder, a man whom I regard as a close friend. Even after an attack I made on the Scots team after the Grand Slam of 1995, Finlay was on the phone asking me up to Scotland for a visit. Or perhaps it was all a trap. Finlay said as an opponent he always preferred to play against Barnes, because you could never get to Andrew. I feel that Rob leads the line well, he is a fearless tackler, and since in recent years he started working seriously on his goalkicking he has been a major kicking asset too. He has an astute rugby brain and a tremendous attitude. To be critical, it seems to me than he can only play one game at a time. He seems either to kick everything or to run everything, showing less flexibility that he might. But I have always felt assured at having Rob in the side.

Stuart's strength, until his retirement in 1994, was always that he spotted attacking opportunities and then had the speed off the mark to make the best of them. For a man who did not actually look very fast in bodily shape, he would be devastatingly quick down the blinds. His weakness was that he was inconsistent with his restart kicks, and a defence not as solid as that of Andrew. And although Barnes did play a big part in the Bath success he was also playing alongside some outstanding players. With Richard Hill inside and with players like Guscott, Simon Halliday and Tony Swift outside, then you really should look a good player.

Barnes came back in a forest-fire of publicity for the Scotland match. At last we managed to cut loose, and were inspired, to be fair, by a brilliant piece of intuitive play by Barnes, who took a difficult pass from Dewi Morris above his head, shot through the Scots and then set Jeremy Guscott free. To see Guscott's acceleration up the middle of the field was a remarkable experience. It was almost a privilege to see it at ground level, as Guscott burned his way past Scott Hastings and the best of the Scottish defenders, and put Rory Underwood in for the try. Tony Underwood and Guscott also scored and we won 26–12, a result which, temporarily as it turned out, lifted spirits to something like the old levels.

In fact, it could have been so much more embarrassing for the Scots. Sadly, we began to struggle inside the last twenty minutes when we really should have been cleaning up. We gave away silly penalties and fell into the trap of being dragged down into niggles and bickering. With the hard work done, we should have been looking to Barnes to unleash Guscott again.

And even though I was now England's most capped hooker, I found that there were still lessons to learn. In my column for the *Sunday Times* the day after, I made a jocular reference to my relatively poor display of throwing in during the match. I believe my throwing in has always been good. It was always Ackford and Dooley, and latterly Johnson and Bayfield, who got the praise when England had a great day in the line-outs. If we didn't have a great day then it seemed that only then did attention turn to me. However, I could put up with it for the common weal.

All I said in the article was that I had been little below par. 'I couldn't hit a barn door,' I said, in what was supposed to be a light-hearted fashion. I learned never ever to criticize myself in the press again. First, because the press always has enough people who are going to criticize you without the need to add to the barrage yourself. Second, because the criticism you make of yourself never seems to be forgotten. That one comment gave rise to a whole series of articles and references and innuendoes, which haunted me for years and still haunt me to this day. Wayne Shelford was soon suggesting somewhere that I could not throw in any more. Other snipers decided I could no longer throw to the back of the line, as if the extra couple of feet between the middle and back made all the difference. And they did not explain, in any case, the big attraction in throwing the ball to the back where stood a back row of Dean Richards, Mike Teague and Peter Winterbottom, a tremendous unit around the field but hardly the epitome of soaring line-out brilliance. But England have, at one time or another, dominated every other line-out with the same thrower-in!

The new attacking England lasted one match. We went to Dublin and the final pretensions of the team to retain the Five Nations title were comprehensively dismantled in one of the heaviest defeats I suffered in any England jersey. We lost 17–3, Ireland swarmed all over us, and there was hardly a period in the match when we gained control. We were under tremendous pressure throughout and the pre-match odds – we were 1/6 on – were proved rather ridiculous.

It was an odd feeling, a sort of gathering, growing desperation. Whenever Ireland scored, or when they so much as earned a scrum or made a tackle, they generated even more passion from themselves and from the crowd at Lansdowne Road. They scored one try, through Mick Galwey, and Eric Elwood, a new fly-half to most of us, kicked the rest of their points.

France ended the season as champions, and as this was the weekend when the British Lions team to tour New Zealand was to be finalized, there were palpitations throughout the England team that players considered to be certain selections might fall at the final fence, might fall victim to a selection policy based on one match only, and to the tortured political selection which traditionally goes on in Lion circles, where selectors lobby, not for the best players, but for players from their own countries. As it turned out, I and a good crop of England players were still chosen for the tour, although political selections still made an unwelcome appearance, and as I explain later, crippled the tour party.

The only saving grace when we returned from New Zealand and yet another unsuccessful Lions tour was that the English contingent had an early chance of revenge, because in November of the same year we opened a new international season against New Zealand, who were involved in an exciting, controversial and high-profile tour. They had won all their games by the time they reached Twickenham, and on the previous Saturday they had murdered the Scots by 51–15 at Murrayfield. Even against a feeble Scottish team there was no doubting the merit of that win or the threat it posed to us; although, as for the tour as a whole, the All Blacks were simply taking advantage of the British sense of fair play. When British Isles teams go to New Zealand they are always quite ruthlessly stitched up by the match itinerary they are given, which unleashes major provincial teams against them in clusters, especially before Test matches, and which is designed specifically to soften up the visitors and, frankly, to injure as many of them as possible.

The All Blacks' itinerary around England and Scotland was typical of our riposte – they played all kinds of soft non-teams, such as Scottish Development, South of Scotland (a procession to the tune of 84–5) and the Combined Services. The Barbarians match at the end of the tour was also a non-event since so many British and French players were not available for selection due to club commitments.

So it must be said that our tremendous victory over New Zealand on a desparately exciting and hard afternoon at Twickenham must be regarded as one of the great one-off performances of the era. By this time Guscott was absent on a year's sabbatical, struggling with a groin injury, and Phil de Glanville had replaced him. Tim Rodber and Ben Clarke were ranged alongside Dean Richards in the back row, and if it did not constitute the fastest back row ever, then it was certainly one of the most powerful. Martin Johnson had emerged from a successful stint as a tour replacement with the Lions, and Kyran Bracken, a young scrum-half from Bristol, was chosen for his first cap. There were a number of injury worries, we had a fractured preparation period and

165

were underdogs in a big way, especially after the slaughter of Murrayfield. And we won, and deserved to.

It should have been more than the single-score margin too, but we did not take the chances we had created to score tries. It was a particular joy for the England forwards that we beat them up front, where they clearly expected to dominate. Victor Ubogu held on extremely well in the scrums, where I felt we had the better of them. As usual, the All Blacks followed their normal practice of hitting hard in the scrum, then keeping the shove on, which is both disruptive and illegal. It is a punishing form of scrummaging but I thought we coped. Nigel Redman had a tremendous game in the line-out, disrupting their ball time and again, and our tackling in the back row and midfield was superb. But perhaps the best feeling was that we were more physical in the loose than the All Blacks. They resorted to snide behaviour, like their endemic professional fouling when in an offside position, and one particularly ridiculous moment when Jamie Joseph stamped on Bracken yards and yards off the ball.

Our preparations to beat them had even extended to the way we received their Haka. I actually love the Haka and the threat and the challenge it represents. But for generations of New Zealand teams it is far more than a theatrical weapon. It has a genuine use in that it focuses them brilliantly. Surely, if an All Black is not focused properly when he takes the field, he must be focused by the time he has been through the ritual of the Haka. It gives you a kind of spiritual feeling, a focus, that the traditional singing of the national anthem cannot match. And if you cannot respond to the Haka as an opponent, then you should really not be out there.

There are many options for dealing with it but we exercised one of the best that day at Twickenham. We took the field wearing our tracksuit tops and we still wore them when we lined up opposite them to watch the Haka. It meant that, when the All Blacks ended the Haka and ran to line up for the kick-off, they found that we were keeping them waiting. We sauntered to the touchline, removed our tracksuits and handed them over to the replacements, before taking up our places. It dissipated some of the fury of the ritual. The crowd began to sing 'Swing Low, Sweet Chariot' as the dance progressed, and it was round one to England.

It did help that the aura of the All Blacks had long gone, and a few more of their reputations went up in smoke too. Jon Callard kicked four fine penalties, Rob Andrew dropped a goal and all the All Blacks could manage were three penalties from Jeff Wilson. The crowd noise had been incredible all afternoon, and when the final whistle went camera shots captured almost every one of the England team jumping in the air. It was a great moment.

In my newspaper column in the *Sunday Times* next day, while congratulating the England team, I also drew attention to a moment which, for me, had been sour and unnecessary. When we hit for the first scrum, Sean Fitzpatrick, in the hearing of me and others in the England pack, racially abused Victor Ubogu. 'Right, let's see how you like this, you black bastard,' he said. I merely wrote that this was unacceptable, and I have always felt, quite apart from the racist overtones, that it showed a complete lack of respect from one international sportsman to another.

A lot of people seemed to take umbrage that I reported this slur. One article said that it was no worse than an Englishman calling a Welsh player 'a Welsh bastard', when, of course, it was entirely different. The equivalent would have been to call Victor an English bastard. A lot of people, New Zealanders as well as British, especially talking through the media, said that I was in the wrong. As usual with these things, they never addressed the actual issue. Did he say it and was it acceptable? He did, and it wasn't. Fitzpatrick did say it and to date I have received no writ. If he hadn't said it, then my comments would have been highly libellous.

Other people said that my comments were being ungracious in victory. I have no regrets whatsoever. Perhaps the only time I became really angry in the whole incident was when I read an article by David Kirk, the former New Zealand scrum-half and captain, in which he said that I was a player 'at home with the tabloids'. He was referring to the fact that, on the Monday after my newspaper article, all the London tabloids splashed on the story. Kirk did not understand that I had spoken to none of them and that every word was a straight lift from the *Sunday Times*. Even some players from other nations said that what is said on the field should be kept on the field. What should also be kept on the field is respect, and Fitzpatrick's comments showed none. If he was hurt, then he should not have said it.

There was a downside of the victory. I had already been embarrassed once by the BBC *Grandstand* Sports Personality of the Year announcement, when the England team had, unfathomably, won the team of the year prize in 1991 after we came only second in the World Cup. Only a few weeks after the New Zealand victory, and at the end of what had been a decidedly moderate year for the team, we were back at the studio for the 1993 awards. Excruciatingly, we were called up again, simply for the one-off victory. This time, members of the Wigan rugby league team were in the audience. They had won everything in their own sport, every trophy there was to win, and here were England being summoned for the presentation. As I made my way to the front of the room with other team members, I tried to apologize to as many people as I could. Everyone muttered afterwards that it had been a political, not a sporting decision, which it clearly had. At the time, the BBC were engaged in a fierce battle for the next contract to televise British domestic rugby, a huge plank of their whole sport schedule. ITV had come into the frame in a major way. To curry favour with Twickenham, the BBC gave us the award – and they won the television contract. All very nice and neat and embarrassing.

All those of us who were a little cynical about the award had further food for thought in the 1994 Five Nations, because we had another extremely poor season by the standards we had set ourselves, lost at home to Ireland, which took some doing, and redeemed ourselves only at the very end. The team was still, essentially, in a state of flux between styles and personnel, the hunger and application were still too low, some of the old feeling in the squad had dissipated. And as I say, my own form had declined too.

We struggled appallingly at Murrayfield against Scotland. In the first ten minutes of the match we played some superb rugby and essentially cut Scotland to pieces. We created what I felt were three glorious scoring opportunities for the backs. On one occasion we had a five–two overlap, which should be a formality at any level, let alone Test level. However, with Guscott absent there was no-one to straighten the midfield play and we squandered every chance. That allowed Scotland to bounce back off the ropes.

In our period of pressure, Neil Back, Leicester's flanker (who was winning his first cap and playing on the open-side flank, arriving at last after a long campaign boosted by his own comments and those of his supporters) was superb. For those ten minutes, when the ball was being run, when there were breakdowns for him to reach, he was highly effective.

169

After that, when both teams and especially the Scots reverted to high kicking, he was reduced to chasing back and forth without too much effect.

Back is certainly confident enough. He has had some excellent matches for Leicester but his performances for England at A and full level, looking back from the perspective of 1995, have not measured up to the very highest standards, although he can perform some of the tasks extremely well. But if you compare his public persona with someone like Andy Robinson of Bath, you find possibly two opposites. Robinson is outstanding in attack and defence, a great player with a record of solid achievement, but you never hear him talking in the media about how good he is. He simply gets on with the job. Bath may well have lost the league title in 1995 by leaving him out for the crucial match against Leicester at Welford Road. Against Scotland back in 1994, and against Ireland a fortnight later, Back was reduced to craning his neck to follow the kicks flying over his head. Perhaps he has been caught in some of the media hype about his position.

Gradually, at Murrayfield, we lost our way. We were shaky under the high ball. Gregor Townsend, the new Scottish fly-half, came in with a reputation as an exciting player and there were reams of publicity, which admittedly we never believed for one second, that he would create a new-style running game. If he was a running player then we never saw it. He simply did what all Scottish fly-halves always do – kicked the ball high in the air for everyone else to chase.

However, Scotland scored the only try of the match in the first half, through Rob Wainwright, the flanker; and then seconds before the end of normal time, Townsend dropped a goal which put Scotland 14–12 into the lead. It was a tremendous kick but it really brought home to us how appallingly we had frittered away what should have been a comfortable victory.

We had one last attack. We won a ball from the kick-off, drove it frantically into their half, and when the Scots infringed, Jon Callard came to kick for goal from around 45 metres. Even a kick from in front of the posts at that stage and in those circumstances would have been an agonizingly difficult assignment, and there were few people in the team who would have swapped with him. There were a few others who simply could not watch him.

As Callard was going through his preparations, I stood out near the touchline to cover any clearing kick if he missed. The Scots in the crowd near to me had a field day. 'Fuck off back to London, you've lost it.' And so on. Callard completed his preparations, looked up at the posts, trotted slowly up and kicked a beautiful goal, surely one of the coolest efforts in the sporting year. It was a great kick. The final whistle went, I turned towards the crowd and bowed gracefully, shrugged my shoulders and walked off. We had drawn the 'get out of jail free' card.

The season's levity began and ended there and then, because I was anxious about the England team. There were new young players coming into the squad, players like Back, Steve Ojomoh, Callard, Rodber and others. I did not fault them for ability, but wondered aloud if their attitudes were quite as hard as they should have been. I stood up before we played Ireland. 'Look,' I said. 'I don't want to sound like an old git, but I want you to understand how bad you will feel if we lose this game to Ireland, and what will happen to you all in the media.' I did not feel that we were any longer bloody-minded enough, that we had a realistic attitude. Some people had probably achieved goals by winning Grand Slams; the new boys had, for the moment, achieved their goals by winning that first cap. We were falling down as a team with our motivation. I was desperate not to give away what we had worked so hard to establish, determined that England's rugby reputation should not begin slipping backwards.

The process did not stop. We gave an abject performance, losing 13–12 to a keen, if mediocre, Irish side. Once again our finishing hardly existed because we did not score a try, whereas Ireland scored one through Simon Geoghegan. We were hammered by a shocking refereeing decision by Patrick Thomas, of France, in the second half. Rob Andrew went down to kill a loose ball, but before he could get up, Geoghegan dived on him. It should have been a penalty to England because you have to allow players to get up and play the ball, but instead the referee penalized Andrew for holding on to it. Yet Ireland could say that they deserved to win, because they showed more tactical nous.

As I predicted, the press gave us a roasting. People discovered how much defeat hurt, and one or two said privately that they were taken aback by the volume of criticism, especially for our lack of style and tries, for what was, after all, a defeat by only one point. Sometimes you realize that people have to learn their own lessons as they gain experience of international sport. I felt incredibly low after the Ireland game. I was hurt because other people got over it all so quickly. I was hurt because I remembered how it used to be. We were looking at a miserable season, possibly even at a wooden spoon.

Thankfully the spur of playing in France was the perfect cold shower for the slumbering inner men. I made sure that the media's usual war of words warmed us all up nicely; we also made sure that no-one was bothered about the jibes that we were a boring, forward-dominated team who had forgotten how to score tries. To worry about expanding our game, I felt, would have taken us down a side road. The vital thing in Paris was to win, to win in any style that was necessary to get the job done. Full stop.

We won 18–14, dragged our season off the rocks, and in truth, won by more than the score suggested. There was a big effort in the line-out by Steve Ojomoh; Rob Andrew kicked all our points; and once again, we kept the forward edge we had built up over the French. They were surprisingly subdued, but a lot of the credit for that must go to the way we played against them. There were the usual sermons about our style being the death of rugby, from self-appointed guardians of the heritage of the game stationed in their pulpits. But we had already left the church to celebrate our win.

The surprise at the end of the season was that Wales came to Twickenham searching for a Grand Slam. They had played far better than for some years, had beaten France and Scotland in Cardiff and won away in Dublin, which was a not inconsiderable performance. It was also the perfect motivation for us because in the team meetings in the week leading up to that game the message was drummed remorselessly in. We cannot let Wales come to Twickenham and win the Championship and the Grand Slam. I was secretly pleased that Alan Davies, the Welsh coach, had been successful because he is a tremendous bloke and a very fine coach. But that did not extend to any charitable thoughts for Wales, none at all.

The press made a great deal of the fact that, since the Five Nations could now be won on points difference, we would take the title if we beat Wales by a margin of 16 points or more. If we did not do that, then Wales would be champions even if they lost the match. The England team did not give a hoot for those statistics. We prepared as normal, to

173

emphasize our strengths and nullify the strengths of Wales, and as far as I can say, no-one really worried about the points margin at all. It was a one-off match, and a match that we could not envisage losing.

We didn't. We won by 15–8, we scored two tries, one of which was a cracker made by quick ball, a break by Phil de Glanville and a finishing burst by Rory Underwood. Tim Rodber scored in the second half when he moved up to the front of the line-out on the Welsh throw, took the ball two-handed and crashed over. I suppose that anyone paying attention to the points difference may have got excited at that stage, because we were cruising along and really should have scored more tries. But Wales came back at the end with a try by Nigel Walker.

There was a bizarre ending. The Queen had come along to present the Five Nations trophy and she looked a little bemused when the team in red came up after the team in white had won. I hope someone explained to her what was happening. Ieuan Evans, the Welsh captain, took the trophy and looked appropriately sheepish, because he and everyone else knew that it had been our day. It was a fitting way to celebrate the 100th match between the two nations.

And a milestone for me. It was my fiftieth cap. The first time I had ever been to Twickenham in 1978, I had watched as Gareth Edwards had led the Welsh team out to mark his fiftieth. My first thoughts when I was asked if I wanted to lead the team on were that I didn't. Then I changed my mind. Why shouldn't I? Dooley and Winterbottom and everyone else who had reached the half-century got to run on ahead of the team.

I duly raced out first. The 50 Club is extremely select, and the happiness for me in joining it lay in the calibre of players and people already there. I was embarrassed by the number of references to me in the speeches that night, but also had a sense of pride. It was an enjoyable dinner and it also marked the end of the reign of Geoff Cooke, who had announced his decision to step down as England team manager. He said it was because he was tired and jaded. No doubt he was, but as I have explained, the treacherous nature of the RFU committee could not have helped. He was to be succeeded by Jack Rowell, for so long a highly successful coach of Bath but a man I knew only by reputation. I felt that perhaps we needed a change, although Dick Best was to carry on as coach. Perhaps we had begun to mark time under that hierarchy.

At the dinner, after one of the speeches in tribute to my fifty caps, I was told that a standing ovation for me was to be led by Graham Dawe. Obviously I had made some progress somewhere. Either that or Dawesy, my great adversary, had taken too much to drink.

8

OTHERNESS

Joy and victory with the British Lions, 1989

The Lions who toured Australia in 1989 were at times the dirtiest team I have ever seen in international rugby.

Bob Dwyer

STEVE SMITH FOR HOOKER. IT WAS LIKE A MANTRA, AND IT MADE me furious. Months of speculation traditionally precede tours by the British Lions, the last great adventure in rugby touring. In the run-up to the Lions tour to Australia in 1989, every pundit, amateur and professional, every last barstool expert, declared that the Lions Test hooker would quite obviously be Smith, from Ballymena and Ireland. The second choice, an afterthought to make the tour party but only as benched understudy to Smith, seemed to be between Kenny Milne of

Scotland and myself. I received about two-thirds of the popular vote to be this sad, no-hoper second string.

The reasoning was based on the fact that Australia's Test hooker at the time was the enormous Tom Lawton, a giant of over 18 stone, the perfect specimen for all those parading the dogma that you have to be a giant to play effective Test rugby in the forwards. A dogma which forgot Jeff Probyn, of course, but dogmas are like that. And if Australia had a giant, then we had to have a giant to match him, everyone said. Smith, who was over 17 stone, was their man. If I was made Test hooker, they all prattled, then Australia would have a four-stone advantage over the Lions in one position in the scrums.

It annoyed me. It really did annoy me. When the party was announced after the 1989 Five Nations Championship, I was in, with Smith as the other hooker and still wedged solidly into everyone's Test team. Nothing has motivated me throughout my career than another hooker competing for a jersey that I wanted to wear. It has been the same in every team for whom I have ever played.

I laid plans. I can remember feeling a consuming motiva tion. It was a hunt with a quarry, a target. Not Lawton, he could come later. First, I had to hunt Steve Smith. It is so much easier to approach a situation in that way, as the outsider, the hungry man. It is a very simple motivation. Effectively, Smith had the job; the only way he could go was down. That creates an entirely different, and difficult, motivational problem.

The way I could win was to maximize everything I could offer, everything I had on Smith. I worked incredibly hard before the tour. I trained twice a day for two months, in the gym and on the Astroturf at Nottingham University, where the all-weather surface was perfect for sprinting. All the bits I could improve, I did improve.

On the tour I focused on Smith and our battle. I stayed out on the field after all the early training sessions, for extra work, a fact which caused a flurry of comment in the media. It was designed to make me even fitter, and it was also designed to be seen by the tour management. I made a conscious decision not to get friendly with Smith and it was only late in the tour that this changed. Otherwise, we either acknowledged each other with a nod so perfunctory that movement of the head could hardly be detected, or simply ignored each other. We both clearly felt that it was not the thing to do to become pally.

I never made up the extra four stone. Smith and Lawton were still giants on the tour. But I achieved what I set out for: I played in all three Tests. Smith, in fact, was a good player, a good striker in the scrum and a strong scrummager; his throwing in was average but he was good in the loose. But when it mattered, I got the nod. In the Test series, we never went backwards in the scrum, we handled Lawton with something approaching comfort. We won the series. End of argument.

When I was a schoolboy, I felt that there was always an otherness, a mysterious quality about the British Lions. They always played away, thousands of miles away, so you never saw them in the flesh. Until as recently as the 1970s, the series they played were never televised and relatively few media men followed them, in contrast to the hordes of today. So the Lions have always had something of an unreal quality, and a heroic quality. It is through the British Lions, rather than through touring with your own single country, that you become one of the gods of the game.

Because of all the demands of the fixture list, there have been doubts cast as to whether the Lions concept should go on. I would be extremely sorry to see them go. It is a particularly challenging and rewarding atmosphere; it is a bigger honour because you have been chosen from a bigger pool of players. It is a chance to find the same glories as past Lions. The two tours I have made, to Australia and then to New Zealand in 1993, have been memorable experiences.

But they were also sharply contrasting in so many aspects, they showed me the two sides of Lions' trips. I can remember the reports coming back from South Africa in 1974, when the Lions went through unbeaten and thrashed the Springboks, by 3–0 with one drawn. But I can also remember the stories from the 1977 and 1983 tours, which were far less happy and which descended into bickering. I am still incredulous that in 1983 the Lions kept choosing Ciaran Fitzgerald as their Test hooker and left Colin Deans out of the side; Deans was the better player by an almost immeasurable distance. Even more incredibly, they left Peter Wheeler out of the party altogether, which was a disgrace. That gave me an insight into the political infighting and the trade-offs which go on among the home unions, a factor in the selection of the 1993 party, when Jeff Probyn was left behind in favour of one inferior Scot and another severely inferior Scot.

And a tour party is an unpredictable entity. The tours of 1989 and 1993 revealed some of the joys and problems on the same lines. Lions tours can be brilliant, united, and the experience of a lifetime; they can also be a grind, full of disloyalty, can become disunited and, in the end, leave a certain bitterness. I've been on one of each.

I am sometimes jealous of Lions of old. They had it easy in those days. All those great players never came under anything remotely approaching the same scrutiny as the players today. There were few media following them as they rambled around New Zealand or South Africa; those who did follow the team rarely wrote anything critical. When they wrote that someone who was playing 12,000 miles away was a great player, you had no basis to judge for yourself. There were very few TV pictures, and above all there were no videos, to replay endlessly, to launch a frantic search for any and every weakness in the game and make-up of every player. People are now scrutinized in a far more technical way, and without that players of old assumed an aura of omnipotence. Gareth Edwards is one of the greatest players in history. I wonder if he had played in the video age whether he would have become bored before every match with a rigorous investigation into the fact that he did not pass off his left hand.

The 1989 tour of Australia was the first the Lions had ever undertaken to that country. That was partly because South Africa were still in the wilderness; it gave all the carpers the excuse to say that, somehow, we were not true Lions because we had not travelled to one of the old strongholds. No-one on the tour gave it a thought. Australia had already begun the improvement which was to lead, two years later, to them winning the World Cup. Some of the midweek games on tour were to have a missionary air about them and they were not too testing; but we were Lions all right. Anyone who regards a three-match series against an Australian national team in any sport as being something of a picnic knows nothing about sport, or about anything.

The party gathered first at London Irish's ground at Sunbury on Thames. The manager was a voluble Welshman, Clive Rowlands. Ian McGeechan, who in 1993 was to become the first man ever to coach two Lions parties, was the coach; Roger Uttley had the unenviable non-post as assistant coach; and the captain was Finlay Calder, the Scottish flanker and captain. We were not quite then into the bitterest years of the England–Scotland feud but enough roots of that feud were showing to make all the English contingent at least a little sceptical of the Scottish captain.

Yet in the months of the tour I developed a tremendous respect for Calder. He is one of the most direct men I have ever met, direct to the point of non-diplomacy. Perhaps it was that which appealed because I have never had much time for the diplomatic routes. On the field, and off the field, he had an iron-hard competitive edge and attitude. When you play against someone like that, it is easy to hate them, you use it to build up an active dislike to take you into a mind set to return the aggression. When England played Scotland, Finlay used to figure large in our plans. We used to say that if we didn't stop Finlay, he would stop us. He would put his body over or around the ball to stop us winning it, or to stop us winning it quickly. He could cause loads of trouble. When you play with a man like that it is very reassuring.

He started the tour slowly because he had niggling injuries. Andy Robinson, the other open-side, was never fit enough to mount a major challenge for the place. Andy had missed training before the tour with injury and simply was unable to catch up during the trip; he must have been bitterly disappointed. Finlay would be the first to admit that he was not the most naturally gifted player ever to become a Lion. But in the final analysis, he was an outstanding player and he would never shirk anything. You could rely on him in the most difficult moments. That is a massive factor in the minds of fellow players.

I seemed to spend a lot of time with him on the tour, travelling and especially seated on planes. We used to discuss the different perceptions of each other's countries. Finlay said that he felt the English held the Scots in a kind of contempt, that they were rough savages from up north. Not really, I used to lie. Calder used to express the view that all Englishmen were anally retentive, that he was always disappointed by our lack of passion. I found it difficult to disagree with that.

As I say, we were in the early stages of the fractious relationship between the Scots and English, a relationship which, for us, had certainly taken over from the Anglo-Welsh ill-feeling as the coldest. As Rob Andrew says, these day the real intense dislike is not for the Welsh, as it once was, but for the Scots. And vice versa. I watched a television programme shortly before the 1995 Grand Slam match in which a Scottish comedian, so called, said that the Scots got together all the dross and perverts, sent them down south and called them English. English people would never be able to make that same jibe in reverse without the Scottish nation rising up in unctuous rebellion, just as we would be unable to make that kind of reference to black people, lesbians or gays.

Rifts deepened after that tour, but on tour, on any tour, you have to maintain a kind of armed neutrality. McGeechan speaks after Lions tours of the good that a Lions trip does for relationships in the succeeding Five Nations Championships. I disagree. I believe that we all simply revert. Mike Teague and John Jeffrey, one from Gloucester and the other from the Scottish Borders, and competing for the same shirt in 1989, simply did not get on at all. Teague, who outplayed Jeffrey and Australia with the form of his life, was given the nickname of Iron Mike. Once, when Teague had made a rare mistake, I heard Jeffrey make an aside, 'Looks like Iron Mike's going rusty.' I looked at him and could see and feel a real resentment.

However, perhaps the intensity of internationals means that clashes are inevitable. We were largely a united party, with no unrest. When you are winning, these things are infinitely easier to achieve. I still keep in touch with Finlay. We speak on the telephone three or four times a year, about news, about games, about savage Scots and the anally retentive English.

And there was something which the Scots brought with them on tour which I admired. This was 1989, and we had not quite reached the era when every player had fully accepted the new preparation culture in England. Certainly, we were fitter and harder working but there was still a residual feeling in English rugby circles, in and around the national squad, that it was still chic to try to get by on little work, to say how grand it was to get by and win, without really trying. The Scots were different. They were used to being intensely competitive. They had to be. They had fewer numbers, a smaller pool of really talented players. They were used to fighting.

In some of the early fitness testing for that tour, I came out as the fittest Lions forward. Finlay came up to me afterwards. 'I was really impressed by that,' he said. It may not sound so remarkable a comment but no one in the English side had ever said anything like that to me. Rigorous training and good test results were things which were not yet deemed fit conversation for polite circles in England. People just shrugged. Being fit had no real cachet in the team.

At the first gathering of the Lions, at a training session at the London Irish ground, Calder, myself and two other Scots were the first out for training. They suggested a game of touch rugby. I was incredulous. I asked what on earth was the point of playing two-a-side touch rugby. They insisted, and we played our two-a-side game. I also learned that a fair bit of this intensity came from the influence of Jim Telfer, their former coach who still exerted huge influence behind the scenes at Murrayfield.

Clive Rowlands was a fascinating character. He is voluble, restless and passionate, Welsh-speaking, and even when speaking English he does so in a rasping Welsh accent not so much laced with expletives, as sunk with them. He can presumably come over to some people as a kind of pop-up pantomime Welshman. Certainly, we all grew tired of hearing his tour joke. He told it at every speech he made for the eight weeks of the tour, and that takes in a huge number of addresses. Of course, that was fine for the hosts who were hearing it for the first time. For the players it was a major trial.

His stock phrase was 'The Badge is getting bigger', which was vaguely inspirational the first time he uttered it, but only vaguely, and not at all inspirational afterwards. But Rowlands was an excellent manager and a tremendously capable man. He was certainly passionate, but he did not engulf everyone in Welshness. He was passionate about Wales but also about everything he did – about the Lions, the tour, the lot. Much of it washed over me in any case but he separated his passion from an overt nationalism. It was the kind of passion you appreciated.

Perhaps the nearest equivalent for passion and rhetoric in the English camp in the same era was John Burgess, the fiery northerner who was president of the RFU in 1987–8 and is still barking to this day. But his passion was not nearly so constructive. He was in the same voluble mould as Rowlands but he became a figure of fun with some of the England players through his over-zealousness, as he banged on about the heart, the Rose, the jersey. It sounded good. It didn't do much good.

Burgess had his finest hour in his presidency before a Twickenham match when all the England team were gathered in the Petersham Hotel, Richmond, our traditional base before a home international. He burst into the team room on the day before the game. 'I just want to say a few words,' he said, eyes and bald head glinting. Everyone looked grimly at the floor. He stood at the head of the room, produced a note-pad with his speech. He was holding a pair of half-rimmed glasses in his hand and he swung them up to put over his ears to read the speech. As he did so, he mistimed the swing and the stem poked him in the eye. 'Bloody hell,' he said. The players did their best not to explode, partly through fear of Burgess's volatility. You could tell that people were desperately holding it in because their shoulders were heaving.

Burgess gathered himself, composed himself and the team were still staring at the floor. Then he swung his glasses again and did exactly the same thing. The room collapsed in hysteria; it was controllable no longer. He ploughed on through his Queen and Country speech but the audience had been lost for all time, in hopeless fits of laughter.

He also developed the habit of coming into the dressing room before the kick-off for a last-minute blast. He would actually go up to every player and kiss them. You could tell how high up he was in the RFU because he had a beige cashmere coat. Most of the committee seem to have the blue cashmere but the top officials graduate to the beige. Before the match against Ireland in 1987, a match for which I was on the bench, he came storming in. Marcus Rose, the England full-back, dipped his hands in a bucket of resin which had been provided to take the moisture from our hands. Rose approached Burgess, was duly hugged in typically fervent fashion. Rose clapped both hands on Burgess's back and Burgess, still shouting his encourage-ment, left the dressing room with two vivid white hand prints on his cashmere. The whole severe atmosphere of the build-up was shattered.

Clive Rowlands was more constructive. Some managers whine on about their own problems. Players simply do not want to know. It is the manager's job to act as a shield. It is his job to sort out all the admin, to sort out why we aren't in a decent hotel, why the coach has broken down, why the flight has been changed. It is his job to deal with the press. Rowlands was the ideal shield, to allow the players to get on with playing.

The tour was my first major contact with McGeechan and he immediately impressed me. He was meticulous, well prepared and committed. He was analytical. He was certainly not infallible and it is ridiculous to imagine that any coach can make a bad side into a good one. People portray rugby coaches as a kind of director of rugby, people who are always right, people who break down the game and reassemble it. In teams where some players have won forty caps and more, that simply does not happen. There is hardly any need at all for basic work. The coach is needed to do the tuning, to be an information source, translating the videos and other information to help that tuning process. Sometimes the coach comes up with a major strategic answer, sometimes not. The image of a dictator with a megaphone belongs to comic strips.

But Geech improved us. At that stage, too, it was possible to be successful in a rather limited style, which is what the Lions achieved. By 1993, the game had moved on a little and I don't believe that he quite kept on top of the changes. But I rank him among the top three coaches I have dealt with – the others would be Alan Davies, with whom I spent my formative years; and Jack Rowell, whom I came across on a formal basis only recently, but who rapidly impressed me no end.

There was one aspect especially where Rowlands and McGeechan endeared themselves to me. It was on their public approach to alleged foul play. It was not to be long into the tour when accusations started that the Lions were a dirty side. We were berated in the myopic Australian press, and that attack reached almost fanatical proportions late in the tour when we were called every name under the sun.

McGeechan's pre-tour strategy was clearly that he was happy with a physical approach. Some coaches are too mealy-mouthed to admit that they want a overtly aggressive game. Rowlands also had the right idea. He had a way of dealing with the whole question, especially if any match threw up allegations against the Lions, that was joy for all the English team who had traditionally been deserted by RFU officials as soon as any trouble started. In private, Rowlands and McGeechan used to tell us not to be caught again. In public, Rowlands would make a measured speech accepting part of the blame, but only part. Then he would turn the blame back on to the opposition, quite rightly on the basis that one man can't have a fight. He would ask the opposition to look at themselves.

In England, we were well used to the disgraceful situation where our officials accepted the blame for any incident. After the controversial match at Cardiff in 1987 we were read the riot act, four England players (Dooley, Hill, Dawe and Chilcott) were suspended, and absolutely no Welshmen. It was spinelessness on the part of the RFU and I found the attitude of our management in Australia in 1989 extremely refreshing.

From the outset, two major battles were fought. There was the aforementioned catchweight contest for the hooking position between Steve Smith and myself. Unbiased on-lookers have told me that I won partly on simple body language, that I turned the argument on its head inside a few days at the start of the tour. Steve, I admitted to no-one at the time, is actually a nice sort of bloke. He did not respond to the challenge in the same way. He was a fierce player when roused but seemed to be roused by external stimuli, by adversity. That is fine, but sometimes you are not in adversity, you are favourite for something. Then you need to be self-motivating. You cannot rely on something happening to upset you.

The wider question as to whether sheer size is of crucial importance in front row selection is one to which my response might be obvious. But I felt that all the hue and cry that to face Lawton we needed someone of Lawton's size, betrayed a lack of rugby knowledge. There are very few times when one hooker out-scrummages another in isolation from the battle of the props. What makes scrums retreat is not a hooker; and provided the hooker is technically competent, providing he can get low, can hook low, then he will not be under pressure if his props are doing their job. He can also, if he is good enough, take the scrum down to where the opposition monster cannot bring his weight to bear.

People who were transfixed by Lawton had not done their homework. He came over with Australia in 1988, played in the Twickenham Test and never budged us an inch. He played against England in Australia earlier that year, when Australia were superior, but again we never retreated in the scrums. When he did decide to work hard and really shove, he could make it very hard work indeed. But not in so decisive a way that it gave credence to the Great Pound for Pound Debate.

The other contest was also fractious. Ostensibly, it was between the Scottish rucking style of play and the English mauling style. Yet it was also a battle between Finlay Calder and Roger Uttley. The role of assistant coach is impossible. You end up taking sessions for the midweek team, never with quite a full complement. But for Roger, it was worse. It was obvious from the start that neither Finlay nor the Scottish contingent rated him at all. The Scots were very dismissive of him and the breakdown of the relationship had a crude and completely unnecessary conclusion at the end of the tour. With some of the Scots as ringleaders, we bought putters for each member of the tour management. With a disgraceful act of churlishness, they came back with a putter for each of the hierarchy, but Roger's was demonstrably cheaper and worse than the others. I believe it was a studied gesture. It could hardly have been otherwise.

The stylistic divisions very quickly came to a head. Back at London Irish, at virtually the first session, Uttley demonstrated a drill for the maul. He asked us to take the ball in, hit with the shoulder, stand the ball up with a big wide stance, and let people get to you. Finlay steamed in immediately. He wanted something completely different. He wanted the Scottish style to become the Lions style. He wanted to hit the opposition head on, deep driving, get the momentum on, wait for the rest to come in behind, then go to ground to set up the ruck. The style, undeniably, does produce good early ball.

But you cannot play it all the time. In Australia, we found the opposition were stealing in and picking the ball up before the ruck developed. Sometimes you cannot put the ball on the ground, you have to stay up and drive the ball and drag the opposition in. Eventually, we veered far more towards the English style. For a start, we found that the Australia Test pack lacked real upper body strength and were unhappy against a team mauling against them. We also had great mauling forwards like Dean Richards and Mike Teague, two pillars of the trip who were to play outstandingly well. We evolved a kind of hybrid version of the two styles. We drove the ball a lot; if a player burst free going forward we rucked it, otherwise it was a maul. It suited us well.

It was a shame that the *rapprochement* of styles did not lead to warmer relationships for Roger Uttley. He and McGeechan maintained the relationship. They had to. But when it became clear that there was potential fractiousness the players took matters in hand. Especially in the forwards, we realized that a lot of the detail was better worked out between ourselves. Uttley, like Dick Best who filled the same unenviable assistant coach position in 1993, was a good organizer of sessions; he made them interesting. Perhaps neither man was a master overall strategist, but although Uttley was limited in that way he did have a vast amount of experience which could have been tapped into in a different style.

The team that staggered out of jet-lag at Perth, our first stop, seemed to me to be potentially very powerful in the forwards, where Paul Ackford was at the height of his career. The backs were not of vast experience, apart from Ieuan Evans, Rory Underwood and Gavin Hastings. It seemed that we might lack authority at fly-half, where Paul Dean of Ireland had not really shown the ability to direct a Test match, and Craig Chalmers was still early in his career. Of the centres, none of John Devereux, Brendan Mullin, Scott Hastings and, especially, Jeremy Guscott had yet turned Test matches by their own brilliance. Guscott showed that at least he had the arrogance to make a top-class player!

Yet in the euphoria of the start of the tour, anxieties were forgotten, and so were supposed enmities. At Perth, the party came together and was to stay together through thick and thin. That helped to make the tour a memorable experience. It showed how a team can gel and how much easier that process is if you are winning. The opposite was to occur four years later in New Zealand.

The Perth stopover set the tone for the tour in another way. The weather was fine, the pitches for playing and training were firm. There was no need to stand shivering between exercises, swathed in five levels of training gear, as the wind howled or the rain lashed down. There was no need to keep moving simply to keep warm. The surroundings were excellent – the Burswood Resort Hotel, where we stayed, was massive and luxurious; it had a twenty-four-hour casino and inveter- ate punters like Dean Richards and Andy Robinson could occasionally be seen emerging from the casino into the breakfast room after short twenty-minute bursts on the tables. Frequently in New Zealand, touring teams are stuck in dreadful, God-forsaken motels. It is not always the fault of the hosts. If a town doesn't have a big hotel then they can hardly build one just for the visit of a touring team. In Australia, our accommodation was top-class.

Perth itself was the perfect stopover city. It is hundreds of miles from anywhere but has most of the country's wealth of minerals. Nearby is that playground of the rich, Fremantle, a former venue for the Americas Cup. The most exclusive part is probably the Royal Perth Yacht Club. One day, we were invited to sail at the Club. Various well-appointed and incredibly expensive yachts appeared and a few of us were embarked on each for a trip. Afterwards, I thanked them for arranging this special trip. They pointed out that it was not a special arrangement, that they did the trip every Wednesday. Serious money there.

One of our temporary crew was Robert Norster, then one of the most effective locks in the world. Bob was a fastidious man. He had an expensive camera with him and he asked one of the Perth men to take a shot of the Lions on the boat.

We duly posed, but after he took the picture the guy dropped the camera on the quayside. Bob groaned loudly. The situation quickly became worse. The quay sloped steeply down to the sea and the camera started sliding towards the edge. The man scrambled desperately across the quay and the camera rolled tantalizingly away. He made a final despairing dive, missed the camera and it dropped, sedately, into the sea. The guy looked at us in horror. As the camera sank to the bottom of Fremantle Harbour to the sounds of gurgling and vast Lions merriment, even Bob's dry sense of humour (drier than his camera, at any rate) began to fray round the edges.

Norster was a talisman for the Welsh team throughout his career. You have to have special qualities to be held in that esteem, you have to earn it. He was a superb technician in the line-out, the only player who ever gave Wade Dooley trouble. He was only about 6'5", by no means massive by today's standards, and he was not massively well built either. But he had great hands, his timing of the jump was brilliant, and for all but the very tallest players, he was a nightmare. On the tour, the Welsh players, and especially the younger ones such as Dai Young at prop, looked up to him, almost saw him as a father-figure.

Another oddity of the international differences came through from the Scots contingent when we were changing for the first match, against Western Australia at the Perry Lakes Stadium. As the kick-off neared, Mike Teague and I were doing our last-minute strapping. In that era, the England dressing room was becoming quieter and quieter. All the bawling and shouting had diminished and a far more constructive and contemplative atmosphere had replaced all the nonsense. But in Perth we were taken back to the old days. As they changed, the Scots players were bouncing off the walls, shouting 'Come on! Get into it.' Incredibly, the two players making the biggest noise were Gavin and Scott Hastings. Teague started to laugh. 'I can't believe this,' he said. 'That's the full-back.' We had to move out and completed our preparations in the next dressing room in case we both burst out laughing. We came back later. One of the fascinations of touring was to compare all the different national traits. There were the Scots still running through the old-style winding up. Even Finlay would take part, though to a lesser extent.

The Irish were not as widespread on the tour, although as ever those who did make the party proved good tourists. Donal Lenihan was able to swallow his disappointment that he was not a strong contender for a Test place by assuming, as the tour wore on, the leadership of the midweek team. Players in the midweek team often feel left out of the main tour, sensing something of a worthlessness. That is a completely mistaken summary. The midweek team is of vital importance, and can indeed turn a tour – it happened in a beneficial way in 1989, and a wholly disastrous way in 1993.

The first two games of the tour, against Western Australia and Australia B, had been quiet – too quiet. The first crunch game of the tour was against Queensland at Ballymore, in Brisbane. Suddenly, the tour took off, the first rumbles of thunder were heard. Mike Hall, the Lions threequarter, had joined the tour late after completing his exams at Cambridge and he was welcomed warmly by Queensland. In one incident at the back of a ruck, Hall was trampled violently by Julian Gardner and other Queenslanders. There was no question of Hall lying on the ball and being fairly rucked out. He was kicked when he was not in the ruck.

While Hall was lying on the ground being treated, Finlay got us all around him. 'That is the last time it is going to happen on this tour. We are not going to allow our players to be put upon like that.' The resolve hardened in that instant and the tenor of the tour changed. There was a recognition that this was the way is was going to be.

It was the start of some lurid tour coverage. As the tour progressed, wilder and wilder accusations against the Lions were thrown – that we had a deliberate policy of rough play and intimidation. We did not. We never formulated a policy, unless it was a policy that we would not start it, but if they started it, we would finish it off.

In that same match, the home hooker was Mark McBain, a horrible little man. By that time our first-choice front row was David Sole at loose head, David Young at tight head, and myself. We were not the biggest front row ever and as scrummagers did not compare with the Rendall, Moore, Probyn front row I played in with England. But both Dai and David were good in the loose, and as a trio we were good enough to get the job done. We had Queensland under pressure in the scrums. They were retreating.

They decided to protect their ball by collapsing the scrum. McBain would hook the ball and then they would bring it crashing down. Collapsing scrums are not usually dangerous for top-class front-row forwards if they are set up low. They are only dangerous when they collapse from a height or if there is some inexperienced player there who is not strong enough; or when one team is going forward, because when that happens your head gets tucked under during the collapse and the locks behind are still pushing. If you can't get your head out it can be extremely dangerous. The Queensland collapsing was extremely dangerous and illegal.

After a few collapses, I took Bob Norster aside during a break in play. I told him to kick McBain if it happened again. It did and he did. McBain came up complaining. You stop taking it down and we'll stop kicking you, I said. He didn't, so we didn't. They whined about it afterwards and you can say that there are no circumstances in which kicking can be condoned. But there is no instance in which we could accept deliberate collapsing, which is a sight more dangerous.

Bill Campbell, the Queensland captain, also contributed to the poisoned atmosphere. He was marking Ackford, who was far too good and too hard for him. We called Campbell 'Shirley' on the tour. He complained afterwards that he was in fear of his life at every line-out due to alleged punching. He was 6'8" and 18 stone. If a man that size couldn't look after himself, who could? I felt that if I was as big as that I would be able to look after myself. Indeed, it would be a pleasure to do so. I would certainly not run to the press to whine, as he did.

Still, it was the start of our reputation as a dirty team and the start of a virulent media campaign against us which abated only when we took off to fly home. Significantly, when Bob Templeton, the assistant coach of the Wallabies, then and still, reflected on that tour during his time in London coaching Harlequins, he was scathing about Australia's action. 'We should have copped it, kept quiet and given it all back,' said Tempo. Once Australians started complaining we felt we had scored an important psychological blow.

The Australian players and media became obsessed. So did Bob Dwyer, the coach. Actually, the Australians usually complain extremely cleverly. Before every game, and not only in rugby, they come out and, in the area they don't like, the area they feel vulnerable in, there will be a complaint about the opposition, not least for the consumption of the referee. When a British team then complains back they are duly labelled whingeing Poms. The Australian sportsman, beyond any question, is the world champion strategic whinger.

Dwyer was usually first onto the soapbox whenever he felt threatened in 1989. Alan Jones, the former Wallaby coach and a great rival of Dwyer, came out at the end of the tour and said that the hysteria generated was designed to take credit away from a superior Lions pack; that was spot on.

We had made our mark, on McBain and Australia, and the tour was on the road. The next stop destroyed for ever my secret ambitions to spend a year off, travelling around the world away from the rugby fields. We were in Cairns, a superb location in the north of Queensland, and staying in the Cairns Hilton, another wonderful Australian hotel. While we were in Cairns, I passed the Cairns Backpackers Hostel. I had a look in. I saw the dormitories with the double bunk-beds, saw the relatively rough conditions, walked back to the Cairns Hilton and knew that I was spoiled for ever, would never do my grand tour. Once you have become accustomed to the five stars, anything else, even a four-star hotel you might previously have regarded as a palace, becomes merely seedy. It ruins your holidays because even when paying your own way you cannot bring yourself to sacrifice as much as a single star – not that I have had many holidays since I became an amateur rugby player.

Cairns was subtropical, steamy and warm. It was only a boat trip from the Barrier Reef, where we went sight-seeing and scuba-diving. We went white-water rafting; David Young, who could not swim, fell in and got into severe difficulties, and Gareth Chilcott dragged him out. We won the match against Queensland Country, and the bond in the team became ever stronger. Cairns was the sort of place where you realized that you like Lions tours very much indeed.

The last major build-up game before the First Test was the match against New South Wales, played at the North Sydney

Oval, just over the Harbour Bridge from the city itself. We won only with a late drop goal by Chalmers. I was particularly looking forward to the game because New South Wales, according to the papers, were fielding a new young hooker. Easy meat. Yet the young man was big, strong and good. His name was Phil Kearns, he was to become Australian captain and his promise was obvious. The home front row of Skeggs, Kearns and Hartill never budged an inch.

We were still winning, showing signs of developing a forward pack, but not the big driving play we had shown glimpses of. We had still not really sorted out a playing identity, or sorted out our backs. There was a lot of kicking and not a lot of continuity. We were winning, but we were a bit lost. And in the First Test, it looked like it. Everyone said that in a three-match series the First Test was the vanishing point, that you could not come back from 0–1. Yet we were well and truly wiped out.

We had some serious injury problems: Teague was unfit and for some unfathomable reason we replaced him with Derek White, the reserve No. 8, when we had John Jeffrey, as a blindside, all ready to play. Yet even with McGeechan and Calder choosing the team he still did not make it. We were short of three centres and forced to team up Hall and Brendan Mullin in the centre. But it was in other areas where we struggled. We scrummaged fairly well but we were murdered in the line-out, Norster had won the vote over Dooley to play in the Test but he and I never struck up an understanding in the match. Steve Cutler had a tremendous game for the Wallabies and we were playing without line-out ball for most of the day. And we were roasted by Michael Lynagh, Australia's fly-half. We would get up from a scrum, and find that Lynagh had stepped back into the pocket, kicked the ball over the forwards and bounced it just inside the

197

touchline, 60 or 70 yards up the field. He did it time and again. It was a brilliant display; Nick Farr-Jones and Lynagh ran the match and 30–12 to them was no flattery either.

The despondency was deep. Calder declared that there would be changes, big changes, and that everyone should get used to the idea. I knew that there was a silver lining somewhere. I did not believe that we had played anywhere remotely near our best. I was also comforted by Lynagh's performance. It was such a faultless thing that I knew he could never repeat it, especially only seven days later. As it transpired, in the Second and Third Tests, the kicks that had bounced so wickedly a few feet inside the touchline before making their way into touch, began to bounce out on the full.

I also felt that in the forwards, we had not made any physical dent in the Wallabies, not gone for the jugular. The Australian view in the aftermath of the First Test was that we might be a good team for kicking people but that we were no good at rugby. It wound us up. The doubts began to lift slightly.

They could so easily have been reimposed in the most grim fashion a few days later. Lenihan's midweek team played the Australian Capital Territories at Canberra between the first and second Tests. At one stage the Lions trailed 17–0, an incredible situation against an enthusiastic but poor team. It was just as well that I was back at the hotel nursing cold symptoms. I could not have stood it. Yet the Lions came back strongly, gradually dragged the game around, and eventually they won 41–25. It was a highly significant comeback. It is always the responsibility of the midweek team to keep the tour on the road, especially before a major Saturday match. If we had lost that match the psychological blow would have been severe, even terminal.

When England toured South Africa in 1994 our early results

had been poor, and in the week before the First Test our second string played South Africa A at Kimberley. All the predictions were that our young side would be thrashed. They did lose, but not before they turned in an inspirational performance, hard-nosed and competitive. The inspiration for our thumping victory in the First Test came from that midweek performance. Let no-one ever tell you that the dirt-trackers don't matter, don't make a difference to the rest of the tour.

Not that motivation for the Second Test was difficult. If we lose, we may as well go home. That was the text for the week. The match was to take place at Ballymore and in the context of the dirty play hysteria that suited the Australian media down to the ground. They dragged up the memories of the Battle of Ballymore, the match played between Australia and England in 1975 which had turned into a war, with Mike Burton becoming the first Englishman ever to be sent off in an international. All of it was rubbish – and motivating.

By this time Rob Andrew had arrived and settled into the party as replacement for Dean and he was teamed up at half-back with Robert Jones in time for the Second Test. When news came that Andrew was coming over, some of the Scots said: 'What's the point?' They did not rate Rob at all. But Rob arrived fit and hungry, he and Robert got on like a house on fire, and he began to direct operations with skill. It was the turning-point of his career.

We decided to make some dents in the Australian forwards, and to turn the screw in pressurizing Ian Williams and David Campese, the two wings, under the high ball. We tested their mettle and they were found wanting. If box kicks are good, as those of Robert Jones were, then all the defenders can do is catch the ball and be engulfed.

The final part of the plan was to bring in Dooley. Obviously

199

Norster was deeply upset, it was a blow to his pride, and some of his fellow Welshmen saw a conspiracy to get him out, which was nonsense. But Dooley was a huge man, even heavier than Cutler and just as tall. He closed the opposition down, stopped them from jumping. He could also take the heavy bumps himself and still win the ball. In the Second and Third Tests, Cutler, so dominant in the First, hardly saw another ball.

Only in the build-up was there something of a sour note. A day before the game, Roger Uttley called a forwards meeting in his hotel room. It was meant to be inspirational and fortifying but unfortunately Roger was not on his best form and some of the comments he came out with brought smirks to the faces. He went through the pack one by one. He came to Wade. 'Well, Wade,' said Roger. 'You are in the team. You are replacing one of the best jumpers in Europe, a man who has everything, great hands, mobility, athleticism. You are in because you are big.' As psychological master-strokes go, it wasn't one.

We came out hungry. It was a great day for the pack because we roasted the Wallabies. By this stage of the tour, Dean Richards was getting fit. Teague was the hungriest of all; he had played brilliantly on tour, missed the First Test and now was insatiable. They both played outstandingly. We had sorted out our hybrid game in the loose and both Teague and Richards made inroads, taking the ball forward and driving.

There were also two major flashpoints. At the early scrums, Nick Farr-Jones found that Robert Jones was standing on his toes. He lashed out and there was a brief bantamweight contest between the two, which was to flare up now and again for the rest of the series. Again, the Australians claimed that we had wound up Robert to target the key Australian player and captain. It was nonsense. You didn't have to wind up Jones. He would wind himself up, all on his own. There was a more lurid incident when David Young kicked Cutler in the head as Cutler lay out of the side of a ruck. He did not catch him particularly hard but it was unnecessary, no accepted form of rucking whatsoever. Tom Lawton came in like a mad, avenging bull throwing punches, and the conspiracy theory of dirty Lions was confirmed for millions of suspicious Aussies.

Gradually we won more and more control. We still did not put points on the board but in the final quarter we took the lead. The position was set up when Campese began to waver under the box kicks. He started by dropping them, then by avoiding them altogether. When we regathered one of them, Finlay and I took possession, Scott Hastings put through a long bouncing pass to Gavin, and Gavin scored down the right-hand side of he field.

Then we made it safe. Jeremy Guscott had been arrogant in a quiet sort of way on the tour to date. He had forced his way into the Test side after ranking last of the four tour centres only a week before. I can recall an outburst of Jerry in Dubbo, the final stopover before the First Test. We had been given a perfectly nice liaison man who had not once bothered us with requests for autographs and the like. Just before we left, he produced two balls to be raffled for Dubbo Zoo. 'Why the fucking hell have you waited all this time?' Jerry asked irritably; the liaison man was clearly shaken. I felt like punching Guscott. 'Look,' I said with all the force I could get together, 'just sign them, will you.'

In the dying moment of the Second Test, Guscott took the ball, ran hard at the Australian midfield, chipped the ball between the centres, raced after it, picked up the bounce and scored. There is arrogance, and constructive arrogance. It was our Test and a great feeling. Up on the banks behind the goalposts the Brits had, typically, mushroomed. They were bawling and shouting from the start, holding up soccer banners and chanting. They came from nowhere. They celebrated too.

The aftermath was predictable. Immediately after the game the Australian media went bonkers over the Young incident. That set off a week-long furore of epic proportions in which they dragged up or exhumed every Australian so-called hard man from the past, who told us how lucky we were that he wasn't still around to sort us out. One column called us the Atavistic Apostles of Anarchy, which was certainly wasted on the average Australian, who could not have had a clue what it meant.

Clive Rowlands stepped in, in typical fashion. He condemned the Young incident, told the media that Young had been spoken to by the tour management and that that sort of incident must not occur again. Then he declared that the Australian camp should look at the reaction of some of their players too, a classic Rowlands gambit, perfectly correct and deflecting.

As we moved on for a few days' break at Surfers' Paradise, which was shut and a waste of time, the storm continued to break. Lawton himself entered the verbal battle. If that is the way the Lions play, I don't want to know, was his gist. 'I have to go to work on Monday and I don't want my brains to be scrambled,' he said. Later that day we were watching a video of the most recent Bledisloe Cup match between Australia and New Zealand. In it, Lawton stepped straight on the head of Sean Fitzpatrick. We replayed the incident and we asked Rowlands to take the video straight to the next press conference, and play it for the world's media as a counter-attack. In the end, we decided against it. The furore never bothered us, it eventually began to amuse us, and it never failed to motivate us.

I took a large part in some of the build-up. I have always found it extremely difficult to keep quiet in team meetings and team affairs. As hooker, you are the focal point. In the scrum, the forwards are all there for your benefit, to make you comfortable. At the line-out you are the key with the throwing in. And the rift between Uttley and Calder left a void. Furthermore, although the Lions pack had developed into an outstanding one, there were few players in it who spoke before they were spoken too. Teague was fairly quiet, so were Young and Sole, even though Sole was later to become a successful Scottish captain. Even Ackford, who read the game well, was not normally a leading figure at team meetings.

The build-up to the Third Test went well. It was a great prospect and a great setting. The Sydney Football Stadium is one of the great venues: it looks great, the surface is great; they even have replays on giant screens, which I would advocate at every sports ground in the world, including Twickenham.

By that time my confidence was high. I had played extremely well on the tour, I had shoved criticism down people's throats, and I felt incredibly fit. Before the game I started my warm-up. Usually I take time to loosen up; sometimes I feel horrible. But I stopped after five minutes because I felt completely loose. It was a feeling I had never had before and never since, but I was ready to play. It was not just the physical thing, the muscles; it was the inner feeling too. I knew that we were not going to lose.

We didn't. It is part of rugby's folklore now that the match turned partly on a horrendous error by David Campese. He ran a kick ahead out of his own in-goal area, and as Ieuan

Evans came rushing up, he flung the ball out to Greg Martin, the full-back. Martin was nowhere near it, Ieuan was on to the ball in a flash and scored. It was the only try.

There were other key moments, apart from that of seeing Campese make an embarrassing mistake. They had a 5-metre scrum with their put-in and it was the perfect position for a Lynagh drop goal. In the scrum, we managed to take it down low, lower than Lawton wanted to go. We got the bump on when the ball came in, Lawton stopped the ball with his foot, but before he could hook it back we drove over the ball and won it. It was a key moment, desperately satisfying for us, and especially for me. I felt, even at the time, that it was a vindication.

Gavin contributed five penalties and we led by 19–18. The last few minutes saw a game gone mad, surging all around the field in attack and counter-attack as the Australians pressed desperately. Our defence was brilliant and it held out. We did a lap of honour around the stadium. I spent most of it hiding behind Dooley, who embarrassed everyone by blowing kisses to the crowd. The feelings were probably too deep for description; far beyond the surface joys. To play a game hard, and to beat the other team up front, is for forwards a great feeling.

We arrived for the after-match dinner at a hotel in King's Cross, where a large group of our supporters were staying. As we entered the foyer, we found them lining the walls, the escalators, the reception area to applaud us through into the dining room. It was a memorable procession.

The dinner was a strange affair in that it was mixed. The Australians could bring their wives and girlfriends; we couldn't since they were 12,000 miles away. I quickly reduced myself to a desperate state. Steve Holdstock, the old Nottingham wing who then played for Manly in Sydney, was at the dinner. I joined him and some Australian friends. One of Steve's Aussie friends asked me to have a drink. I took a bottle of wine, gave another to his friend. 'Right,' I said. 'I'll drink this one and you drink that one.'

The guy's wife went white and told me not even to try. I said: 'Come on, you soft Aussie bastard, drink it.' I drank my bottle straight down in one. It was an average red. Steve Holdstock's mate got about two-thirds of it down, sank to the floor. Steve told me later, when I tried to piece together subsequent events of the night, that I tried to drag him back up to finish the bottle. 'Leave him alone, you animal. Haven't you done enough?' said the wife. I then finished the other third in the second bottle.

I am told that I survived about another twenty minutes, then I knew that I had to get out of the room; I also remembered that our hotel was down through the city, across the Harbour Bridge on the North Shore. Later that evening, David Hands of *The Times* and Terry Cooper of the Press Association were driving across the bridge; in the back was Bob Weighill of the Four Home Unions tours committee. They had found him leaving the dinner at the same time and gave him a lift.

Apparently, they saw this figure weaving back towards them down one of the lanes of the bridge, doing aeroplane impressions. They found that the figure was familiar. They stopped and picked me up, took me back to the team hotel. I have no idea how I came to be on the Bridge, whether I had taken a taxi or walked all the way. At the hotel, I threw up in a big way and went to bed. I was therefore asleep when the piss-up after a major Test series victory was warming up. It had been a performance of major immaturity, I had been obnoxious to the wife of one of the dinner guests; it was stupid and macho. If I had paced myself I could have savoured one of the great victories. Still, the fact that I did not savour it did not take the victory away.

The last week was a lap of honour. We played a country team in a desperate place called Newcastle, we beat an ANZAC team at Ballymore. It was an unnecessary week but at least our victory could not be tarnished by it.

The tour scored highly on all counts. The fact that we were allowed to play with an unapologetic, physical approach suited me down to the ground. We were not under the silly restraints of so-called good behaviour, our management recognized that we were engaged in an international rugby series. We played with a free rein. It made for an upbeat tour, the formation of a formidable pack. Socially, there were no bad apples in the barrel.

It was also, to me, a perfect venue. I can remember training on just one wet field; otherwise, it was firm, dry and warm. Australia became one of my favourite places. I remember travelling over on the ferry from the North Shore into Circular Quay one morning. Everyone else, the daily commuters, sat with their heads down. They had seen it all before. I was thinking: 'God. That is the Sydney Harbour Bridge. God, that is the Sydney Opera House.' It was a lovely place, and a lovely feeling to know that you had beaten their rugby team.

9

ONE TEST, ONE TEAPOT

The failure of the 1993 British Lions

To tour New Zealand is the ultimate physical test in rugby,
perhaps the ultimate physical test of any sport.

Ian McGeechan

TOWARDS THE END OF THE 1993 LIONS TOUR OF NEW ZEALAND, THE
Land of the Long White Cloud (though most of them are not
long and white, but long and black), we were becalmed in
Hamilton, which is a sprawling and featureless town in the
North Island and which seems to be an endless succession
of poor motels and used-car lots and drive-in fast-food outlets.
It rained incessantly during our stopover, it was a bleak place
with few social graces or opportunities.

We stayed in a shocking motel; no offence to New Zealand

hoteliers because there is hardly any point in a place like Hamilton constructing dozens of five-star glass palaces. Or even one. This was the place where the tour reached a low point because the dirt-trackers, the Lions midweek team, a group which to a large extent had stopped bothering with rugby and started drinking in a big way, ended their active part in the tour with yet another shocking, almost cowardly performance against the local side, Waikato.

I sat in my room in Hamilton, listening to the rain hammer on the thin walls of the building, debating whether to risk some uninspired food in an uninspired hotel restaurant; and I thought how wonderful the All Blacks must find Britain when they come over, staying in the Hilton and Caledonian and Berkeley Court and St Ermin's, and the other big five-star establishments, and the cultural diversions.

The most obvious contrasts between the wonderful memories of top-of-the-ground touring with the Lions in 1989 in Australia and the reality of my second Lions trip, to New Zealand, were that the place was greyer, the pitches softer, the weather colder and wetter, the diversions fewer, the facilities inferior. It was also a much harder tour. So many people say that New Zealand is the hardest place to tour, they speak ruefully of the incessant pressure on the field and off, the lack of escape and respite. True, all true. New Zealand may not be a heaven on rugby's earth but it is a compelling place to play if you really want to retire having experienced the whole range.

I found the whole tour a gloomy experience. I had never been to New Zealand before, and the place is the very stuff of Lions legend, full of glorious deeds but, from the British point of view, relatively full of abject defeats. It still amazes me that people used to tour there and be away for six months, people with jobs and families. People used to break their legs on tour and still be fit again for the last few matches. Half the time away was spent sailing back and forth. A modern-day team would be sick with boredom after one day afloat.

New Zealand society is a macho world but in a different, more oppressive way to macho society in Australia. New Zealand is also refreshing. The best thing about their rugby is the complete lack of cant about the game and especially about rucking. If you are lying on the wrong side of the ball in New Zealand, not only do you get vigorously rucked out but you also get penalized. There is no big attraction in lying around trying to kill the ball, to say the least. Players do not hang around because it is dangerous to do so and you might also give away points. It is not worthwhile trying to stop the flow.

In the United Kingdom, we have completely lost sight of that among the rhetoric and hand-wringing of the debate about rucking. People simply have no idea of the practicalities and technicalities of it. They spend too long talking about aspects of safety and the image of the game. The fact is, if vigorous rucking was allowed here then players would get out of the way and the game would flow so much better, and have a better image. The other fact is that the safety aspects are not nearly as worrying as they might look. We would also stop giving a clear incentive to the player who is on the floor lying around the ball. At the moment, we are paying too much attention to the players trying to ruck to clear the ball and not enough to the player lying on or near it.

By comparison with New Zealand, the game in the British Isles can be stop-start. It is no wonder that touring teams from New Zealand find touring here a frustrating experience on the field. There are easy bench-marks to differentiate between fierce rucking and violence. Fierce rucking must be allowed throughout the game and it was good to experience the New Zealand attitudes to it all.

That does not mean I could necessarily stand playing my whole career down there. I find the typical All Black extremely surly (and appreciate that the typical All Black might well say the same about me). It was incredible how often Kiwis came up to us on the 1993 tour telling us how they hoped we would beat the All Blacks, thrash them. 'They are such arrogant bastards. We can't stand them,' was the gist.

Individually, I did not find them arrogant, but as a collective not riveting company. Sean Fitzpatrick, the captain with whom I have crossed swords since and whom I met again recently in the semi-finals of the World Cup in South Africa, was their epitome and still is. He is a very good player, a good hooker, a good thrower-in and very physical about the field. You do not have to like the guy particularly to admire his play, which is just as well. But if you are going to win in New Zealand, you have to take on players like Fitzpatrick. You have to be dedicated enough, brave enough and good enough, week in week out. You have to set yourself, individually, for the challenge of your whole career. Any weakness in any touring party will be ruthlessly sought out and exposed.

That is precisely what happened to the 1993 Lions. We did give one of the great one-off performances in Lions history, we did play some outstanding rugby; but we finished by losing the Test series, with a poor overall record, and with more than a taste of bitterness. And to be frank, that great one-off performance stood between us and a shambles. We were tested and were found out.

And perhaps one nationality in particular. Towards the end of the tour, Ian McGeechan, the first man ever to coach two Lions tours, was asked by Robert Armstrong of The

Guardian if he was disappointed by the performances of the Celtic players who had made the trip. 'No,' said McGeechan. 'I think Gavin Hastings has captained the party very well.' It is debatable whether McGeechan actually meant to damn the Scottish contingent with faint praise, but faint praise was actually far more than they deserved. For if the 1989 Lions were a one-for-all party, then some of the 1993 Lions, at the end, could hardly look one another in the eye.

For some, it was difficult from the start. The issue of tour selection was vexed, the anti-English mentality was abroad, and so was the propensity for the selection to be carved up so that all the selectors, rather than choosing the very best team to make the most difficult tour, contented themselves with dragging enough of their own countrymen into the squad to pad it out.

We in the English contingent did our cause no good at all by being thrashed by Ireland at Lansdowne Road on the eve of selection. That gave the carpers more excuse. But what happened was a travesty. They went for players who had played well once or twice during that season, who had flashed in the pan, instead of players who had proven international records over a period of time. They chose players like Peter Wright, Andy Reed and Damien Cronin of Scotland and Mick Galwey of Ireland because they had exceeded expectations in that Five Nations – no matter that those expectations were tiny in the first place. When the party was announced there were sixteen Englishmen, seven Scots, five Welsh and two Irish. The anti-English backlash in the Celtic press, who have representatives in their own countries and many others in England, was fierce. They really gave some of the England selections a hard reception. When the party came back there was a dead silence on those issues.

My own selection would have contained more English players, not less. In one of the trade-offs, they chose as the tight-head props Paul Burnell and Peter Wright, two players never in the same league as Jeff Probyn. As the tour unfolded, that selection became embarrassing in the extreme and they had to haul Jason Leonard over to the tight-head from the loose just to shore up the scrum and the ruinous selection. Possibly there was a case before the tour for players like Peter Clohessy and Neil Francis, but in any case those were not the areas which the Celtic press were complaining about.

As it turned out, some of those bad selections did not actually affect the top team, the combination which appeared in the Tests – at least, not in personnel. But they did affect the Tests and the whole tour by the disgraceful collapse of the midweek team, which almost surrendered as the tour drew to a close. That did not do wonders for morale. Some of the vaunted Celtic contingent dishonoured the Lions jersey.

It was a tremendous honour for McGeechan that he was asked to take charge of his second Lions tour, but in the end the trip probably did not embellish his reputation. He is still probably one of the three best coaches I have played under, along with Alan Davies and Jack Rowell, but it seemed to me that for all his untiring efforts he had not moved on too much between 1989 and 1993. The game had moved forward a little quicker than Geech. The laws had changed, and in British rugby we were still running behind in the race to encapsulate the new theories. In 1993, we did not know precisely what was needed.

We started by playing to a certain pattern but New Zealand countered it. We did not move on to the next step. Geech was bitterly disappointed at the end of the tour. New Zealand has always been his favourite enemy, so to speak, and he saw a chance to take them on their own territory. We failed, his countrymen let him down badly on the field and became a joke, and it became just another defeated Lions tour, like most of them.

Geoff Cooke, the manager, did what he does very well – organizing, attending to all the background details, and occasionally having an input on the technical side. He had a large say in team affairs. Dick Best, the assistant coach, filled the same sort of role as had Roger Uttley in 1989 – the non-role, where you are always searching for your real purpose in life as the tour goes on around you. He was a very good sessions man on tour, far more inventive than most coaches. He felt badly let down by the Scottish players who gave up the ghost, and as usual with Best the way he got across his anger was not subtle. His distaste was quite apparent, which did not go down well. But the players he was attacking should have looked inwards, instead of outwards.

The seasons prior to the tour had been dominated by England and all the speculation before the 1992–3 season began was that Will Carling would be tour captain. But as we began to lose momentum in the Five Nations, and as the Celtic anti-Englishness reached a height, things changed rapidly. By the time of the announcement it was almost a foregone conclusion that Gavin Hastings would lead the team. I suppose that a predominantly English party led by Cooke, the English team manager, would have been unacceptable to the Celtic fringe. Gavin it was, and to be frank, the political situation was such that it was always going to be him, even if we had kept ourselves together and won the Grand Slam under Carling. Trade-offs are one of the unhealthy things about Lions tours.

On the tour, Gavin struck me entirely as he had always

struck me – as a nice bloke, rather than the deep and mystical leader his legend describes. His anti-Englishness, if it is there, is better disguised than in many of his contemporaries and he had a spell with London Scottish, so he is not like some sort of Border farmer who never set foot south of Hadrian's Wall. He has an aura about him that suggests he is one of the greatest players ever and he has certainly done wonders for some poor Scottish teams, but he has also made howlers like everyone else. He can be brilliant and he can be very ordinary, and in 1993 we saw both sides. There was a lot of speculation as to how he and Carling would get on; it seemed to me throughout the tour that they were not bosom buddies and they had harsh things to say about one another after the trip. There is definitely no love lost.

Carling had not played well in the domestic season and the loss of form was well documented. It seemed to me that at some points of the season and tour he was even a little bored. There seemed to be times during the tour when he had a knock in games and just wandered off; it was difficult to know whether the injuries were psychological or something more serious, but essentially, he just drifted out of the tour.

Perhaps it was this public airing of the blip in his career which gave him the necessary kick in the backside because he did eventually respond well. He had the dire fate of being relegated to the appalling midweek team where he even, for the Waikato match, became captain. He soon found that only a few players, like Stuart Barnes, Richard Webster and one or two more, were still playing with pride. Will did his best in adversity when it would have been easier for him to limp off home, to say, stuff it, I don't have to prove anything. He had a poor tour, the first downward dip, it seemed, on his career. But at least he stuck it out till the end.

If the final record was atrocious, there were still some

brilliant players on the tour. Peter Winterbottom was in his last season before retirement but he was still a great player, he still had the total respect of everyone who played with or against him. He had huge commitment, he would never let you down and he was a superb all-round flanker. Ieuan Evans was brilliant in his running, he had the kind of electricity that the All Blacks backs could never ever dream about. Jeremy Guscott also impressed me; he came out of a hard tour extremely well. I suppose I had always regarded him as a bit flash and a man who does just what he wants (and I have never been disappointed in that latter aspect of his character!) but he seemed to set out to prove to New Zealanders that he was a physical player as well as a brilliant runner. He did a lot of the dirty stuff, he tackled well, dropped on the ball, he rucked and mauled. He could easily have hid in safety, because it is easier for backs to do that. But to see him pile in made him go up considerably in my estimation.

What no-one in the management could do was to engender the same spirit which took us through in 1989, the kind of selfless commitment which characterized the earlier trip. It was not all their fault, because the players themselves must take the Lions' share of the blame. But in 1993, there was an atmosphere that everyone would do their own thing rather than everyone pulling together. It was almost a throwback, because some players came with the attitude (or at least developed the attitude when they did not figure in the first string line-up in the big games) that they would do as well as they could while still having a good time off the field. The iron will to succeed never existed in a large section of the party.

It is so easy, when the bad apples are in the barrel, to become enticed. You can get infected by the kind of atmosphere which prevailed on that tour and I am not absolving

215

myself. I was chosen on the bench for the Otago game, and the day before the game three of us went to lunch. We were soon joined by three others. We ordered a conservative single bottle of wine between us, had one glass each and the bottle was empty. Three players left. The remaining three of us had another eight bottles between us, staggered back to the hotel as dark fell, staggered straight into a team meeting feeling completely out of it.

I was not playing in the match and I did not get called up as replacement during the game but that is no excuse. I should not have become involved. Rugby players are social animals, and in the modern era that fact has been buried by the desire for victory. However, it lurks below the surface, waiting to be exposed for a party and for any weakness in characters who find they are not up, mentally and physically, to a New Zealand tour.

There were sporadic efforts during the tour to get the team off the beer. Before the match against Southland in dreary, dark and wet Invercargill, there was a meeting called by Cooke of senior players. Cooke spoke up. He said he thought there was a problem, that the boys were drinking too much. His school of thought was that we should go back to the lads and pass on the management's rebuke. I declared that the rebuke should come down from on high, from the management itself, that it did not matter if it sounded heavy-handed, because it all needed to be thrashed out. I told Cooke that it was his job to sort it out.

Cooke said that he admired my frankness but I was outvoted. It was left to us to pass on the message, and one way and another that message never got through. The midweek team all but disintegrated into a giant piss-up. But the way the tour was going, even an edict from on high would have dragged the lads back on to the straight and narrow for a week, or less. Then the right hands would have been put back to bad use. It is not as if everyone was too drunk to play. But a Lions team needs complete concentration. In 1993, concentration wavered fatally.

It was in some senses an enjoyable tour. Although by the end, as I say, it was difficult to look some of the team in the eye, there were some genuine good tourists, and I even seemed to get on well with the Welsh contingent, Robert Jones, Tony Clement, Richard Webster and others. Webster was a complete one-off (thank God). He was by the end of the tour the biggest open-side flanker we had seen. He must have weighed in at well over 18 stone.

There was still, as usual, the frustration of watching the All Blacks appearing in all sorts of advertisement campaigns and promotional and marketing opportunities which the authorities all around Britain were flatly denying to us. It made a joke of it all. Good luck to the All Blacks for making the most of their market value. They are a good side and they deserve their profile and the opportunities which come their way. But why on earth are British authorities surprised when we come back from Down Under in militant mood because of what we have seen? The announcement in 1995 of the massive, Murdoch-inspired injection of cash for the three major Southern Hemisphere unions is just another twist in the tale which leaves us in Europe ever further behind.

Old-style officialdom impinged on the tour in a more direct way. After the defeat in the First Test, we moved on to Invercargill and there came the awful news that Wade Dooley's father, a man well known and respected in the England squad, had died. Wade immediately left for home and was replaced by Martin Johnson. Technically, replaced players cannot return to the tour because of some boring subsection in the tour agreement, but the New Zealand RU were kind enough to say that Wade was welcome back as a member of the party whenever he felt ready to return.

A few weeks later, Wade did feel ready to return. To the fury of the team, the blimps on the Four Home Unions, who organize Lions tours, dragged up the subsection and, even though the hosting union and the management and players of the tour party wanted him back, they still refused, sticking to the letter of the law, even for a man who had given everything for rugby, given everything on the tour, and who had to leave to attend his father's funeral. The players would have been overjoyed to have him back, there was great affection for him, and even if he had not made the Test side, which is debatable, then at least he would have refused to let the midweek side fall apart.

The great thing about rugby union laws in the eyes of the game's officials is that they are phrased in vague terms. This allows them to exercise what they claim to be the spirit of the game. If there is a law set down apparently in straightforward terms which says something that they do not like, they invoke the 'spirit of the game' hidden clause to interpret it in a different way, as it suits them. Then, when they come to a law which is clearly meant to have some leeway of interpretation, you suddenly find that the spirit of the game is out of the window and they interpret the law to the letter. Here, there could surely never have been a better opportunity to invoke their beloved 'spirit of the game'. Dooley was a tremendously wholehearted servant of the game, he did so much work for so many good causes; he was ruled out of the career climax he had earned by a bunch of hidden bureaucrats in London.

Their blimpish representative who did come out, Bob Weighill, was quickly on the defensive, claiming, when some of the tour party could bring themselves to talk to him, that he was only the messenger, trying to make people feel sorry for him as an injured party. If he was only the messenger, as he said, then did he get straight on to the phone and demand that the ruling be changed, that he was a dissenting voice? No.

Then, with the pig-headedness which only rugby officials can summon, there were even calls for Cooke's dismissal as manager because he had backed Dooley to the hilt and complained in public about his disgraceful treatment. It was yet another example of a bunch of old men putting their own structure and procedures above the game itself. I asked myself the question I have asked so often before and since. Who on this earth do these people think they are?

The battle for the hooking jersey in the Tests was also entirely different. This time the contenders were myself and Ken Milne, the Scot. But the mind set was completely different. I had been goaded into what amounted to a constructive fury in 1989 by all and sundry declaring that Smith was huge and therefore was bound to be the Test hooker. The adversity was not the same in 1993, the mind set was not the same. Milne was, basically, a nice bloke and a good hooker, there was nothing to get the mental teeth into for motivation. He can be a little bit passive, but he goes through his job in a quietly effective sort of way, is determined and, however hard I tried, rather difficult to dislike. I could not work him up in my mind into a demonic figure as I had worked up Smith in 1989.

Things changed quickly, however, because Milne was chosen ahead of me for the early big games, and quickly became favourite to play in the Test matches and made the Otago side for the Saturday match immediately prior to the First Test. When it became apparent that I was out of the nominal Test team then the mind set changed again. It came too late for the First Test, where I sat on the bench, in a quiet anger. Australians have a term called 'death-riding' which means that the players on the bench wish ill for the players on the pitch, and I admit that for the first part of the First Test I wanted the Lions to lose.

But they were hit hard by the referee, Brian Kinsey of Australia – we had never rated him one bit in the England camp – who gave Frank Bunce a try for nothing when it seemed that Ieuan Evans had reached the ball first; and as the game wore on and the stakes grew, and especially when the Lions took the lead not long before the end, I began to react in a different way. By the end, I was rising from my seat and cheering like the rest. However, we were robbed of the Test by another bad decision by the referee, when he penalized Dean Richards for what seemed a perfectly fair tackle on Bunce which robbed Bunce of the ball at a key stage, and Grant Fox kicked us to defeat with a penalty.

My plans to recover the position were laid. I decided to be seen to be hungry and heavily involved in everything. I decided to come over as more belligerent, and also to do my own thing. In the matches I had played until then, I had been totally team-orientated. I decided that I would spend more time impressing the selectors by being, if you like, more visible.

Yet all those of us in the midweek team who were trying to get into the Test team had a built-in disadvantage because some of the players were not true Lions. We were always pushing off a weak base. We had played Southland in Invercargill before the First Test and I sank to my lowest point on any tour during and after that match. It was so bad that I spent almost an hour in the bar that night talking to the press, the sure sign of impending madness and depression.

Jason Leonard and I were anxious to break into the top team but all we had to help us out in the front row in midweek was Peter Wright, who was so far out of his depth in the loose play, where he stood around trying to catch his breath with his hands on his hips. Because of the shape he made when he was wheezing away, hands on hips, he was called Teapot. Here we were on a Lions tour, and we had to tell the bloke how to scrummage, had to tell him to get the scrum low. I looked at Wright, thought of Jeff Probyn sitting in his chair at home. Any good tight-head can take the scrum low, holding it on his right shoulder, coming in to try to put pressure on the opposition hooker. Wright's form on that tour would not have got him into any English First Division club side. He was also tetchy when we tried to give him advice, even though we were just trying to get the best out of him – albeit, admittedly, for selfish reasons.

We managed to beat Southland but struggled in the forwards, even though they were only a Division 2 side. We could not even sort out the trouble that they started. I looked into the eyes of some Lions forwards during that match and found no-one at home. Before the game, some of the Scots were walking round the dressing room shouting 'concentrate, concentrate' and banging the tables. We would have liked to, but some idiots were shouting 'concentrate' at the tops of their voices and interrupting our concentration. People like Damien Cronin were unfathomable. His weight ballooned on the tour. I could never understand why he went off the rails because he had some good games for Scotland. 'He's hungry,' Geech told me of Cronin before the tour. That was certainly true, because he must have spent half the tour eating, judging by his weight gain.

Just after the First Test, with neither Burnell nor Wright up to the job at tight-head prop, McGeechan asked me if I thought they should switch Jason to the tight-head. I said yes immediately, and although the switch was belated at least McGeechan had been honest enough to face the embarrass-ment of the original selection. Jason and I played in the midweek game against Taranaki, when we played well in a good match, and we were chosen to play in the Saturday match against Auckland, obviously in a Test trial. So I had made it back to the Test team; better still, I had escaped the increasingly feeble midweek team. If I had been stuck in that team for a week longer, I would have faked an injury and flown home.

Before the Auckland match, McGeechan came up to me with news of the selection. 'You are in for Auckland,' he said. 'We need competitors and you are a competitor.' I nodded, turned around and walked away.

The tour had begun in a riot of back play, with lots of pace. It was odd in a way because it was not the sort of thing that British rugby was famous for at the time. Players like Ieuan Evans, Scott Gibbs, the two Underwoods and Jeremy Guscott were playing superbly. There was an incredible match against the Maoris at Wellington, always a difficult place to play because there always seems to be a strong wind to add to the problems caused by the slope. Before the start, Gavin had been in belligerent mood. A lot of talk of the regeneration of Maori culture was in the air, lots of Maori songs and different sorts of Haka. 'We are going to go out there and shove their Haka up their backsides,' he said.

That really inspired us. We were down 20–0 in what seemed as many minutes. The Maoris caught us cold and ran us ragged. At around this time, during a pause in play when we were trying to work out what had hit us, Mike Teague piped up: 'When are we going to start shoving their Haka up their backsides?' We then made a fantastic comeback to win 24–20, inspired by magic from Ieuan Evans and the backs.

These were heady days on the tour. But it all came unstuck when we played Otago in Dunedin a week before the First Test. We won a lot of ball but we turned shedfuls over to Otago and we were well beaten. I felt strongly at the time that we were turning too much ball over, and while a policy of playing open rugby was all very well, we needed to play with far more precision throughout the team. I wanted a more restricted game at that point and I said so in the team meetings; but although there was a lot of talk at that time and again at the end of the tour that I had been one of the prime movers in cutting back on the back play, it was more a general feeling that we needed some reassessment.

I was probably wrong to be so cautious, and realized so at the end of the tour. We should have kept the ball in the hands more, especially as our backs were far better than New Zealand's; all the Kiwis did behind the scrum was to play a kind of hard-running, up-and-down style while we had far, far more to offer. Perhaps I had the natural caution of an English forward.

We were still poor for the Auckland game, and by the time the Second Test came around we were 0–1 down, had lost to Otago and Auckland, and were having a hard time in the papers in both hemispheres. Gavin was hobbling with a hamstring injury (he gave away a try in the first few seconds of the match after dropping a high ball). McGeechan and some of the rest of us had become ever more cautious despite the successes of the early matches, when we played with some gas. We were one match away from what would have been, had we lost, the end of the tour bar the shouting.

And from that unpromising beginning came one of the great performances in Lions history. I doubt if there has ever been a better performance by a British Lions pack on any tour. On that day in Wellington, thankfully bright, dry and without the normal Wellington hurricane screaming down the pitch, we shut out Sean Fitzpatrick and his pack totally. We shut them out in the line-out, when Martin Bayfield ruled, we drove at them in the loose, we tackled superbly. It was also a massive psychological boost for us that we scrummaged well too. I had no doubts that Jason would do a good job on the tight-head because he is so strong.

There were two key moments. The All Blacks had a 5-yard scrum near the left-hand touchline and when we went down you could feel and hear them setting themselves for a pushover. They went for the double shove, first holding the ball, then getting the weight on. We held them out, then actually got a nudge on ourselves; it was just a foot or so, but it was a massive boost. They lost control of the ball, they tried to recover but we knocked them over, the ball went into touch and we cleared the lines. Those sorts of goal-line stands make a massive difference. It is far more than the fact that you did not concede the try. They give a huge lift to the team and they give you confidence in the forwards that you can take whatever the other pack can throw. You have faced them down.

The other moment came when Fitzpatrick, who had a poor game, knocked on. We recovered the ball, Dewi Morris and Guscott sent Rory away down the left wing outside John Kirwan to score. It was the killer. As we waited for the conversion, the sporting New Zealand crowd started throwing cans at us from the Millard Stand. One of them, which turned out to be full, just missed me. I opened it, took a quick drink, saluted the crowd and toasted our victory. I was the last to join the celebrations that night, because I was selected for the random drug test and had to spend some time in my dehydrated state trying to summon up a sample. But I soon caught up with the others. It was difficult, considering what the victory meant to the team and to me personally, to keep tears from the eyes.

But perhaps it was not all good news, because in the euphoria of that day we thought we could win the deciding Third Test in Auckland with the same style of play. New Zealand went away and did what they do so well – they analysed the failure at Wellington to set their goals for the decider. That kind of analysis and improvement is one of the massive strengths of All Blacks rugby.

They paid us a kind of compliment because for the Third Test they reverted to a game plan so similar to ours in the Second Test that it was almost the same. They concentrated on the line-out, they kicked loads of ball into the box, they kept the ball on the field so as not to concede line-outs, they became far more physical, especially in the line-out. We basically did not move on tactically, we assumed that we would dominate the line-outs again.

There was just that final midweek match against Waikato at dingy Hamilton. On the previous midweek match, against Hawkes Bay in Napier, the team had fallen apart to a ridiculous extent and were hammered after leading well. Some of the Lions were miserably bad and even McGeechan, who rarely criticized players in public, said that 'some of the Lions have to examine their attitude'. Some people were quite surprised after the Second Test victory when I emphasized the importance of a strong effort in midweek, but it was necessary to keep up morale, to keep the mood building, let alone the fact that for most of the team it was the last chance they would have to play in a Lions jersey. Yet again, however, the team were pitiful, with a few working hard and others hanging round waiting for the end.

The pre-match speculation was that the All Blacks would come at us like the crazed dogs of hell; which they did. But the irony of the whole match, and of our defeat, was that after the opening passages of play we were 10–3 in the lead, chiefly thanks to an opportunist try by Scott Gibbs. Yet this was not to be our day and it was certainly not to be Gavin's. He picked up a loose ball and kicked, but instead of putting the ball long he kicked it high, and it went straight out. The All Blacks had a line-out where he had kicked from and they kept so much pressure on that they scored two tries. If we had just put in ten minutes of consolidation work after the Gibbs try we would probably have won.

But in trying to chase the game we dropped into the wrong rhythm. When the Lions were playing well on that tour, there was first-phase ball, then second-phase ball, then from the third phase there would be some sort of tactical kick or move. But when you are not taking the ball through the phases, when you are taking the ball into rucks and turning it over to the opposition, when you are not getting that rhythm, then it is terribly hard. At half-time, I said to the boys that we must work on developing the phases.

But we defended badly in the second half, there was a sinking feeling in the last quarter of the match and we were well beaten. Fitzpatrick, who had been quiet as a mouse for the first two Tests, especially when playing badly under pressure in the Second, suddenly started piping up in the last few minutes. 'You've lost it, you can fuck off back home.' He waited until he was sure of winning, he wasn't able to say anything when it was all in the balance. I told him how extremely brave he was being now he was on top.

The feeling at the end was one of desperation. It was an experience to tour New Zealand and to experience their intensity, even though large parts of the trip were a bore. But we had worked hard to no lasting effect, we had not toured as a united party, some of the team had effectively bottled out. And we had missed a chance of glory, a chance given to very, very few people.

10

NO WIGS, NO GOWNS, NO PAKISTANIS

Hard life in the law

*No brilliance is needed in the law. Nothing but common
sense, and clean fingernails.*
John Mortimer, *A Voyage Round My Father*

IF I WAS FIRST ATTRACTED TO THE LAW AS A PROFESSION BY AN
ambition to emulate the colourful, fighting speeches, the
dramatic delivery and the victories against the odds won on
Crown Court, and a hundred other soapy televised courtroom
dramas, the reality set in like a quick and cold blanket.

Early in my law career, working for a firm in Nottingham,
I was the duty solicitor, on call to go to police stations to
represent the interests of the ranks of the arrested. The idea
is to make sure that the police keep to the rules concerning

the interrogation and other procedures. Some policemen in my experience fastidiously keep to the rules, others fastidiously ignore them. But I must confess to a certain sympathy for the police, especially when they are dealing with professional criminals.

I was called out in the early hours to a police station in Newark. The police had trawled up a gang of professional housebreakers whose sphere of operations ranged up and down the A1. The custody sergeant told me that my client was in one of the cells.

I entered the cell and found a rather rough and angry-looking Liverpudlian. I told him who I was, I explained that the police had arrested him because they said he had been involved in a major burglary, that they had a positive identification, and that three people had been arrested.

'Who the fuck are you?' he said with a biting sneer. I repeated my preamble.

'Fuck off,' he said. 'I don't want you. I want my brief. My brief is on his way.'

I left the cell and went to see the custody sergeant. I asked him if the accused had made any phone calls. The custody sergeant, responsible for all the administration and all the movements of the arrested guests, told me categorically that he had made no calls of any kind to anyone. 'But he says his brief is on the way,' I said. The sergeant told me that there was no way.

I went back into the cell. I asked him how his brief could be on the way when he had made no calls whatsoever. 'Fuck off,' he said. 'I don't want to speak to *you*.' I was tired, frustrated and pissed off. I looked around. There was no-one else in the cell. I got hold of him and pinned him against the wall.

'Don't you ever speak to me like that again,' I said. He

229

was taken aback. He lost most of his swagger and went white. 'I don't mean to be rude,' he said. 'I just want my own brief.'

Sure enough, a few hours later a solicitor turned up. I asked him how he knew about the arrest. He claimed he had been telephoned. I told him that I profoundly doubted his story, and pointed out that no calls had been made. He intimated that it was none of my business. It was quite obvious when the bail application was made that they were indeed a team of professionals. I never discovered how the solicitor came to arrive out of the blue. It may have been prearranged that he should come unless he heard from the gang that things had gone well. Or something. That sort of thing rather turned me off the criminal law. I didn't mind helping people with genuine remorse, but to some criminals, it was all a game.

Any dreams of becoming a barrister had died even sooner. A clerk in some barristers' chambers in Nottingham took me aside when I had finished my law degree at Nottingham University. He told me he would be willing to offer me a trainee pupillage as a barrister in his chambers. He added his rider to a generous offer – he would be able to offer me the position provided I would do nothing more than play club rugby for Nottingham. He knew what the answer would be, because at the time I had high sporting aspirations.

He was merely trying to warn me. Barristers are essentially self-employed; they build up their names and their practices in their first two years when, not to put too fine a point on it, they take all the dross, all the lesser jobs the major barristers don't want, such as hack criminal stuff, family work or simple common law matters. I would probably have spent much of the first two years away on the rugby circuit – away, and therefore not even available for the dross. And if you are given work by a particular firm of solicitors, who want you to appear tomorrow in Crown Court in Cardiff or Manchester, then you can hardly say that you're very sorry but you have to go to training. If you do, they will not ask you again.

So I became a solicitor, which involved more day-to-day running of cases, preparing sets of papers for barristers with an outline of the case, relevant statements and relevant evidence, with occasional appearances as an advocate at the magistrates' courts – whereas as a barrister you have the equivalent of the lead singer's role in a pop group, appearing to lead the case at the Crown Courts and above, in your wig and gown. It is partly attractive, but there is no contact with the client until the day of the case, and probably none after the case ends.

It is a perception of the courtroom dramas that barristers can make a world of difference to their cases. They can make a difference if the cases are arguable, in the balance. But if you have a weak hand from the start, there are very, very few barristers indeed who could make a difference. So many of the facts tend to speak for themselves.

There is also racism and inverse racism. I once instructed a barrister from London in a drugs case. The barrister was black and defending our client, also black. He never failed to give ringing denunciations of racism wherever he felt it had occurred, either in the case or outside the courtroom. I found him, in fact, a complete prat unable to grasp the basic facts. I remember when we were going through jury selection, he objected to two Asian jurors, for no reason that I could see.

'Why did you object to those two?' I asked.

'Well, we don't want any fucking Pakistanis, do we?' he said.

There are also imponderables, such as how your witness will perform. Time and again you think that cases you have prepared are cast-iron, only for the witness to come up with something completely new which they had never even mentioned. When you ask them why they never brought it up before, they invariably come up with the same answer. 'Because you never asked me.'

I once appeared in a magistrate's court on behalf of a defendant who had been charged with assault. My plan was to establish that he was anxious and frightened when the complainant had approached him.

'Would you say you were anxious?' I asked in court.

'No,' he replied, pulling the rug from under my feet. After the case, I asked him why he had said what he said. 'I don't know what anxious means,' he said. That was my fault, and not his.

The alternative to nasty surprises is to coach witnesses, but that is very dangerous. You can take people through in outline some of the questions they may be asked, but if you coach them on specific answers, laboriously trying to get them to learn their lines, things usually start to go wrong. Their answers sound unnatural, parrot-fashion. They sound coached. You also find that when coached witnesses are cross-examined they get pulled apart very quickly, and often they only remember half the answer you may have given them.

Criminal work is the most accessible to the new solicitor so it is the kind of work you are mostly given. Initially, despite everything, it can be quite rewarding. I can still remember the first time I appeared as an advocate in court. It was an assault case, perhaps strangely involving two women who had been fighting. Even though I was up against a junior barrister on the other side, I won. The magistrates accepted that it had been self-defence, which is quite rare.

Contentious work has always appealed to me, because unlike wills and conveyancing it is adversarial work, you end with a winner and a loser. There is certainly, even now, a build-up of adrenaline when the verdict approaches. A victory is extremely pleasing, whether it is won in a small court or the House of Lords, especially as so many cases never actually come to court. The adversarial nature appealed to my own nature, just as did rugby. But gradually I passed into the field of civil law for good.

After two and a half years with Browne Jacobsen, a Nottingham company involved with civil work, I decided on a change – of club as well as career. I left Nottingham for London and approached Harlequins. The club's excellent machine for finding City posts swung into action. They raised the possibility of leaving the law and entering corporate finance with a merchant banking firm. At the time, as an assistant solicitor I did not have the variation and management responsibilities that come with a post at partnership level. I also believed that a year or two in corporate finance would do no harm in the long term for a legal career – the door back to law was still open. In 1990, I joined Rea Brothers.

They were a good company. They supported me through my own court case in Nottingham. But at that time corporate finance was in a rough period. Deals were simply not being done and it meant that those deals which were being done were extremely important. You had to throw all your resources at them night and day until the thing was finished. It was famine or feast work. They could not really put people into teams who might then have to disappear for two days, or two weeks, or even six weeks. I stuck it out for eighteen months but it did not lend itself to someone with my commitments. I also came to realize that corporate finance is easier for people with an accountancy background than for lawyers.

I discussed the future with Edwin Glasgow, a highly

respected QC who is a member of Harlequins. He mentioned to me a legal firm called Edward Lewis. He felt that they were a company who were going places, that in ten years' time they would be up there. He predicted that it would be a wise move to get in at the start.

It was. I joined Edward Lewis in 1991, became a salaried partner eighteen months afterwards, and in June 1995 I was made an equity partner. It was somehow appropriate that, on the day when I was made an equity partner, I was in South Africa with England, preparing for a match in the World Cup, roughly 8,000 miles away from Edward Lewis's offices in the City. The aspect of the firm which appeals to me is that they do not have a City mentality, they are not dominated by public school and Oxbridge people and are all the better for that.

The arrival of the equity partnership has changed the stakes in a big way. I now have more supervisory and management duties and a more proactive role in bringing work into the firm. Effectively, it means that you are self-employed, that instead of drawing a salary you share the profits, and it is technically possible for companies to make a loss. It has happened recently in other City firms, where concerns with huge turnovers found that liabilities exceeded the income with disasterous results.

The law is no longer a soft touch, as it was once considered. Previously, non-contributors were sometimes kept on. 'Old so-and-so, he didn't have a very good year. But we'll keep him going.' The profession is now in the real world – although watching the ludicrous trial of O. J. Simpson, perhaps that is an exaggeration.

The extra commitments of my new post originally caused me to contemplate retirement from rugby, and in May I actually announced that I was going to stop playing after the

World Cup. I already had all sorts of problems trying to combine sport and business and personal life, even before the extra demands of the partnership. It was starting to chip away so that it was becoming 95 per cent of both. Perhaps other people did not notice the missing 5 per cent, but it certainly mattered to me. I did not want to let the team down, and most importantly the clients. It has taken some serious juggling and sacrifice to go back on my original decision to retire. It also illustrates what I have always believed – that the line peddled by Dudley Wood and the RFU that rugby is a passport to business prosperity is rubbish. It is, in fact, a retardation of a career – and many of the current England squad have discovered that to their cost.

The Newark Burglars are now something of a distant memory. In 1991 I took on a case which started as a small affair on a point of law, on behalf of a major insurance company. The case, Giles versus Thompson, was on a principle called maintenance and champerty. It started with thirty cases under the one umbrella, then grew at a rapid rate until there were hundreds and hundreds. The work began to take over days and nights and weekends. It was all I could do to take Saturday afternoon off for the match itself. As I have said before, it affected my form markedly, affected my build-up and play in the 1993 Five Nations.

It concerned the point of whether it was legal or not for car hire companies to offer what they said was free car hire for people involved in accidents which were quite clearly not their fault, in return for a promise that they would get their money back from the other motorist's insurer; and if that did not happen, then the person who had been offered the loan of the car would assist in pursuing the claims through the courts. It is a convenient scheme, but what happened was the car hire companies, knowing the motorist was not at fault and would win if the case went to court, would inflate their rates significantly.

Originally, the insurers said they would pay up. But then the claims began to build up, the rates continued to inflate and all the solicitors instructed to act on the claims were charging their fees too. So everyone was winning in a big way – except the insurers, and ultimately anyone who paid premiums. I represented the insurers. The judgement was given while I was away on the Lions tour in 1993; but the case went on to the Court of Appeal – who showed no qualms at all in passing the buck onwards and upwards – and ultimately to the House of Lords. To see the skills of the advocates facing the law lords was quite something, as well as watching the law lords file in, dressed in civilian gear as per tradition, to deliver their verdict.

Ultimately, we lost the case on the issue of public policy, which was disappointing, although as with all cases from small criminal to major civil, all you can do is prepare to the best of your abilities. At least the media did not blame me.

11

WARS IN A PARALLEL UNIVERSE

Amateurism and bitter battles with the RFU, 1990–5

*Money can't buy friends, but you can
get a better class of enemy.*

Spike Milligan

THE DOCTRINE OF AMATEURISM WAS EFFECTIVELY IN RUINS IN THE 1980s because as well as the thousands of hidden abuses at various levels throughout the world, from money in the boots of Welsh club players to the growing signs of almost overt professionalism in South African provinces, there were the major scandals. When the New Zealand Cavaliers, effectively a rebel party, broke the boycott of South Africa with a tour in 1986, the whole rugby world knew that the Cavaliers had been richly rewarded for their trouble, and good luck to them.

In 1989 the South African Rugby Board celebrated its centenary, and even though it was impossible for a single country to tour at the time, long before Nelson Mandela's release was even on the horizon, they made strenuous efforts to bring in some kind of composite team for the celebrations. I was on tour with the British Lions in Australia in the middle of 1989 when a summons was received. Would the whole party, the Lions *en bloc*, come to South Africa later in the year to play celebration Tests against the Springboks?

The approach was on two levels and it remained on two levels until the end. The formal approach was merely for us to come over and play, within the current laws relating to amateurism. The other approach recognized that we would be extremely unlikely to make the tour, with all the other commitments and with the fair-sized storm of protest we might have to go through, and therefore would have to be well rewarded. So background figures waved their cheques. We assumed that the authorities in South Africa were fully aware that other people, fixers, were working in tandem with their invitation.

We held a meeting in a hotel room on the Lions' tour and all thirty Lions sat down to discuss it. We said: 'Right. We don't go for less than £20,000 per man.' And when you get a group of players together, inevitably the amount soon shoots up. At one stage of the meeting we were going to demand £100,000 per man. The debate suggested that because it was such an obnoxious regime we would need that sum. We would have to bar our doors, some people would have to give up their jobs and so on.

Mike Teague raised his voice of reason from the back of the room. 'These figures are just stupid,' he said. Bob Norster had done some snappy mental arithmetic and worked out that it would cost the organizers £3 million to get us there at those rates, in basic salary alone. Even for the blue-chip companies who were sponsoring South African rugby at the time, that was a major sum. The sensible point of view was taken that £20,000 might be a base figure after all, when in your working life would you ever manage to save that amount, especially in one go, with the competing demands of mortgage and children? If you actually got £20,000 in your hand it would be nice, and to get a little more would be even nicer. Four of the Lions, Finlay Calder, Donal Lenihan, Norster and myself were appointed as negotiators and talks took place with Barney Oosterhuizen, an agent of the sponsors. He made it clear that he had nothing to do with the official negotiations, although official channels must surely have been aware of him.

While we were still considering the options out in Australia, John Kendall-Carpenter, a friend of South Africa and a former president of the RFU, flew to Australia to broker and encourage some kind of official deal, telling us that if we went we would not be penalized by our unions because it was an officially sanctioned IRB tour. He pointed out in earnest tones that the normal tour allowance would be available, which was then about £12 per day.

Everyone did their best not to snigger loudly. I often wondered if Kendall-Carpenter knew about the parallel universe which was offering thousands of pounds. He did say, and it was the view expressed by others, that some kind of tour had to be arranged for the South Africans because if they had no-one to play, they would dynamite the concept of amateurism by making rugby an open game, leaving the IRB and paying whoever they wanted to come in.

Details were gradually thrashed out with the real

negotiators – which offshore bank the money would come through, and that the players would all be responsible for their own tax. I received an anxious call from Sandy Sanders, president of the RFU, telling me that he had heard rumours of big money being made available for players, and that in his view anyone who had even discussed money would have professionalized themselves. I told Sanders that his view was unlikely to be upheld in a court of law. 'Are people being offered money?' he asked. 'I can't say,' I replied.

I spoke to Will Carling who said he had been assured by the RFU that anyone who toured would never play for England again. I said this was complete nonsense because the RFU had in effect sanctioned the tour by passing on official invitations. Moreover, unless they could prove conclusively that someone had taken the South African shilling then there was nothing they could do about it.

Eventually, no decision was made for the Lions tour to make the trip as a party. We decided to leave it to individuals and then the South Africans could group any player who wanted to tour under any banner they required. In the end, the party was drawn from several countries and was known as the World XV.

My final offer from the shadowy parallel universe was £40,000, for a three-week tour. I sat down for a spot of serious contemplating. I was then in a solicitors' practice in Nottingham, I had just taken ten weeks off for the Lions tour, and if I accepted would need another three weeks off. I was only an assistant solicitor, albeit one with prospects. The partnership secretary told me that some of the partners would be in favour, others, with strong views on South Africa, would be against. He estimated that I would be granted the time off but that it might cause lingering bad feeling. In the end I decided not to go, partly on the grounds that it could harm any prospects of a partnership in the future. Money by itself has never motivated me, and I reasoned that in the long run an equity partnership would far outweigh the sum offered.

And regretted it. I should have taken the money. I left the firm shortly afterwards anyway and the boys who did accept had no problems, the payments were completely legal because they broke no law, and the Inland Revenue were only concerned about their due, not about what sporting regulations might have been broken. It was a lot of money and I should have banked it. The players who did go have a special handshake called the First National Bank handshake, in honour of the sponsors who enticed them to South Africa.

The most hilarious aspect of the whole thing was when Kendall-Carpenter addressed the troops after they had gathered in South Africa, troops drawn from around the world. The money even had to be upped late in the day because not enough players were attracted, and it took some last-minute recruiting of leading Welsh players and dramatic helicopter dashes, but eventually the party and the terms were all settled.

Kendall-Carpenter rose. 'Thank you for coming,' he said gravely. 'I believe you have just saved rugby's amateurism. If you had not come here, the game would have gone professional.' It was a wonder that the whole room did not break out into uncontrollable laughter. Did Kendall-Carpenter honestly believe what he was saying or did he know precisely what was happening? I am cynical enough to believe the latter.

I can just about summon rueful laughter about the money I passed up, about the hypocrisy of the whole affair. But there was nothing terribly amusing about the remainder of my collision with the antiquated by-laws of rugby, the battle

241

which I, and the rest of the England squad, waged against the appalling intransigence, rudeness and hypocrisy of the RFU over the past five years. It has been a time in which I encountered more opposition from my own union than from the teams of France, Scotland and New Zealand combined. It is an episode which I look back on with considerable anger, regret at all the wasted time, and very little sense of triumphalism now that outright victory is in sight.

By 1990, the demands on the leading players round the world were already reaching prodigious proportions and yet most of the rugby unions, especially the RFU, were still stridently in favour of retaining the strictly amateur concept – even though the abuses which went on around the world were numerous. They preferred to pretend that none of these were happening so that they could fool themselves into believing that there was still something left that was worth defending, that amateurism was actually the great thing in the game, without which there could not be a game. Their stances have become ever more ridiculous.

But the attitude of players were changing rapidly. The commitments were vast and making it impossible, even in 1990 and before the quantum leap in fitness and other squad sessions was made, to balance home and business life. The world, and especially the rugby world, was becoming rampagingly commercial. There was also jealousy. The Southern Hemisphere unions simply turned a blind eye to the activities of their leading players, who were already either bringing in decent money from inflated expenses, or simply taking advantage of the commercial opportunities available to them in their own countries and cashing in on their names.

Good luck to them, but it was grossly unfair that the same avenues were denied to us. In the 1970s, some straight cash had become available to players when companies like Adidas paid boot money, but even that had stopped. The England squad was now being used increasingly by the RFU, and by Twickenham's powerful money-making commercial machine, to drag in huge amounts of cash from all kinds of major deals. It was all done on our backs, and especially since we had started achieving, through sheer hard work and application, the results for which English rugby had been praying for years. We were used unashamedly.

However, it was widely predicted that, when the November 1990 meeting of the IRB reported, it would relax restrictions on players earning money off the field. There was no way it would allow pay for play, but many of the unfair restrictions on players earning from ancillary activities were, quite rightly, at risk. The meeting was eagerly awaited.

It was the view of some of us that we should be ready to take advantage of those freedoms, just as the Southern Hemisphere squads had their plans already laid. During 1990 I came down to London from Nottingham for a number of meetings with various people interested in representing the England team. However, I soon realized that the RFU would be fanatically obstructive, that even when the freedoms were announced they would still be obstructive, and that they would interpret the new by-laws in the most twisted way to stop us.

Even then we could see the first smoke of the battle, so it was absolutely crucial that we were united as a squad. The RFU had shown themselves willing to drop players for all sorts of reasons, and unless we stayed together in the battle against the silly strictness of amateurism, they would pick us off. At that time, there were influential RFU presidents of the old school, the climate was a world away from that of today. If the Carling Affair, when Will Carling was sacked and then reinstated in May 1995, had happened in 1990 it is quite likely that Will would have been sacrificed on the bonfire of their vanities and prejudices, and the squad would not have been powerful enough to stop it, as we stopped it in 1995.

Gradually, working chiefly with Will and Rob Andrew, I helped to formulate our strategy. We set up an England players' company, which we called Playervision. The players signed up to contract their promotional services to the company, the company would sign deals with sponsors and companies keen on using the England team in any commercial capacity. We paid from our own funds for a top lawyer to draw up the contracts. Originally, we thought that around twenty-six England players should sign, but then we extended it so that roughly the top thirty-five players in the country signed, just to make our force a little stronger.

Jeremy Guscott was the only leading player to hold out against signing for some time, but eventually, once we had pointed out to him that it did not affect any deals he did outside the England squad, and that we needed him for solidarity, he signed. That solidarity was to be a feature of the next five years. At least the unity was a rewarding experience. I put an incredible amount of time into the set-up phase, literally hundreds of man-hours. It was all very demanding for those of us who were still trying to train and play, go to work and live our lives at the same time. It added another draining element to the mix.

Dudley Wood, the RFU secretary and the die-hard defender of amateurism, immediately tried to intervene with warnings. This was still before the 1990 IRB meeting but I had shown the IRB regulations to a leading commercial lawyer, who shared my opinion that, as far as they stopped players from earning income legitimately under the law, they could never be upheld in court. I told Wood that the IRB regulations were so woolly anyway that if the players formed a company and did off-the-field activities, then there was nothing that the RFU could do about it.

'I think you will find,' said Wood, 'that the RFU can do pretty much what it likes.' I disagreed. 'I don't think that you will find the RFU are above corporate law, Dudley.' But the battle lines were already drawn and it was perceived throughout the years of bitterness between team and union that it was Dudley Wood and I who were the protagonists. I admire the contribution Wood has made to some aspects of rugby, but I have always felt that his role in the amateurism debate as it affected the England team was disgraceful, even rude, and always obstructive.

When the IRB announcement was made, it effectively opened areas where players could be rewarded: the field of communication, so that we could be paid for media work and books; and it also allowed certain forms of commercial activity for which we could be paid. They added a rider which stated that the activity could not be 'rugby-related'. When pressed, they explained in their tortuous fashion that you could not appear in an advertisement for washing powder with your England kit on, but you could appear in your civvies. The clause, because it was imprecisely worded, caused a tremendous amount of controversy. The Southern Hemisphere unions interpreted it freely, others did not. But at least it crossed the rubicon for the first time, players could legitimately cash in to some extent on their hard work, their profile and the profile of the game.

The reaction of the RFU was almost vicious. Their view, even though it quite obviously was at variance with the spirit and letter of the IRB changes, was that because we were rugby players, then everything was rugby-related and that effectively, apart from the communication clauses, nothing would be allowed. I spoke to Wood after the announcement. 'These changes are very small,' he said. I agreed. He told me that he felt his executive would rule that players could not appear in promotions or advertisements because they were rugby players. 'That makes a nonsense of the law change,' I said. 'Yes, it rather does, doesn't it,' Wood replied.

But the RFU were shaken because after the announcement all hell broke loose. They were running around desperately trying to learn all about our plans, trying to scupper them, finding every avenue they possibly could to hold us up and kill potential deals. You might think that, with certain commercial activity now allowed, just as some tiny recompense for all the effort we put in and the profile we had given the RFU, they would have been gracious and done their level best, as did other unions, to maximize our opportunities. Instead, they tried to strangle the income until it choked completely.

Before the IRB meeting, Playervision had engaged a company called WHJ, run by Bob Willis, the former England fast bowler, who were to approach companies to set up associations with us. Will had said that he wanted one squad under one agent rather than everyone having separate and divisive agents (that was shortly before he joined Jon Holmes, his own agent, but you could see his point).

When we launched the association there was vast suspicion from the RFU, who spoke disparagingly about 'agents hovering around the game', which was insulting for Willis. The RFU then revealed what amounted to a delaying tactic. They offered to market the squad 'in house', saying that Mike Coley, their marketing manager, would act as manager in the commercial world on our behalf. I met with Will and Rob. 'Do we trust them?' we asked ourselves. It was no reflection of Coley's commercial abilities but on the attitudes of masters

Uncorking the celebrations after the final leg of the 1991 Grand Slam, with France safely despatched. *Colorsport*

A forceful point to fellow Harlequins in our triumph over Northampton in the 1991 Cup Final at Twickenham. *Bob Thomas Sports Photography*

The ultimate feeling of being alive. Celebrating the final whistle after the fierce World Cup quarter-final in Paris in 1991. *Times Newspapers/ Chris Smith*

Trying to break past Simon Poidevin of Australia in the 1991 Final, when we missed our date with destiny because of tactical misdirection. *Mike Brett Photography*

England's finest trying not to look bored at another Moore tirade, as we thrash Ireland in 1992. From left: Winterbottom, Probyn, Skinner, Rodber, Moore, Ackford, Dooley.
Mike Brett Photography

I tried to dislike all rival hookers. A rare moment of harmony with John Olver, whom I disliked less than most. And Graham Dawe, with whom years of warring gave way to mutual respect.
Popperfoto
Mike Brett Photography

My large friends, Bayfield and Dooley, offer assistance as Jeff Tordo of France and myself take part in the grand staring championships in Paris, 1992. *Times Newspapers/Chris Smith*

One of the greatest days for forward play in the British Isles. Peter Winterbottom, myself and Nick Popplewell take the game to the All Blacks in the Second Test in Wellington – a wonderful victory. *Colorsport*

IT'S NOT THE WINNING

NIKE

Brian Moore. Harlequins & England.

IT'S THE TAKING APART

The Nike adverts which caused trouble amongst the paranoid. *Simons Palmer*

NIKE

THESE MEN ARE DANGEROUS

DO NOT ATTEMPT TO TACKLE THEM

Martin Johnson, myself, Dewi Morris and Martin Bayfield with tongue-in-cheek. *Simons Palmer*

Sewing up the ball against the All Blacks at Twickenham, and Sean Fitzpatrick can only hang around on the fringes and wait. *Colorsport*

Johan le Roux has made an impression on me and my England jersey during the Springbok comeback in the Second Test at Cape Town, 1994. *Allsport/David Rogers*

A great moment for President Mandela as he is introduced to me at Loftus Versveld before the First Test against South Africa in 1994. *Empics/Ross Kinnaird*

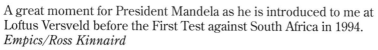

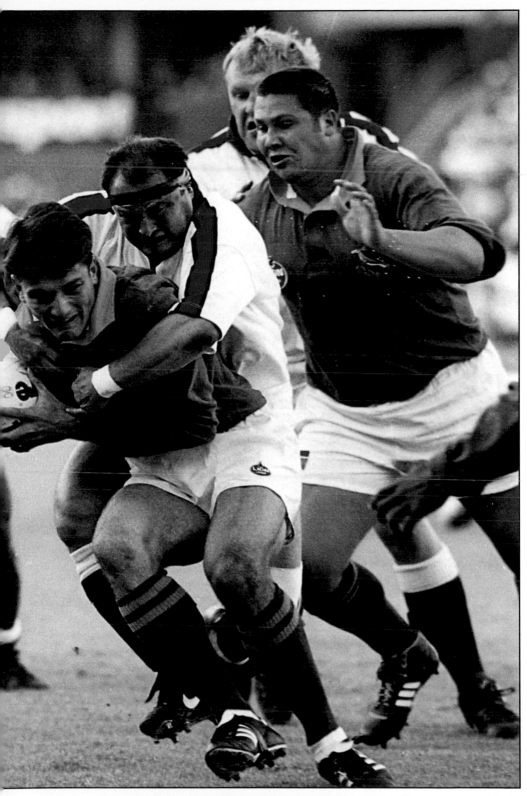

Pressurizing Joost van der Westhuizen after a line-out in the First Test. We recovered this ball and the move ended in our first try of the match. *Empics/Ross Kinnaird*

The World Cup, 1995.
Evading Willie Ofahengaue
in the emotional victory
over Australia at Cape Town,
hard fought and won late by
Rob Andrew's sensational
drop-kick. *Colorsport*

A symbolic moment of the
semi-final and the
tournament. Jonah Lomu
has thundered through our
cover defence, Tony
Underwood was the last line
to fall. *Colorsport*

when we all decided that no, we didn't trust them. Not one inch.

Before we actually gave Willis the nod to seek deals for Playervision, we had to go through one more RFU charade. They said they wanted to see presentations from other companies before they would agree to the appointment of a company to market the players. There were two rather significant problems with this. First, it had nothing whatsoever to do with them, the appointment was not at their behest. Second, we had already signed with Willis, signed a legally binding contract. But we went though a farce at Twickenham when Rob and I, together with Coley and Wood and others, sat in a room at the RFU offices and gravely listened to pitches from various companies, including First Artists.

When they had all presented, I raised the point that we had signed with Willis anyway. The RFU, after due consideration which was utterly meaningless, chose Willis. The other companies who bid had no idea they were taking part in a charade. I am sorry they wasted their time.

There is no question in my mind that the RFU had no intention of marketing us seriously if we had indeed moved under their own banner, but that they merely wanted to keep tabs on us, to turn down most of the deals. If they had offered to market us then it was their solemn responsibility to maximize our income. They had no intention of doing that whatsoever.

Things had come to such a state that, for one meeting which Jeff Probyn and I had with Coley in the Barbican, Probyn went secretly miked up to record the conversation. We had found that after previous meetings with RFU people, they had gone away to report back to the full committee and had reported back an entirely different conclusion to the one we had thought we had reached. Probyn, sitting at the table with one arm slightly raised to point the microphone in the right direction, and with wires trailing under his shirt, looked the unlikeliest secret agent I have ever come across. I kept wanting to laugh. Sean Connery, Roger Moore, Jeff Probyn . . . ?

The squad would greatly have preferred to stay under the RFU banner; they had a natural suspicion of outside agents. We understood their feelings and we shared them. But when we explained what exactly the RFU tactics were, that we felt they were trying to lay a wet blanket on proceedings, they changed their minds.

We always felt that the ideal thing would be partnership between the Union and the team. We would approach possible sponsors together and do deals that would effectively lock in the team and the Union, and would make it impossible for companies to get into the sport any other way – they would have to pay a premium for their association with the game. A large percentage of the money would go to RFU coffers and some to Playervision, in exchange for players' appearances and other promotional work on behalf of the company. We knew that the amounts raised would be greater for both sides if we acted together; and it would have saved us years of fighting, in which neither side emerged with its image enhanced. It is the most bitter irony that the kind of deal we suggested is now about to happen, with the shirt deal currently being finalized. Why did it have to take five years?

Dudley Wood dismissed our joint approach out of hand. 'I think you will find that the committee would not wish to share any money that should be going to the good of the game,' he said. But what he and the RFU have never grasped is that there are many companies who do not actually want the central involvement of the RFU, do not want to put money into junior rugby or to sponsor a particular competition. Instead, they want involvement with the players, the famous faces, to use directly the profile of successful sportsmen. This is money which can never be obtained by the RFU for the 'good of the game' or otherwise.

It was only when Willis began to market the team in earnest in 1991 that the RFU really began to pull out the stops. Understandably, because the new regulations were so complicated, companies who were interested rang the RFU to see if the deal Bob had suggested was 'legal'. Twickenham merely said no to every request. The company would then not wish to proceed.

Then there was the Cardiff incident, at the Wales–England match at Cardiff in 1991. Before the match, Willis approached the BBC to ask for a payment of £500, essentially token, for Playervision in exchange for a whole season's co-operation with interviews and the like, centred around the Five Nations. The BBC rang Twickenham to check the deal and Dudley Wood's reaction was that we could professionalize ourselves if we took the money, even though in the eyes of everyone else it was merely a perfectly legitimate action under communication for reward. We were incensed and devised our media boycott after the match. During the fuss, some of the general sports writers contributed articles under the general heading: 'Was it all worth it for £500?' Our answer was that of course it was worth it. It would have been worth it if the sum involved was two pence. We had to expose in some way the RFU's position and that is precisely what we did.

The next spiteful act of the RFU was to pull out from the match programme for the subsequent England–Scotland match of 1991 an advertisement for Timberland. The Timberland company approached us offering some clothing, though not money, for the players if some of us appeared in their programme ad. We did, with no mention of rugby, wearing no rugby kit. Scandalously and with breathtaking cheek, the RFU concluded that the advertisement was rugby-related because it was in a programme for a rugby match. This was an untenable position, utterly at odds with the IRB's interpretation of their own law, and it made the RFU and the England players an object of amusement in the Southern Hemisphere. Even the conservative Scottish RU allowed the Scotland players to appear in the same kind of advertisement for the same company. The reality was that the goalposts were being frequently moved to suit the purposes of a group of increasingly frightened men.

We decided to part company with Bob Willis for various reasons shortly afterwards, but I felt genuinely sorry for him. He was the first to dip his toe in the waters and it was always going to be a thankless task, given the barrage of abuse and obstruction he had to deal with.

Our next move was to link with the Parallel Media Group (PMG) and we signed with them after leaving Willis. Together, we decided that we would change tack, to try to avoid all the fall-out. We realized that the RFU were trying to torpedo the whole thing so we sought to build a bridge with them – not for their support, but for their neutrality, to stop putting people off.

We formulated the 'Run With the Ball' campaign. PMG would bring in companies as supporters of the squad and we would promote the campaign and the game itself through advertising on billboards and in cinemas. We would also conduct training camps for young players. We felt that might persuade the RFU that, by giving them something for nothing, by promoting the game, they should lay off so that companies were not put off. That was all we were seeking.

Virgin, Wilkinson Sword and others joined the scheme.

Before we announced Run With the Ball at a London hotel, I asked every player to contact the RFU committeemen in their area to explain the whole thing, to emphasize that they would get promotional input and coaching time for free. I got the feedback from players – X is a 'yes', Y is a 'no'. We found that a substantial majority was in favour of our scheme and had no objection.

Then we attended a full committee meeting of the RFU. Six players together with representatives of Parallel Media sat down to seek what was effectively RFU approval. There were Paul Ackford, Rob Andrew, Simon Halliday, Peter Winterbottom, Will Carling and myself. The anti-player ranks had obviously worked out a strategy beforehand. They came at us from all angles, firing questions that had obviously been worked out in advance to try to cause the maximum discomfort. They came from people we thought of as the usual suspects – Don White and Jeff Addison, and others. You always knew when the line had been thrashed out beforehand, because questions never overlapped as they would in off-the-cuff questioning, and there were no short silences while the next question was formulated. They came rapid-fire.

The PMG people fielded the questions extremely well. I was told later that the voting showed 75 per cent support for our plan, which was a gratifying margin and illustrated that perhaps the more vocal anti-player representatives had less support that they believed. It was late in the day, we had not really left enough time for proper approaches to companies, but we felt that at last we had a free rein, that the RFU would not block our aspirations. They had already cost Parallel Media thousands of pounds.

Astonishingly, we then began to hear stories, through Robert Dodds of PMG, that Dudley Wood was still telling prospective companies that not all parts of the Run With the Ball campaign were acceptable despite a formal endorsement by the full committee. This was disgraceful and it made me furious. If a company secretary misrepresented the view of his company then he would not be there long. At roughly the same time, Wood spoke in the press about the supposed evils of professionalism, then pointed out that of course this was only a personal view, which again was supremely disingenuous.

I raised Wood's attitude with Mike Pearey, the president. Pearey had the respect of the players because he was always scrupulously fair. He was put under enormous pressure from past presidents and the frightened old guard and I felt very, very sorry for him. His offence was trying to listen to both sides in the dispute. I said to Pearey that Wood should be sacked. Pearey said that everyone was entitled to their opinion but that he would have a word. The damage had been done, however. Pearey, meanwhile, sat in when we first met with a company interested in sponsoring Run With the Ball. He came along to demonstrate RFU approval and that was a gesture which he did not have to make, but which endeared him to the players.

Dudley Wood then asked for a meeting with PMG at their offices in Knightsbridge. We sat down across the table from him, and he said that before we started he would like to say a few words. He them rambled on for about twenty minutes about how huge the RFU was, how much money they needed for their upkeep, and allied supreme irrelevancies. Then he came to the presentation that we had made to the full committee. He was blatantly and, I believe, purposely rude about it. He said that in his career with ICI he had seen a good few presentations and he would give ours about two out of ten. I was terribly embarrassed at this stage for the PMG people. Robert Dodds had always been highly successful in his field and I was worried that he would react in anger at this unwarranted attack. However Richard, like me, wanted to give Wood no excuse to go back to the RFU and rubbish us, by saying that he'd spoken to PMG who were rude and dismissive of the RFU and their staff. We believed he had come to goad us and was seeking ammunition to blacken our reputation. Robert patiently heard Wood out, answered all the criticisms, thanked him courteously for coming and the meeting broke up.

Wood, as a paid employee of the RFU, should have come along mandated to make the thing work. Surely, if he had such fundamental objections and was so intent on obstruction, the honourable course would have been for him to resign. Run With the Ball ran for a year, and to be frank it was not a success. It was set up well after the optimum period for marketing, after companies who showed interest had allocated their budgets. The stock line from them was that if we had approached them eighteen months before, then they would have come in, but for now all they had left in their budget was X and we would have to accept that. Run With the Ball also had start-up costs which were heavy and the whole thing actually made an operating loss. Contracted items of media spend had to be delivered and this cost could not be avoided.

Eventually, and chiefly because PMG waived their commission, the players made around £2,000 each for the year, paid in two instalments. They were angry, and it took a good deal of explaining. They wanted to know why we had wasted money given to us by the joining companies on poster campaigns to promote the game. I tried to explain that this was to head off the RFU's malevolence, and was the price for approval of the campaign by the full committee.

I was distraught that so much effort had shown little

reward. Many of the players were also highly critical of PMG's performance. People like Mike Teague, a great friend but who had taken part in none of the set-up activities or the promotional activities, wanted to know, basically, where all his expected thousands had gone. Other players who had not really been party to the whole sorry mess of dealing with the RFU merely asked for their money. I became a little heated, asked Teague precisely what he had done to earn a large sum. But I could understand the frustration even though I appreciated from the sharp end the difficulties we had to overcome. With the benefit of hindsight we should not have established any promotional campaign, but at the time it seemed the only way forward to obtain RFU neutrality. What history taught me was that it was far better to just go ahead and do things, leaving the RFU to react, rather than to try and accommodate them.

One tactic which they used successfully for a number of years was to bog players down in working parties. Taking time away from their daytime jobs, a number of players would turn up for a meeting which usually went amicably and which seemed to have made progress. We would then find that what we thought had been agreed had in fact to be ratified by the Amateur Status committee. In turn, this had to be ratified by the Executive committee, then in turn by the Full committee. As these meetings stretched months into the future 'agreements' were nothing of the sort. In fact, they could be changed at any one of those junctures and the whole process would have to start again. We wasted hours and hours talking to people who had no mandate to settle anything.

At least we had taken part in the promotion of the game and we kept our promise to conduct coaching sessions. We organized, and paid for from our funds, a whole week of coaching for children from all over the country, staged at

Richmond Athletic Grounds, timed to coincide with the World Cup in the autumn of 1991. We even paid coaches to take part and the players attended as often as they could. It was a great success and the RFU are still using a video produced by the players. Alan Black, the national promotion officer at Twickenham, obviously loved all the promotion and the coaching; it cost him nothing from his own budget. At the end, I never received one single word of thanks from the RFU committee.

The path ahead was now obvious. We decided we were no longer going to do anything for the RFU, we were going to move into straight commercial work and we were going keep all the money. We approached companies through PMG, said this is what we can do for you, this is what it will cost. We had a stronger hand in that the worst RFU resistance was easing simply because the regulations were being thrashed out as we went along, and because opinion in the press and among the general public was always massively in our favour.

Periodically the RFU would come out and say that they had received scores of letters praising their stance on amateurism and decrying player greed. There was a deliberate attempt to portray the players as nothing more than mercenaries, when in fact all we have ever wanted was some recompense for the extraordinary commitment which International players give. In fact, I never believed there was such a preponderance of mail. I would have been confident of an overwhelming majority if this issue had been put to a referendum of all rugby supporters, players and administrators.

Over the last four years, the link between PMG and Playervision has gone from strength to strength, the deals have got better and better. The basic deal is a package to tie up with major companies as supporters of the England team, and in exchange for their support they are free to use players

255

in trade dinners, company days, product launches, golf days, the whole realm of commercial activity. It has become apparent that, especially in these years of high profile, the players can deliver major media exposure. The structure could not expand too much more because there is a limit to the amount of free time in which the players can be available for promotional duties.

We have excellent relationships with our sponsors, who include at the moment Courage, Isostar and Scrumpy Jack Cider. Scottish Provident sponsored us for our tour of South Africa in 1994 and Cellnet took over at the 1995 Rugby World Cup, and both firms received substantial media exposure. None of the companies we have been involved with have been disappointed with the results, and the commitment of the squad, albeit relying heavily on the London-based players, has generally been outstanding. We can see from our register of players' appearances if anyone is not really pulling their weight. We have delivered for everyone. We are sometimes bedevilled by outside agents claiming they could have made us all millionaires, but they are usually talking pie in the sky.

The present expectation is that the players would make a basic sum of roughly £7,000 per year, plus considerably more in World Cup year. It may not seem a vast amount, and indeed, in the next few years, as the revolution accelerates, the sums will rise massively. But it is a bonus over and above salaries and above what the players can achieve with their own deals outside the squad, which in many cases is considerable. The staple of Playervision is that everyone takes the same, from the high-profile goal-kickers to the reserve prop; so a hard-working fringe player like Graham Rowntree would take out the same sum from Playervision as Rob Andrew or Jeremy Guscott. It is a principle which I believe is very important.

There is also a gross misconception of how much money

is paid for off the field activities. I was involved in two poster campaigns for Nike and the first one in which I appeared did not benefit me at all. I put the money into the team pool, believing at the time that this was right and proper. When the second advertisement with myself, Martin Bayfield, Martin Johnson and Dewi Morris came along, the fee again went into the team pool. In fact, the second advertisement caused a major furore. We were all featured in identikit style on a poster which bore the legend: 'Warning. These men are dangerous.' It was purely tongue-in-cheek and very effective. Incredibly, RFU people and others rose up in a pompous fury suggesting the poster was some sort of celebration of violence. 'I don't think that reflects well on you,' someone told me. 'It depends on whether you have a sense of humour,' I replied.

I suppose that there might be a little jealousy at Will's earnings, which are vast and dwarf the amount he takes from Playervision; but that is simply the way of the commercial world. Jealousy is a human emotion and Will has put in no less and no more than anyone else. Yet I sometimes ask myself if I would feel any better if he didn't earn the money he does, and the answer is no.

The RFU recently underwent a sea-change, with Dudley Wood retiring and being replaced by a man with considerably more adaptability to the current era in Tony Hallett, a former high-ranking naval officer. The RFU are still not whole-hearted in support by any means, but whatever they say they have made accommodations on their precious principle all the way along the line. They are now desperate to keep the principle of no pay for play; that has become the focus of the latest myopia, the latest attempt to tell themselves that the real world is not happening. The final frontier. And soon that bastion will fall too.

The announcement in June 1995 of a massive injection of

257

money into Southern Hemisphere rugby by Ruper Murdoch's News Corporation changed the face of world rugby for good. Murdoch bought TV rights for Southern Hemisphere rugby at national and provincial levels for the next ten years, paying over US $500 million. Much of the proceeds are said to be earmarked for the leading players, to keep them in the game and ward off the threat of rugby league scouts.

As a result, the Northern Hemisphere, which has laboured under the pedantic and increasingly ridiculous semantic interpretation of archaic rules, has been put starkly in the dock. Just what are they going to do to ensure a level playing field?

We said all along that the RFU should be planning for the inevitable day of professionalism. However unpalatable that route might be, the game does not have an option and it would be far better to control things than be dictated to.

The situation was complicated even further by the introduction into the equation of three proposed alternatives to Murdoch. Kerry Packer, Murdoch's bitter business rival took a different route to try and establish his influence on the game. Whilst Murdoch did deals with the Unions in the Southern Hemisphere, Packer went right for the heart of the product: the players. The intention: to create a professional circus throughout the world, involved an ambitious plan to create a Super-10 competition in both America and Europe, effectively replicating the successful competition in the Southern Hemisphere.

In addition to this the leading English clubs, tired of the millstone of the RFU committee and indeed other purportedly 'senior' clubs, put forward an initiative of a European Club competition. On top of that there was a widely touted initiative for a World Super Clubs competition. The common denominator in all these schemes was that players would be paid. The professional ethic was accepted and amateurism was dead.

Predictably, the RFU response to these initiatives was panicky and ill thought out. Desperate meetings took place between the Players committee and RFU representatives, which thrashed through various alternatives, all of which involved the RFU throwing money at the problem. We made it quite plain that it was not only money, but the overall structure of the game which needed to change, to enable players to compete against their Southern Hemisphere counterparts both financially, and, more importantly, on the field of play. It was quite obvious that the RFU representatives, though committed to change, simply could not grasp the wider picture of a totally professional game.

This failure did nothing more than bear out my experiences of the last five years. I was always told that the further the game drifted from true-blue amateurism, the more people would drift out of the game, and that many committee men would resign. I was always utterly sceptical. I remember predicting confidently to Cliff Brittle, a hard line RFU member, that no committee man would ever resign over this issue. I have kept a close watch on the list of resignations; to date there have been none. So much for that principle.

In fact, the game will be fully professional within two years. However you dress up payment in the game, it is actually about the stepping on the field, regardless of whether you also deliver any media value off the field. In effect, the top echelon of the game will be run very much like rugby league, with the remaining 98 per cent of people continuing to play for fun as they have done and always will do. This division works in every other sport without difficulty. I simply do not believe the RFU claim that vast swathes of players and administrators in junior clubs will leave the game if the top end is professional.

At all levels, unions and teams will have to pay what they can afford either on a professional or semi-professional basis. Referees will have to be paid and so will administrators. As people go down the scale, there will be an effective divide between paid and unpaid. Someone once warned me that if the game was fully professional at top level then the RFU would not be able to gather fifty-seven people to administer the game. Wonderful. Why do you need fifty-seven people in the first place? The fact is that a small band of paid executives could achieve the same result, and, moreover, you can sack people you pay, whereas you would find it very difficult to sack amateurs, no matter how incompetent they are.

The advent of a professional game will bring much needed reward for the time and effort put in at the highest level. It will also give people not blessed with mental capabilities the opportunity to earn a decent living out of their physical blessings. And yet, there will be a down side. People involved in professional careers, such as doctors, surveyors and lawyers, will find it very difficult to pursue a career. Accommodations will have to be made and they will have to give up, at least temporarily, advancement in their careers. This is a sad fact, but again it is inevitable.

In addition to this, professionalism will exact a price from players in other ways. There will be no room for complaints about tiredness or pressure. Training will no longer be haphazard. Importantly, the relationship with the crowd will change. Once people know their admission money is linked to your salary, they feel they have the right, almost an obligation, to make their feelings known about your performance at every point. When it goes well it is wonderful. When it goes badly it is savage.

If these are the down sides then there will certainly be up sides. Fitter and more athletic players will provide a faster and more furious game, provided the lawmakers and referees can keep up to speed. The danger of foul play, a card often used by the RFU, is largely illusory. Suspension and fining will be a severe deterrent, and, provided that the disciplinary measures are severe, professionalism could well benefit the game in the way that it has done in golf.

Rugby is a unique game and will remain as such. The huge physical commitments involved will not lessen the camaraderie and social life for the vast majority of the game. At the very highest level this will subtly alter, although I do not believe these aspects will be lost forever. The challenge for rugby union is to maintain the best aspects of the game and limit the worst. I am not blind to the pitfalls of a professional game, but believe this is the logical end once unions accept money. It has happened in every other sport and rugby union will not avoid it.

Unfortunately, at present it looks like the change will be forced instead of managed, something we have continually advised the RFU not to allow. The dominance of money interests in athletics, tennis and so on has come about simply because their own bodies took a similar stance to the RFU. 'This will not happen in our game' was the cry and it did, time after time. In fact, the RFU refusal to prevent this occurring in rugby is even worse than ruling bodies in other sports, because they were quite clearly told of the threat and had living proof that it would occur – yet they did nothing.

When Dudley Wood trumpets the achievements of his last ten years as secretary of the RFU he will probably point to the vast new stand at Twickenham and the great regard in which rugby is held in England. He should also reflect on a few other matters. Just how much of this would have been possible without the success of the England team, which was based squarely on the hard work of its players? Further, and more importantly, now that he has stepped away from his paid post, where is the sensible plan to move forward into the professional era? A secretary's job, for which he is paid handsomely, is to give advice to the union at various levels. The inevitability of professionalism was such that Wood should have been openly pushing the RFU to examine the whole issue thoroughly, and to put forward a blueprint for the future, even if publicly attempts were made to prevent professionalism occurring. To me the way in which Wood has acted is very similar to that of a Minister of Defence in 1933, refusing to make preparations for World War II. Nobody wanted the war, but everyone knew it was coming, and would it really have been sensible to refuse to plan for battle?

On reflection, I don't begrudge all the time I have spent in the creation of Playervision, nor the hundreds and hundreds of hours involved with this subject. However, I do resent the totally unnecessary bitterness which has pervaded the whole issue. There were times when I was so overwhelmed with various commitments that I actually made the decision to step aside. But then I realized that this is precisely what the RFU traded on. They knew that all players have a shelf life, but that they are in power for twenty or thirty years. They also knew that younger and less-experienced players would be afraid to speak out against what was happening for fear of losing their places. To step back would have meant leaving the younger and more exposed players at the mercy of bullying and intimidation. Myself, Andrew and Carling, and indeed a number of others, were determined to see it through. There were times in the early days when we were protected from dismissal only by the solidarity of the squad and our excellent results. I am proud that I did see it through, not so much to outlast amateurism, but to outlast hypocrisy and intransigence.

12

CONTINUITY AND REVOLT

The World Cup build-up and the third Grand Slam

It is never difficult to distinguish between a Scotsman with a
grievance and a ray of sunshine.
P. G. Wodehouse, *Blandings Castle and elsewhere*

IT WAS THE SPORTING EVENT OF THE YEAR, AN INDICATION THAT
the growth of rugby was still headlong. I always believed
that the third rugby World Cup would be bigger and better.
South Africa was always going to be a special venue, provided
that optimism and patience survived among the different
races there. When England toured South Africa in 1994, a
privileged visit just after the first elections had brought
President Mandela to power, the air of optimism was palpable; but in the year before the World Cup started, there was

always the chance of a backlash, either from the far right, or more probably from disaffected non-whites who had found that having the vote, having elected a black president and a global hero, had not, for the moment, affected their standard of living in any profound fashion.

However, the optimism was indeed retained, the progress of the Rainbow Nation had obviously continued and, perhaps best of all for rugby, the tournament itself seemed to accelerate the progress and reconciliation.

South Africa's return would obviously galvanize the rugby side, because before the tournament it seemed obvious to me that there were now five major contenders, in Australia, South Africa, New Zealand, France and ourselves, and any one of those teams could beat the others if it hit the ground running and kept the streak of form. I also disagreed with what many observers were saying about the so-called lesser nations. I knew that they would not be wiped out. Teams like Canada and Italy may not have enjoyed spectacular results but with the focus of the tournament I knew they would all improve and try their best to sink their teeth into the more illustrious teams. That is precisely how it turned out. England's fortunes were not so predictable. I knew from a year out that we could beat any other team on our day, if we had good fortune with the refereeing, and if we stayed ruthless rather than slipping into an all-too-familiar mind set when we accepted one great victory instead of putting it behind us and going hell for leather for the whole prize. It had happened before.

However, there was still the massive period of build-up to get through first. The rather neat figure of Geoff Cooke had been replaced by the rather gangling figure of Jack Rowell just in time for our expeditionary and exploratory tour of South Africa in the summer of 1994. To see how Jack went about assessing the squad and imposing himself was fascinating. My first impression in early squad meetings was that he was deliberately trying to make everyone nervous, to sow doubt in people's minds about their place in the team. Sometimes he would chew people out, sometimes crack a joke about them in public and sometimes in private, sometimes he would attack someone with a blunt comment or perhaps a word behind the scenes, or perhaps, most bewildering of all, no word at all. It was no more than good man management but it had not existed in many teams I had played for. Geoff Cooke's approach tended to be more homogeneous, he did it all inside the team room in a fairly structured way.

Jack certainly had his desired effect – on Will Carling, to name one. He was definitely a little unnerved early on, until he and Jack got used to each other. Carling started making references to the need to end a comfort zone in the England team. I looked round and tried to work out who he thought was languishing in one, because I certainly had never been there.

Jack was less organized than the formidably organized Cooke, or that is how he liked to appear as we built up for the South Africa matches in 1994. He would occasionally arrive at team meetings, look round and ask: 'Well, what's happening then?' We would look blank. He would select one player and point out that he had told him to organize this or that; the player would not have suspected that he was supposed to take the whole session, would drag himself to his feet and with a good deal of stuttering start the meeting rolling. It made you think and it made you prepare fully just in case he called on you next.

I was immediately impressed by Rowell as a coach, and indeed my conclusion at the end of an enormous season, which stretched from the start of the 1994 tour to the end of the World Cup, more than twelve back-breaking, rigorous and high-profile months later, is that Rowell is one of the best coaches I have been involved with, a man of talent and charisma, a man who lives up, for good or ill, to everything his former charges at Bath used to say about him!

The 1994 tour began in a sweat. We opened against Natal in Durban, where we were to be based a year later for our pool matches in the World Cup. The humidity was extraordinary. I was sweating from the moment I walked into the dressing room until the time I returned after the match, so much so that the ball was slippery and difficult to handle.

In the early games England did not play well, did not cause South Africa to quake at the prospect of what we would do to them in the two-match Test series and the World Cup a year later. We lost to Natal, lost to Orange Free State at Bloemfontein, the (horrible) Garden City; then we lost to Transvaal at Ellis Park, Johannesburg.

Rowell had come in with a brief to accelerate the English game, to improve continuity. Against Transvaal we were given a glimpse of what we hoped would be our own future – Transvaal were dynamic, they played astonishing rugby. Perhaps it was also the effects of altitude but I have never played in so fast a game, a game where the opposition made so few mistakes, even when handling under pressure. Incredibly, it was less than two years since I had first played against the South Africans, on their tour of France and England. At that time they were hidebound, muscle-bound, old-fashioned. Here, suddenly, they were bang up to date. It was quite obvious that the priceless cross-pollenation of the Super-10 tournament had worked a kind of magic on the country's rugby – and in record time.

Yet we lost only by 4 points. Will Carling had a try

disallowed when he touched down behind the Transvaal line, only to find that Ian Rogers, the referee, had turned his back and already awarded a drop-out, which was a shocking piece of refereeing. The criticism in the press both at home and in South Africa reached a peak, increased by the fact that we were losing our games. There were elements of triumphalism and arrogance in the South African media as the Tests approached. Yet I always felt that the pressure of a Test match would mitigate against Transvaal's fast-flowing style, that we were gathering strength.

And as so often happens, a midweek match inspired us. People who write off midweek matches as being of no significance never realize how much they influence the mood of the tour, the mood of the party. Our second-string team played South Africa A in Kimberley three days before the First Test. It was not really the England Second XV because the tour selection had brought in some of the more promising young players at the expense of players who were towards the end of their careers, yet who might, strictly speaking, have been the current second choice for the England side.

The South African A team was loudly trumpeted, people said it was a team of incredible talents. They also fielded a bunch of forwards who, to say the least, have never cared where they put their feet or their fists – James Dalton, Kobus Wiese and especially Johan le Roux, the ridiculously excitable prop from Transvaal. I was not surprised in any way to learn that le Roux was sent home in disgrace from a tour of New Zealand later that year after graphically biting Sean Fitzpatrick in a Test match.

But although the attempted intimidation was obvious at Kimberley, our team stood up to it extremely well, with forwards like John Mallett, Simon Shaw and Steve Ojomoh facing them down. We did lose the match, chiefly due to a hotly disputed try, but we stood our ground in some toe-to-toe exchanges, and all in all it was an inspirational performance. When we prepared for the First Test, to be played at Loftus Versveld, Pretoria, I was convinced we could upset all the predictions.

We were probably helped by the fact that, for South Africans, it was a massive occasion as well as a Test. President Mandela was present to meet the teams and there was a great sense around that rugby was changing and becoming less of the ogre to the non-white population that it had once been. It was a special moment when I shook hands with the President, but while all the pre-match fuss was going on, while helicopters were flying over in formation and the show proceeded, we kept very firmly focused, while possibly the Springboks were swept along with the extraneous matters.

For the first twenty minutes we played some of the best rugby of my time in the England team, we scored two tries, and soon we were playing to the sound of silence. Loftus Versveld was eerily quiet. I remember two crucial incidents in those opening stages. They knocked down a line-out ball which missed Joost van der Westhuizen, the South African scrum-half. I caught him in possession as he tried to recover, turned him over and we won the ball. It was moved left and later in the move Ben Clarke drove over for the try. The second came when Francois Pienaar, the South African captain, tried to come around the side of the scrum. Tim Rodber, Dean Richards and Ben Clarke played superbly in that Test in the back row, and when Pienaar came round he was tackled, he was hit by the forwards driving as one, knocked back yards, and we were given the scrum. Deeply satisfying. Rob Andrew kicked brilliantly in that match and also scored a try by following up his own kick, leaping high over the Springbok line for the catch and falling back to earth for the score.

South Africa tried to stage a comeback but we coped with their storm and for the last fifteen minutes were attacking again, and could have scored at least one more try. It all constituted one of the best Test victories in which I have been involved.

The significance of rugby in the fabric of South African society was made obvious to us in the aftermath of that Test. The national reaction was vast and wounded. Every newspaper carried inquests on its front page, demands for action, appeals for calm. Every paper carried editorials, one saying that we had taught South Africa a lesson in rugby and in humility. Rugby may have grown enormously in Britain but I could not imagine *The Times* or *Telegraph* containing weeping editorials on the occasion of England defeats.

I suppose that in the week after the Test, a week which ended with the Second Test at Newlands, Cape Town, we once again showed what could be termed the English rugby disease – a failure to maintain complete concentration and ruthlessness to turn a brilliant one-off into total victory, or at least something more lasting. Perhaps we allowed our feelings of euphoria to go on a day too long. Certainly there was a monumental party in the evening after the game, one in which many players, including myself, overindulged spectacularly. When you look back you feel we could all have been more focused – although that is with hindsight's benefit, because at the time the focus felt roughly the same.

By the time we reached Cape Town we had lost Dean Richards with injury. Tim Rodber, who had suffered the emotional upset of being sent off three days before the Test in a violent match against Eastern Province and then suffered a physical upset too, had been outstanding in the First Test but had a quiet match in the return. And we lost the match, eventually overwhelmed and forced to concede a drawn series.

We had expected the Springboks to come at us with vast intensity and emotion. Their backlash was abrasive, the physical onslaught fierce. Johan le Roux had been brought into the team to bring in his particular brand of hysteria, and if that was what the selectors wanted then he did not let them down. Le Roux had bitten Paul Hull in the Transvaal match; within seconds of the kick-off in Cape Town he had stood on Hull's head. At times, with his eyes rolling wildly, he was running around bawling, 'I love it, I love it,' at the top of his voice, a man completely gone. He was completely unable to differentiate between acceptable ferocity and plain lunatic play. He is a man who, basically, should not be allowed on to a rugby field.

We had managed to hold out against some of the worst blasts of the storm in the first half and it was only 3–3 when Rory Underwood burst away in space. A try then might conceivably have turned the tide but Rory was hammered by a superb tackle by Adriaan Richter, the South African No. 8. Then towards the end the pressure told, and they ran in tries through Hennie le Roux and, after an attack from deep down the left wing, through André Joubert.

The feeling after the match and after the tour was that we had demonstrated the ability to beat anybody, but in the year until the World Cup had ample scope for improvement; that we could beat any of the five top teams, but also we could lose to any of them. At that time, we all regarded the emergence of Paul Hull as the individual success of the tour – not that it did Paul much good. He never even made the World Cup squad, held back by the fact that he was not a regular goal-kicker.

I felt my form had been good. I did have a shocker against
Natal, but I played well in the First Test, and in the Second.
When it was all hands to the pumps, I tried to do my fair
share of tackling and grappling along with everyone else. I
did feel valued by Jack Rowell throughout the tour, because
Rowell seemed to give me far more of a central role than had
Cooke. For some reason, Jack even let me escape from the
various remonstrations he had with the rest of the squad in
the cause of grabbing their attention and ensuring they were
on their toes. Perhaps he realized I was on my toes already.

The tour had ended on notes of considerable sourness after
the Eastern Province match, which became known as the
Battle of Port Elizabeth. The other provincial teams we had
met warned us that Eastern Province would be dirty and try
to upset us, and the match became essentially a running
battle, perhaps not the worst I have ever seen but very close
to it. Tim Rodber had gone on as a replacement, was
provoked and retaliated with a flurry of punches. After a
period of confusion when a desperate referee tried to make
his decision known, he was sent off. The cheap shots from
Eastern Province came thick and fast. The worst was a boot
to the head of Jon Callard from Elandre van der Berg, the
home forward. Callard had two extremely nasty cuts near his
eye and went off to have lines of stitches, badly shaken. I was
desperate to get on to the field. Graham Dawe was in the
heart of the battle, and when he was hit from behind by his
opposite number temporarily went groggy. However, our
bench were equally desperate for me not to go on, because
they foresaw a repeat of the Rodber incident, with the
replacement losing his cool. Dawe battled in another strong
forward performance and we won.

I thought we lost the plot a little after the match. Rodber,
to the fury of many people appointed as guardians of the

game, was let off with no punishment and so was available for the Test on Saturday. To demonstrate the appalling attitude and violence of the Eastern Province side, we allowed John Mallett and Lawrence Dallaglio to be photographed. They had livid stud marks on their backs and those pictures were suddenly winging their way across the world.

I was unhappy about that. I have always drawn a distinction between raking to the head and to the body: the first type is always unacceptable, the second is usually a result of vigorous rucking and simply unfortunate. We were correct to make a protest but we should have concentrated on Callard's injuries, which were bad enough.

That, for the moment, was South Africa. It had been a good tour, a useful tour to kick off our World Cup preparations and the new era under Rowell and his new chief lieutenant, Les Cusworth, who took charge of the backs. I found the whole country fascinating, especially the contrasts – it differed widely, from Pretoria to Durban, from Durban to Cape Town. Every town differed in terms of climate, social mix, atmosphere. There was the hideous Bloemfontein and the grandeur of Cape Town. It was and is a great place to tour, with the rider that tours should always do their best to bypass the murder capital of the world, the evil Johannesburg.

The tour was also notable for the impact it made on the travelling RFU representatives who were with us. I have to take the word of others for that because I made a point of not talking to any of them at any point of the tour. But these men who had always claimed that our stories of widespread professionalism in South Africa were exaggerated were now confronted with the evidence. The Eastern Province president spoke in public of needing more money to keep his squad in the province. Louis Luyt, the SARFU president, made various speeches condemning England's stand on amateurism. There was also the universally accepted fact of massive expenses paid by all the major provincial teams.

I am told that many of the RFU camp followers were genuinely taken aback. At least that gave them some sort of right to be there. I simply could not understand why they all invaded the tour party proper, why they had a right to be on the team bus, to be at the team hotel and team dinners. 'We are part of the committee,' was their explanation. 'So fucking what?' was our response.

No-one would accuse England of being underprepared for the World Cup when it eventually arrived. The domestic season 1994–5 involved six Test matches, interminable squad sessions and personal training, including a stack of sessions at Marlow Rugby Club in Buckinghamshire. And before the players based in the west country and the north began to complain that the southern-based players were therefore training on their doorstep, we had to inform them that to get to Marlow from my London office usually took around two hours, less than the trip from Bath.

The staple of our preparation was to work on achieving greater continuity, using the back row to make space and retain the ball and then handing on to the backs to exploit it. That was the theory of our game, the one Jack Rowell espoused the whole season; it worked to varying degrees of success in the domestic internationals; we did score a lot of tries during the season. The only other priorities were to win the Grand Slam and the World Cup.

The two pre-Christmas Tests were perfectly graduated. We began by overwhelming Romania, after a sticky start on a dark Twickenham autumn Saturday; we scored more than 50 points against Canada too, which was a very fine effort. Canada may not have been quite at their best that day but they showed how competitive they are in the World Cup to follow, and for a good half-hour at Twickenham they were highly physical and energetic. They had a heavy pack, they won line-ball through Norm Hadley in the middle, and by throwing the ball long to their back row. They disrupted us and they knocked us backwards. It took a tremendous kicking performance by Rob Andrew to subdue them and we made our scores later on, cashing in on good groundwork and good approach work. We were affected, as we were to be affected later in the season, by the fact that Canada were quite prepared to concede a penalty and 3 points to stop a possible 7 for a converted try.

It was an indication of the changed perceptions of everyone in English rugby that we were expected to win the Grand Slam in the 1995 Five Nations, that anything else would have been a kind of failure, whereas when I came into the side we would always have settled for two reasonable performances in our home games and a mid-table position. I was concerned that, under the pressure which the Five Nations always exerts, not to mention the weather conditions of a European winter, we did not retreat into our shell, we did try to keep the ball in hand and keep the flow and continuity.

And the opener, in Dublin, was the perfect test. It was played in the worst weather conditions I have experienced. High winds are more disruptive than heavy rain and the wind simply howled round Lansdowne Road. It was also bitterly, bitingly cold. If you placed the ball on the ground it would simply roll away on the wind, and with throwing in to the line-out I had to take a wider stance because the wind threatened to blow me off balance. The only type of throw relevant to the conditions was hard and flat – any lobbed throw would have blown at least 5 yards off the straight.

It was a notable effort by England to subdue Ireland in

conditions which were essentially suited to the spoiling Irish tactics. We won 20–8, with tries from Carling, Ben Clarke and Tony Underwood. I was also thrilled that we clearly had the better of Ireland in the scrummages. By the time of the match I had heard enough about the Irish front row. A new hooker in Keith Wood had arrived in the side, between Nick Popplewell and Peter Clohessy, the props. As a unit they had played against the United States and for the Barbarians against South Africa, and they were receiving what theatre impresarios tend to call rave reviews – especially Wood, who showed lively ability in the loose play. The confrontation between the front rows and between Wood, this new pretender, and myself was built up for weeks.

On the day before the game, I conducted a forty-minute press conference with members of the media. I was – perhaps strangely for me – conspicuously fair, extremely careful not to say anything which could demean the Irish. I said that it was too early to judge Wood and his colleagues, because they had only met the USA in a Test; and that while they had played well against what was the second-string South Africa front row for the Barbarians, a Barbarian match was a world away in intensity from a real Test. I then concluded by saying that the Irish might turn out to be the best front row in the world but it was a little too early for the final assessment.

Next day, I read the headlines. 'Moore Aggro' was one. 'Moore warns Irish' was another. I realized that there was no point in trying to be measured and even-handed, because people were going to write whatever they wanted anyway. In the team meetings before the match I felt my own motivation and anger growing, as the latest eulogy to the Irish front row poured out in the papers. At the final team meeting the boys were asked one by one where they thought the main threat would come. Dewi Morris stood up. 'Well,' he said, 'I think Keith Wood is a threat, he is a lively player, takes the ball up well.' Phil de Glanville was next. 'Keith Wood has to be their main danger, an outstanding player, drives the ball well, the focal point for the Irish team.'

The next man called upon mentioned Wood as well for a torrent of praise. I had heard enough, I was just about to get to my feet to attack this gushing nonsense when I saw everyone fighting back the laughter. The room then collapsed. Apparently, they were watching me when the praise for Wood started and I looked angrier and angrier. I had fallen hook, line and sinker for the wind-up.

But I did have the last word. We were so superior to them in the scrum that we could have had a penalty try when they collapsed. But we drove superbly, our control was excellent and we came out well satisfied.

The French came to Twickenham with huge expectations. I was absolutely delighted that they had won the Test series in New Zealand in the previous summer. It was a great thing for the reputation of rugby in the Five Nations and the Northern Hemisphere and they were excellent value for their victories. And they were obviously so desperate to keep control of themselves, not to rise to the usual baited line about their indiscipline, that they lost the balance in the wrong direction, they came in almost too apologetic and too passive.

I had kicked off the traditional media barney the day before the match. It was just after Eric Cantona, the Manchester United footballer, had dramatically attacked a spectator at Crystal Palace. 'The French,' I told the media, 'are like fifteen Eric Cantonas. Brilliant and brutal.' Paul Ackford called it the most irresponsible comment he had heard that year, so at least I was on form. The fact that I had uttered the line as part of a much longer, and jocular, reference to the prospects for the match escaped most readers, and most newspaper sub-editors too.

England were also in form. We beat France by 31–10, it was one of the best performances of our whole long season. Jeremy Guscott broke what had been a scoring drought since his return from injury against Romania, with a try near the posts, and towards the end we scored two superb tries, both touched down by Tony Underwood. One was direct from a scrum in a blindside attack, a move we had practised hundreds of times in training, and it was made by a burst from full-back by Mike Catt, a player whose talents gave us another dimension. The French scored a typically brilliant try, counter-attacking from deep in their own right-hand corner and sending Sebastien Viars over in the diagonally opposite corner. It was breathtaking as well as typical, but in the final analysis we had maintained our dominance over France, and the French forwards in particular. They must have been furious.

The next adventure was to carry our emotional baggage back down to Cardiff. We may have broken the spell of Cardiff, where successive England teams were bewitched, but there were always enough memories, enough history and sociology, enough pressure involved in playing there, and anyone who believes that Cardiff will ever provide easy pickings for an English team does not understand international rugby, or life.

I was genuinely sorry, however, at the problems facing Alan Davies, my old friend. Wales, who had won the Championship in the previous season, had been savaged by injury and had lost their two best players, Scott Quinnell and Scott Gibbs, to rugby league. It was ridiculous that Davies was singled out for criticism, and jettisoned before the World Cup. Very few of the Welsh problems were in his control.

We beat Wales by 23–9, with tries from Victor Ubogu and Rory Underwood. We again found a team prepared to spoil us by conceding penalties, and we really should have awarded Garin Jenkins, the Welsh hooker, a cap for England, so often did he seem to be around our side in the scrum-half position, stopping the flow. Again we attempted to keep some ball in hand, to maintain our drive to a game of more continuity; again we had some partial success.

Elsewhere, the Scots had been toiling through their season and then shocked the rugby world, no doubt including themselves, by winning in Paris for the first time since the dinosaurs died. Although they were assisted by some poor French play it was still a momentous victory for them, one sealed by Gavin Hastings running through to score at the posts. It set up a repeat of 1990, a true Grand Slam shoot-out at Twickenham; for me, the perfect motivation. And for the game yet another burst of spectacular publicity and hype. The media were besieged again by rugby for the whole two weeks before the match.

We were also well motivated by various insulting articles in the papers on the morning of the match from Scots with a chip on both shoulders. John Jeffrey called us Barboured yobs, which seemed to me to fall short of outstanding technical analysis about a rugby match. He said that the Scottish team always suffered abuse from the car park crowds when their team bus arrived at Twickenham. The poor dears. In my experience Twickenham is the mildest crowd around, and whatever they do dish out is nothing compared to the invective we have to put up with when we visit Murrayfield.

We duly completed the Grand Slam, my third as a member of the England team, and saw off Scotland to the tune of 24–12. But it was deeply unsatisfying. We had set out to play a new-style game but Scotland had decided to play an entirely negative game. The penalty count against them was 19–9 and Brian Stirling, the referee, could easily have penalized them completely out of sight. However, as the Scots know well, referees can only award so many penalties, otherwise they become associated with appalling matches and no-one asks them to referee again. All our points came from kicks: whenever we threatened to take the ball through enough phases to make space for the backs, a blue jersey would come lolling over the top and the whistle would go.

When I came off I was bitterly disappointed. It was a lovely day, a perfect stage, with millions of people looking on. I felt very sorry for the people who had expected more of the match. I was dragged into the interview room to speak live on BBC to Nigel Starmer-Smith. Some people would have given the PR answers to Starmer-Smith's questions, but I have rarely bothered with the PR response and I was in no mood to start. I merely said what everyone in the England dressing room was talking about in private – that Scotland had come to kill, that they had done well what they had come to do, which wasn't much, that they had ruined the match and that I felt sorry for the spectators.

Up in the *Grandstand* studios, John Jeffrey had his fit of apoplexy. This was the man who had dished out abuse to England as a country in the morning, reacting in fury to what was, at the end of the day, technical criticism of a rugby team rather than abuse of a nation as a whole. When we killed the 1988 Calcutta Cup match stone dead at Murrayfield, Derrick Grant, the Scotland coach, quite rightly berated us all over the media. It was perfectly acceptable for a Scotsman to do that, but not, apparently, for an Englishman to return the compliment.

Enraged Scots jammed the BBC switchboard and I received mountains of mail in the next week or so. There were two common denominators: all the letters were abusive, like Jeffrey, and like Jeffrey none actually addressed the technical issues I had raised, none tried to set up a cogent counter-argument. One letter, easily the funniest of a hilarious bunch, was nine pages long and was still swearing away by the time it reached the ninth page. I also came across a hilarious article by John Beattie, a former international who has never spoken to me, which simply raged on abusively and could never actually bring itself to steer anywhere near any of the issues whatsoever.

My friend Finlay Calder came quickly on to the phone. 'This is your only friend in Scotland,' he said when I answered. 'What you said was true,' said Finlay, 'but did you really expect us to do anything else?' I replied that of course I had expected nothing else, it was what England would have done if they were similarly outplayed and outgunned, but why should I take all the stick for bringing up the subject in public. We had a good laugh about the whole thing. 'When you come up we'll go out and do some missionary work,' said Calder. 'You are in dire need of a better image up here.'

Notwithstanding the last round-up, it had been the least satisfying of the Grand Slams. We had done it before, it was no longer new. The differences in perception meant that it was not seen out in the country as a momentous act. There was also the strong feeling in the squad that the job was only half-finished, that the prize was the title of World Champions, that it was a realistic goal, and that we would soon get over the flat feeling left by the spoiling Scots.

The departure for the World Cup was still two months away after the Grand Slam and we were able to step up our preparations at Marlow out of the public glare, and we moved into a stage, to be frank, where the preparations were beginning to pall, and the burst of freedom represented by the real thing in South Africa was being keenly anticipated.

At the start of May I went back to Yorkshire to attend the Old Crossleyans dinner, and to look up some friends. On the Saturday I was at the house of David Bradley, my best man, to watch the live coverage of the Pilkington Cup final between Wasps and Bath. At the Crossleyans dinner, a fair few people brought up the subject of a TV programme which had gone out that week in which Will Carling, as part of a rather jokey and throwaway line, had called the RFU committee 'fifty-seven old farts'. Apart from remarking on the accuracy of the line, I dismissed it. 'He was only being light-hearted,' I said. I was amazed that so many people thought it a big deal.

I was watching Gary Lineker's Football Focus on *Grandstand* next day when Gary referred to the fact that Will Carling had been sacked as England captain over the issue. I was, at first, almost stupefied. Then I began to laugh. I found the whole thing absolutely hilarious. The RFU had pompously overreacted, and I knew immediately that their position was completely untenable, that they had blown it in a big way and would quickly became a laughing stock. I knew that everyone would refuse to take the captaincy, I knew that they would have to reinstate Will.

I was also staggered, not so much by their thin skins but by their timing. It was then less than two weeks before we were to depart for South Africa, so they might clearly be seen to be interfering with our World Cup preparation and our chances. And I could imagine well the suppressed anger of Pilkington, the faithful sponsors of the Cup. That Saturday was the big day of their whole year. And here were the RFU spoiling the party, distracting attention from the final completely, so much so that most of the leading rugby writers were diverted to covering the Carling Affair, leaving their understudies to pen a few short paragraphs on the big match itself.

It was an astonishing tactical blunder and a desperate overreaction. They could well have carried it off, say, eight years ago. But this was 1995, the RFU no longer wielded the power it thought it did, the public and media were almost solidly behind Will on the whole matter – indeed, I contemplated for a time the theory that it was all a giant publicity stunt cooked up by Jon Holmes, Will's agent, to increase his man's popularity.

The team stayed solid – although Ben Clarke did break ranks in his *Telegraph* column to say, rather diffidently, that he might accept the job – an admission for which he was rigorously pilloried at the next team meeting. This time, it was not me who orchestrated the team but Rob Andrew and Dean Richards. They issued a careful statement asking the RFU to reconsider, effectively offering them an escape route as public anger grew. Desperate though I would have been to accept the captaincy if offered, I would also have turned them down flatter than flat – not that they would have approached me even as a last resort.

The capitulation was rapid and it was total. On the Monday we were due to train at Marlow. Will and Dennis Easby, the president, had meet at Twickenham in the morning and devised some kind of statement which purported to have Will apologizing and being warned as to future comments. Then, in what must have been a rather stilted journey, they drove to Marlow together to meet the squad and make the formal announcement.

Easby must either be very thick-skinned or very courageous – and I tend towards the latter. He fronted up at Marlow, had to walk past members of the public holding banners in support of Will. He announced that Will was reinstated, tried to explain the capitulation in terms that made everyone snigger; the whole reaction from the players showed the contempt in which elements of the RFU had come to be held on the part of the squad. It indicated to anyone still clinging to the thought that the RFU were fit rulers of the game that they should perhaps think again.

13

SCHIZOPHRENIA

The 1995 World Cup, and five minutes that changed the world

How do you stop Jonah Lomu? I've no idea.
I suppose an elephant gun might help.

Bob Dwyer

IT WAS NEAR THE END OF THE QUARTER-FINAL, A MATCH ALMOST drowning with emotion. Australia set themselves for a scrum near our 22, on their left-hand side of the field and, it seemed, in a perfect position for Michael Lynagh to drop what would almost certainly be the winning goal. When the scrum went down my thoughts flashed back to a game in Paris early in my England career, when Les Cusworth had gone for what would have been a crucial drop goal; however, the French scrum had wheeled their own back row nearer to Cusworth and the open-side flanker charged down the kick.

I called a wheel to our left, which would take George Gregan, the Australia scrum-half, further away from Lynagh and would bring Ben Clarke, on our open-side, nearer to him. Phil Kearns struck the ball for Australia and we put the wheel on. I could see the ball at the feet of the No. 8 at the back of the Australian scrum. Then it disappeared and I listened for the thud as Lynagh made contact. But it never came. He had not dropped for goal; he said later that the circumstances were not quite right. Later in the same move, however, David Campese took the ball, looked up at the posts and dropped for goal with his left foot.

Time seemed frozen. I swear that, from the time I saw Campese shaping to kick and before I ever saw the outcome, I was able to think: 'Oh no. Not him. Anyone but him.' I also had time to formulate the next day's newspaper headlines. 'King Campo kicks England out of Cup' was my best effort. The kick almost hit the corner flag, we were still alive, and King Campo had made a king cock up. I scrapped the headline. Later that day, in newspaper offices around the world, they were dreaming up headlines to describe another drop-kick.

Symbolism and intensity. The tone was set from the start. We sat in our headquarters hotel in Durban and watched the opening ceremony from Newlands, and the first match itself, between Australia and South Africa. The ceremony was colourful and symbolic, and ended with President Mandela, loudly acclaimed by the mainly white crowd, declaring the tournament open.

The match was exciting, incredibly hard-fought and fast, and South Africa deservedly won 27–18. All those of us grouped around the television knew, indeed we had known for months and months, that provided we got through our pool matches as champions, we would meet in the quarter-finals the loser in the opening match. So Australia it was to be.

It seemed to be a view universally held that this was bad news, that we wanted to avoid Australia, the champions, and therefore we should be disappointed that they lost. I never shared that view. I was glad immediately that we had avoided the Springboks. Of course Australia would prove a painfully difficult proposition, but to me, South Africa held more deadly dangers. We had discovered on our tour in 1994 that rugby in South Africa is far more than a pastime, that parts of the country live and die on the fortunes of the Springboks. If we met them in the quarter-finals they would be one match from ejection from their own tournament, an intolerable position, one which would have shaken the country and the team to the core, and made them play with almost a madness.

The first opposition for England were the organizers, Rugby World Cup. They had already forced us to downgrade the hotels we had arranged a year in advance after considerable research from our planners; they also ordained that all the teams qualifying for the knock-out stages should take part in a silly travel pantomime in which we were forced to stay in Johannesburg, rather than the cities where our matches were taking place, and travel down on the eve of the match, coming back immediately afterwards. It was all an unnecessary nonsense and made a supremely exacting competition even worse.

But RWC were already off to a good start in their battle to make team preparation as difficult as possible. They ordered all teams, wherever in the country they were staying, to attend an opening banquet near Cape Town a few days before the action actually began. For us, it meant a pre-dawn call and a full day's travelling. When the teams arrived, no-one really wanted to be friendly with people they would soon be trying, metaphorically (in most cases), to tear apart. I could have understood if there were hordes of sponsors' guests. At least that would have conveyed some spurious sense of purpose. It seemed that it was all an exercise in RWC patting themselves on the back while the players perfected some long-faced scowling. It was a complete waste of time and money.

It was such a blessed relief after the endless preparations when the release of the first game loomed, but I was well aware that our group matches, against Argentina, Italy and Western Samoa, would constitute anything but a lap of honour *en route* to the finals. And we duly had to battle our way through three extremely hard and physical matches against three highly competitive, hard-hitting and well-organized sides.

The relief for me after the opening game, on an amazingly dull and equable day at the giant King's Park, Durban, was that I already had behind me the most difficult afternoon in the scrum I was likely to face either during the tournament or anywhere else on the planet. The Pumas have always been a powerful scrummaging side, but in time for the World Cup they had even put coals on the fire. They had switched their best-known prop, Federico Mendez, to hooker and teamed him with Patricio Noriega and Matias Corral.

It was like scrummaging against a tractor in low gear. I have always been disparaging about non-hookers converting to fill such a specialist position, but against Mendez and his friends, we had to fight hard to hang on when it was our put-in, and on their feed we could simply never get anywhere near them. They hit hard, shoved their way over the ball and that was that. It was an extremely draining experience and I was comforted by seeing the damage they did in the scrum to other teams they met – they clearly had outscrummaged Australia when the teams met in a short series before departing for the tournament. The Pumas also had a front jumper of high class in German Llanes, their lock.

Yet Argentina were not a force as an all-round team, almost as if all their energies had been concentrated on building up their scrummaging. We won 24–18, never played with continuity, and indeed had to rely on Argentina missing a load of their goal kicks. Argentina, in fact, scored two tries and all our points came from kicks. But there was no panic or dejection – the evidence had already been seen, that the so-called lesser sides would put up powerful opposition, that with the exception probably only of the Ivory Coast, they were fit, well organized and highly motivated. Tonga gave France all kinds of problems, Canada dominated phases of their matches against South Africa and Australia, Japan could have beaten Ireland.

There were no hiding places anywhere in South Africa. The combination of improved fitness regimes, better organization, growing experience, video assessment and incentive had narrowed the gap so that there were some close-run affairs. By the time of the next World Cup in Cardiff in 1999, there could be some genuine upsets, some victories for the emerging teams.

Their other boost lay in the new laws. Nowadays, if you can field an accurate goal-kicker and an effective line-out, you are more than half-way there. As David Campese says, the midfield is now crowded with forwards because of the law changes, and the stupid turnover law means that you have to give up the ball to the other team even if they have a vastly inferior ball-winning capacity and do not deserve possession.

We had trouble with Italy too, beating them only by 27–20 in what was again a flawed performance, but against a vastly underrated team. Both Underwoods scored a try, Rob kicked 17 points to keep us in front and just out of danger. We again conceded two tries and our second unconvincing effort on the trot convinced the media that we were struggling badly and on the verge of panic. It was rubbish, but we needed a good performance in our last pool match against Western Samoa.

And we produced it. The Samoans were powerful, but also clever, footballers. They were uncomfortable to play against because they hit hard in the tackle and high enough on the body to be on the borderline of legality. But they were a positive team, and while Argentina and Italy had tried to kill the action, it suited Samoa to keep the game flowing – and that suited England. We won by 44–22, with two more tries from Rory, one from Neil Back and a penalty try. Jon Callard kicked some nice goals and both John Mallett and Damian Hopley won their first caps for England.

The match was also remarkable for featuring the smallest back row in England history. Graham Dawe had been chosen as hooker, for his first cap since 1987 and a tribute to his staying power. But we suffered some injuries during the game, and towards the end the England flankers were myself at open-side, and that notable hard-hitting back-row man, Kyran Bracken, on the other side. Still, it was another cap, and it meant that I played in all six of the matches that England played during the World Cup.

The Samoan match restored confidence and set us up for the knock-out stages. But as we prepared to leave Durban, our home town for so long, to enter the sudden-death stages, we knew that we had to find a good deal more if we were not to suffer the sad fate of premature ejection.

*   *   *

People asked me in the preamble to the match if the Australia quarter-final loomed as an opportunity to win revenge for the defeat they had inflicted on us in the final in 1991. They kept on asking. The answer was still the same. No. It had no bearing, it was a different match played by different teams. There is no extra incentive needed than to imagine yourself departing for home if you lose, and on the next Monday taking the tube to work at rush hour, or clocking on to your job with reality bursting out, painfully, all over. If we lost, we knew that history would judge our campaign not so much a failure as a disaster. I told myself that there was no way we could possibly contemplate losing.

Jack Rowell had used me as pack leader ever since he arrived as team manager and I spoke to the forwards on the evening before the match. I told them that we were up against a team in which many of the individuals could be considered as among the best, or even the very best, players in their position in the world game. I said that therefore, if we took up the challenge and we all beat our opposite number, then we would win the game, because rugby is still decided up front, first, last and always. We planned to be overtly physical in the first twenty minutes.

It was a tremendous match, emotional, anxious, sternly competitive and, until the very dying seconds, impossible to call. It was among the most memorable matches I have ever played – and not simply because England won, broke the mould of Australia's domination, and reached the semi-final.

We pounded them hard in the first quarter and at one stage, just before half-time, we had pulled away to 13–3. We scored a fantastic counter-attack try after Michael Lynagh had fumbled the ball near our 22 and Andrew, Guscott and Carling had sent Tony Underwood away on a long and electric sprint down the right-hand touchline. But we were hit hard by

Australia either side of half-time. Lynagh kicked a goal at the end of the first half to make it 13–6 and then Damian Smith scored for Australia will a brilliant high leap and take of a kick ahead from Lynagh. It could, and should, have been a numbing moment for us, because Lynagh's conversion made it level at 13–13. But we did show character. We kept falling behind to a kick, drawing level with a kick of our own, and suddenly extra time was looming with a spectacular lack of allure. Then came Australia's scrum, the attempts to jockey Lynagh out of position, and then Campese's mishit, just when he seemed set for a Campo-style deadly thrust.

Shortly afterwards, with normal time expiring, we were given a penalty near our 22. Mike Catt could have been forgiven if he had contented himself with blasting the ball into touch three feet up the field. It was not the time for misplaced speculation to give away the whole tournament. But he kicked a superb long touch, giving us a line-out throw near the Australia 10-metre line. As I trotted up to take the ball for the throw-in, I had no doubts. Drop goal. Drop goal. Drop goal. I repeated it in my mind, a mental mantra.

At the last three line-outs, I had called for a throw to Tim Rodber, with Martin Bayfield hopefully throwing the Australia jumpers off the scent by dummying to come forward while the ball sailed over his head to Tim. But to our intense frustration, John Eales, the brilliant Australia four jumper, read all three throws and won them all. Later, we were to find out why – they had cracked our line-out codes and Eales knew precisely what was going to happen.

I decided to call a ball for Bayfield coming forward. In that way, even if the Australians knew where the ball was going, a perfect throw would make sure that Martin won it anyway. I threw, the ball banged into Martin's palms and he brought it down. We made a desperate surge so that we could bring

Rob Andrew within range for a drop goal. The maul seemed to be struggling to a halt at one stage. I panicked, because I could envisage the referee, David Bishop, ruling that the maul had stopped, the ball was hidden, and therefore it was an Australian scrum under the ridiculous turnover law. 'Give it back, give it back,' I started shouting.

Dewi Morris saw it differently. He wanted the drive to continue. 'Not near enough, he needs more room.' So the drive came to life again, we made an extra five yards. The ball went back to Rob via Dewi, I stuck my head up and I saw the kick all the way. I knew immediately that it was over, and the only check on the galloping euphoria I felt as the team went mad around me was that there was still time remaining.

The closing stages were something of a nightmare. There was one occasion when two Englishmen tackled an Australian simultaneously, fell on the floor. I could envisage a penalty, as jumpy referees often give in those circumstances. 'Get off him, get off him, give him the ball,' I shouted. One last Australia move broke down, Dewi Morris drilled a superb kick down the blindside and the final whistle blew.

It was a momentous victory. It suits various people with vested interests to write down such occasions, by claiming that the opposition had gone. That would have been very unfair to the Australians, and to us. It was a win over a Southern Hemisphere giant, never to be sniffed at. We had played well under crushing pressure, we had kept our heads, the forwards had taken on and cancelled out one of the best packs of the era. It was a tremendous feeling.

If it had always been difficult to call the quarter-final then it is fair to say that New Zealand were favourites to beat us in the semi-final. They had played some highly effective high-speed rugby in the tournament, and they had also produced the man who was beyond any doubt whatsoever the star of the whole thing, one of the most arresting sportsmen of the whole sporting year in any country in any sport. Jonah Lomu, who only made the final New Zealand squad with a late burst of fitness work, was a devastatingly powerful runner, possibly the most devastating the game has ever seen. He had cut great swathes through the tournament, quickly become the media darling. Everyone came up with a pet theory on how we were going to stop Lomu in the semi-final – everything from shooting him with an elephant gun, to sticking Steve Ojomoh in on the wing as the man with the size and some of the pace to compare.

The truth was that you had to rely on existing defensive patterns, on first-time tackling. We laid whatever plans we could, emphasized that even if the first tackle did not exactly deposit Lomu in the eighth row of the stand, then at least we should hold on to him until reinforcements arrived. Otherwise, I felt that we prepared well, prepared hard. I felt strongly that if we were at our best then we would win. To be brutally frank, the expectation probably was to last less than five minutes of the semi-final, five minutes which, in effect, changed the world.

First, there was the highlight of any pre-match ritual against the All Blacks, the Haka. It was during the knock-out stages of the tournament that I asked for a meeting with Jack Rowell. The circumstances surrounding my retirement announcement, when I said in May that I would retire when the England World Cup ended, had changed. I wanted to know from Jack what his philosophy would be on selection for the new season, 1995–6. Would he base his choices on form and experience, or would he be looking to start building for the next World Cup and look for young players. He assured me that he would be selecting entirely on merit, full stop. I decided privately that I would play on, and announced the decision shortly afterwards.

And I knew it was the right decision when I lined up with the England team to face the Haka at Newlands. I stood opposite Mike Brewer, the All Black flanker. I have always liked watching the Haka and accepting the challenge which the All Blacks throw down. I watched Brewer and the others as they wound themselves up for the final leap. Where could you ever get a feeling like this, I asked myself. Where do you face someone in that mood? It was a feeling that caused a sensation up my spine, it was something that I realized, then and there out on Newlands, you should never pass up unless you have to. When the Haka ended, Brewer advanced towards us, mouthing some threat or other. Some people found his posturing ludicrous. But for me, it was part of the theatricals, and it appealed to me just as the whole thing appealed to me.

The appeal quickly waned. New Zealand switched their kick-off, towards Lomu on the left wing. For a few fleeting microseconds, it seemed that Will Carling and Tony Underwood would actually reach the ball first with some space to burst away; but they collided, New Zealand won the ball and the opening was both surprising and successful for them. In the final against South Africa, they tried the same switch kick-off. This time, the ball only travelled 9 metres, they were called back and dumped back in their own half with a kick from Joel Stransky, after the ensuing scrum at half-way. Fine margins.

New Zealand won the next ball, retained it through two or three rucks, and after the move almost broke down in midfield, they set Lomu free. Lomu simply battered his way through three tackles and scored. There were only two minutes gone. It was not a strategic collapse on our part. There were three players in the cover and he simply ran through all three. You cannot legislate for that in a game plan, we simply have to rely on the tacklers themselves.

We kicked off, pressurized them under the falling ball, Bachop flung a pass which missed Andrew Mehrtens and went direct to Walter Little in midfield, who was, for the moment, struggling on the back foot around his own 22. Yet Little, who had a very fine tournament, accelerated and broke out of a tackle by Jeremy Guscott, who rarely misses tackles. They attacked in numbers, Josh Kronfeld backed up and crashed over for the try. We were still inside the first five minutes of the match, the deficit was already in double figures. These were devastating blows, stunning and bewildering. Any moment you expected to wake up, sweating but safe, in your bed.

Not long after that, Zinzan Brooke picked up the ball around 45 metres from the posts, looked up and dropped an amazing goal. That was the instant when I knew it was fated not to be our day. As the ball went flying over, I looked at Sean Fitzpatrick, my old adversary and the New Zealand captain. He shrugged.

At one stage early in the second half we trailed by 35–3. Both Will Carling and I tried to turn the tide. I said during one break in play that we were not going to troop off the field at the end feeling humiliated, that we had to start taking the ball to the All Blacks. I told the lads that I didn't care how we did it. I did not even care if someone was sent off. We had been outplayed and out-muscled and it was time to strike back.

From that point on we did take the game to the All Blacks. We reduced the margin from the low/high point of 32 points and we lost by a margin of 16, by 45–29. We scored four tries, two each from Rory Underwood and Will Carling, who scored a clever individual try with a chip ahead and chase. There was no suggestion that the All Blacks were relaxed and prepared to allow some consolation tries. They were bawling, 'They must not cross the line, don't let them cross the line,' throughout the second half.

In the second half we showed that we could play effective all-round rugby, and that the All Blacks were no more comfortable than any other team when the ball was being run at them. If nothing else, our heads did not go down; at least we were not too stupefied by the shattering opening period when our dreams of winning the World Cup died.

All kinds of motivational tools were paraded before our eyes to try to guarantee that we would be up and fighting for the final match of our World Cup. Instead of taking the high road to Johannesburg, for the finest hotel in the country and for the grandeur and spotlight of the final, we took a side road for Pretoria. France were just shaded by South Africa in the first semi-final in Durban, played in a monsoon, and we had to meet them in the third-place play-off.

We heard many theories why this was a game of towering importance. The team which finished third in the tournament would not have to pre-qualify. And of course, we would be desperate to win to maintain our long run of success against the French. Neither argument really made it. They were just not mental tools of any significance. The qualification for the next tournament was not in our minds; it concerned, to be blunt, another group of players at another point in history. And to win to keep a run of success is not a goad, not a mind set to make you play out of your skin.

The truth was, too, that I was incredibly tired for the French match, having played a formidably hard semi-final three days before and having seen aspirations crushed under the hooves of Jonah Lomu. We were not used to playing at altitude, it was our first game in the tournament which had not taken place at sea level. Not even the prospect of a lively, and dangerous evening, match with my French friends could really stir anything deep down, even though on the surface we all felt as if we were ready to play and determined.

France duly won, ended their losing run against England, and qualified for the finals proper next time round. The score was 19–9 in a very poor match, and they scored tries late in the match by Emile N'tamack and Olivier Roumat. We gave a shambolic performance, and our scrummaging was the worst I have ever experienced in any England team. The forwards didn't win much ball, the backs tried to ship it across the pitch. Just spraying the ball round, especially against a back line containing a tackler as powerful as Philippe Sella, was inviting disaster. So the record books said that in the rugby World Cup of 1995 England finished fourth.

An optional squad trip to the final was arranged. I simply could not face it, could not face the pain of the realization that the party we had been planning for years would now take place without us. South Africa won by 15–12, breaking a long deadlock in the second period of extra time with a drop goal from Joel Stransky. That was the signal for the whole nation to go mad; and it was significant, and clear even over the television, that a sizeable percentage of the non-white population was celebrating hard as well.

It was probably not a great spectacle for the casual watchers, for the people dreaming of a fast-flowing epic. But I found it a fascinating contest and a spectacular occasion with President Mandela taking the field to be introduced to the teams before the match, wearing a Springbok cap and a

No. 6 jersey borrowed from Francois Pienaar; and afterwards almost dancing on the podium after he had presented the Webb Ellis trophy itself to Pienaar.

There was still the check on enjoyment because it was all happening to someone else. There was a schizophrenic feel to our performance when I looked back, on the flight home. I was terribly disappointed with the outcome, and in truth I looked back at the vast amount of preparation we had gone through, the huge sacrifices we had made, and realized that in one sense it had not been worth it.

There was a great deal of criticism that we had not developed our all-round game and shown so little in the backs – although too much of the criticism was simplistic. It is now impossible to attack from first phase and even from a few phases after that. The field is now so crowded due to the misguided new laws, that you have to launch the back row up with the ball and try to set the backs going when space eventually appears. It is just too simplistic for words, especially in the World Cup, to talk of running rugby for the sake of entertainment. It just does not happen like that.

Certainly, although Rowell did impress me and is obviously the man to retain the job as manager/coach, I would be looking to him to take it all forward again in the new season, 1995–6. The challenge for him is to emulate the success he achieved with Bath even though he will only have the squad together infrequently, not week in week out, even day in day out, the luxury he enjoyed in his Bath years.

On the credit side, I felt that we had improved as the tournament progressed, that we had played extremely well against Australia and for much of the semi-final against New Zealand. We had coped with a very hard pool and a very hard draw, and at least we proved that at our best we were indeed a match for anyone else, if not consistently. The nightmarish spell against New Zealand was certainly enough to banish anything approaching euphoria.

But at the end my chief memory and my chief regret surrounded a different game at a different time. After South Africa 1995, I began to feel a profoundly deeper regret about England 1991, and our defeat in the final of that year. South Africa had so many advantages in 1995. It was their tournament, their crowds, their home. The support factor gives everything a massive extra dimension. They were in a situation in which they were enveloped by an almost religious fervour.

Just as we were in 1991, when it was our event, our crowds, our fervour, our home. Everything was in our hands and we had blown it, we had blown the tactics in the final, won forward superiority and not cashed in on it. It felt bad at the time. With the depth of perception afforded by what I saw four years later, it now felt even worse. It opened old wounds. That was our chance, our time. It is conceivable that not for generations will we ever have another like it. Something to think about when contemplating that empty space on all our mantelpieces.

14

THE VIEW FROM RICHMOND HILL

An English rugby retrospective

IN ONE SENSE (AND IN ONE SENSE ONLY) I AM LOOKING FORWARD to a sedentary later life, for the perspective that the passing years bring with them. It is difficult to assess the significance of episodes of your life when you are actually living through them, and although I suspect I know most of the answers, it is difficult to quantify precisely what rugby, and especially playing rugby for England, has meant to me. It is difficult to quantify when you are still nose-down and trying to maintain concentration, passion and life and limb against the global and grim fraternity of the front row.

By the end of the World Cup, I had won sixty-nine international caps, sixty-three as hooker for England, five Tests as hooker for the Lions and one as replacement flanker for England against Western Samoa. I was hoping, after initial thoughts of retirement, to add a few more to the pile in 1995–6. Sean Fitzpatrick was one ahead as the world's most capped hooker by the end of the World Cup. He stood on seventy, but had matches in the Southern Hemisphere's winter of 1995 to pull further ahead. Good luck to him. I admire him for his commitment and achievements. No doubt he sometimes feels as tired as I do.

And as privileged. I have said many times that bald statistics fade into insignificance, fade against the honour and the thrill of playing in the most successful era in England rugby history, in which we were contenders for the Grand Slam in almost every season, in which we reached a World Cup final – albeit to live with the sadness that we clearly should have won it – and in which we won three Slams in all. And this in an era when rugby's profile grew massively, when rugby players became household names in non-rugby households. None of this could be bought with the value of all the sporting statistics in the world. And as for seeking personal glories, I do not believe that anyone I have played with would accuse me of putting my interests above those of the collective.

It has indeed been a draining experience. Usually, to juggle the competing demands of business and domestic and sporting matters has been particularly exhausting. But there has always been enough to spur me on – challenges from physically superior opponents, from the next pretender for my position, or the next young gun in the other team; from the critics, from the whole issue of amateurism and the RFU's bitter rearguard action, when I knew that I had to keep going or they would reimpose their control, and the interests of the players would be submerged. I am always looking for the next challenge. If there is not one looming, I tell myself there is, I invent one. I think people are better in adversity.

I am profoundly thankful for the accident of birth which ensured that I did play in this era. In past eras it would have been possible to have won fifty caps for England having won say only seven matches. I could not have gone through seven consecutive defeats, which is what some England players had to do in the not-too-distant past. I have no idea how on earth they kept going, kept themselves from madness.

There have been highlights among highlights. I loved the spectacular win over Australia at Twickenham in 1988; the hard grounds and the tough forward battles with the successful Lions in 1989; the sense of headiness and danger against the French in the 1991 World Cup quarter-final; the crushing of the Springboks in Pretoria in 1994; and the stirring victory over Australia in South Africa in the recent World Cup. Occasionally the boot was on the other foot. I have had uncomfortable times, notably against the electric Australians in Sydney in 1991, the fighting Irish in Dublin in 1993, the avenging Springboks in 1994 in the Second Test, and the All Blacks in the explosive first five minutes of the semi-final in 1995.

Perhaps heroes are for followers rather than players. There are players I have admired greatly, but you are usually too busy trying to combine with them, or else stop them in their tracks, to hold them in awe. There are a few scattered exceptions. Peter Winterbottom would certainly be my hero. He was rewarding for his astonishing courage. He is the hardest man I have met; nothing seemed to faze him, nothing seemed to bother him. He was a great technical flanker, and at the end of his career his previously fallible hands could be relied upon. He was quiet in team meetings – in fact he was quiet, full stop. No-one got to know him, and that is part of his mystique. I certainly never grew to know him, despite all the matches for club and country and for the British Lions. He just went out and did it, all the time.

Dean Richards would not be far behind. He has less of a mystique about him than Winters, not only because I have come to know him so much better, but because a less mystical person could not be imagined. Dean is rewarding for his complete lack of pretension in anything. He was and is a great player, with few weaknesses; never particularly dynamic on the ball, but he created platforms which the opposition could never dismantle. I was always anxious if Dean wasn't there, I would never have willingly gone into a game without him.

Wade Dooley was the most honest player of my era. He did all the donkey work, the stuff that gained no kudos except with his colleagues. He pushed, shoved, grappled, hit rucks and mauls. He did it all selflessly, week in week out. If there was a crisis, an argument, a flashpoint, whether during the match or off the field, Dooley would step in alongside you, probably in front of you. The writer who called him 'the heart of England' was getting close to the essence of the man.

I could not really afford to have heroes in the opposition, and nor, to be frank, in that species called backs. To my mind, the game is a forward exercise, always was, and it is now becoming even more so. The other lot just seem to stand there and hang around. Jeremy Guscott is the most talented back, the most complete talent, to step on a rugby field, ever. But I tolerate backs, rather than grow to like them. Perhaps it was the fact that they never seemed to bale us out when we had a bad day, as we had to bale them out so many times.

England, in my time, have never approached the situation which Welsh forwards enjoyed in the 1970s, when they could win 30 per cent of the ball and still win games through the brilliance of numbers 15 to 9. We in the forwards have often wondered why backs of other teams did to us what we never seemed to do to them.

I used to listen to our backs in some bewilderment. Their thought processes seemed to change from year to year, even from month to month. At one meeting, they decided that we were not sucking enough people in, so we were asked to take the ball on further. Then they concluded that they were not getting enough quick ball, so we had to release quicker. Then we weren't doing enough to get the ball into midfield quickly, and so please could we deliver ball off the top of the jump in the line-outs? Then they didn't want the ball from 5-yard scrums, because the tacklers were all lining them up. Then they did want it from 5-yard scrums, because although the defence was tight, it only needed one slip or one break and they were in. You felt like lifting your head and asking them what the fuck had changed from last week to this week.

The only forward who used to speak up was Jeff Probyn. He was duly shouted down for being a complete dinosaur. He did have a point, because most of their theories were mutually contradictory. We forwards, all rather simple people, were left to wonder if they knew what the hell they were doing, international cream or not.

There is no doubt as to the identity of the most famous back of all – indeed, the most famous player in England rugby history. I am always acutely aware that Will Carling could accuse me of jealousy, of being plain envious of his post as captain, his high earnings from the game and his massive profile – and there are elements of truth in that. If I am honest, I am envious. I have been both critical and admiring of him elsewhere in this book, and have to admit in the end that, although he is a colleague with club and country, I

have never really got to know him – perhaps a fuel for my
envy!

There is a polarization in the perception of him. One view
appears to be that he is the greatest thing ever to happen to
post-war English rugby, a brilliant leader of men and player;
the other is that, basically, he is especially lucky, not more
qualified than several others to be captain, and with a rare
arrogance. Both perceptions are unfair to Will. The truth is
that there is less to him than the image. He is not the mystical
communicator of legend, he has put in no more and no less
to the success of England than Wade Dooley, Jeff Probyn and
many others. I have always thought that, purely because a
captain is praised too long in victory and criticized too loudly
in defeat, any one of four or five of the senior players could
have led England to the same results. It was essentially
a rattling of the squad sabre against the RFU, rather than a
gesture made chiefly on Will's behalf, when we united to keep
him in the captaincy for the World Cup after his justified
comments about the RFU.

Yet nor is he the aloof and pretentious beast of his
contra-legend. He has done wonders, in his measured behaviour, for the image of rugby in general. The RFU have
never acknowledged that contribution.

I would have to say that he is less selfless than he
sometimes appears. He has a particular sense of where he is
going and what is right for him, a sense developed in
conjunction with Jon Holmes, his agent. In fact, I do not
believe that he should lead England again in 1995–6, purely
because it is time for a change. Everyone has a shelf life in
a certain job, and then the law of diminishing returns begins
to apply. What used to work on the team will no longer work.
Fresh face and fresh voice needed. I would imagine that, as
his reign wore on, even Montgomery became a bore to his

troops. Still, like Montgomery Will can walk off into history with the list of achievements of his troops posted on the consciousness of the nation.

The other highly significant drawback to life as an international sportsman became apparent to Will Carling a long time ago. At the time, I could never really understand what his problem was. Did he want to become a new Marlene Dietrich? Now I have total sympathy because, to my surprise, I have been going through the same thing.

Rugby has always been a sport in which ordinary people from all parts of the game mixed happily, with no star system. There would usually be an Oxbridge element in most gatherings, interpersed with a few chippies and builders. There has never been, until recently, an echelon famous well beyond the game. It has been possible for the best players to remain down to earth in character because, even at the start of the 1990s, players would only be recognized in public by their friends, by rugby aficionados.

The 1991 World Cup changed that for ever. It became impossible for Will to emerge in public without being besieged, and to a lesser extent the wider public recognition came the way of Jeremy, Rob, myself and others. Millions of new followers tuned in, women found that they liked the sport, began to follow it. There was an amazing sea change. For the first time, people would stop me in the street, people would know who I was, would feel free to give me their frank opinion of where I had gone wrong in any recent match. Media attention grew in remarkable fashion, there were more demands on the players and more appearances on the TV and in newspaper profiles. I found it, in large part, gratifying and even exciting, although occasionally intrusive. I was aware that many people affect to be put out by being recognized, by adulation, but in reality are extremely put out if they are not recognized.

But the boom in the game, the recent England successes, and then the 1995 World Cup, have transformed the situation once more. It is certainly no exaggeration to say that the leading England rugby players are now as familiar to the general public in this country as the leading footballers. For me, things have now long gone past the pleasurable stage, have tipped over the edge of normality and level-headedness. It is extremely difficult to keep your feet on the ground when you are the source of constant attention from people coming to shake your hand, telling you what a great bloke you are, even people trying to punch you.

What happens is that you feel invigorated for the wrong reasons. You almost feel you can do anything you like. You find it difficult to keep a perspective on life and what actually matters. Compared to the elevation of your sporting life and the recognition, many fundamentals of ordinary life seem, by comparison, dull. In fact, they are not dull; they are reality. For some reason I have never been able to fathom, I once appeared on the appalling *You Bet*, with Matthew Kelly. The true, unsatisfying ephemera of celebrity, of being famous for being famous, was everywhere.

I recently met Rob Andrew and Dewi Morris for a chat in London. We sat in a bar and it is no exaggeration to say that, in all the time we sat there trying to thrash out some heavy matters, we did not have a moment to ourselves. People sat down next to us, women came over. One bloke came over to say that he wanted to shake us by the hand because, as he said: 'I think you three are gods, you are gods. You have done so much for English sport.' It was flattering, deeply embarrassing and deeply intrusive. I was also picked out by a girl. When I felt unable to raise a smile to mark her constant barrage of inane questions, she told me to tell her all about it, what was bothering me. I told her that if I had known her for twenty years, rather than two minutes, I might well have confided in her; but as I hadn't, then it was not appropriate.

I am fully aware that I have never shied away from limelight, and that I am in a situation that I have assisted in creating, that I was the most famous player in the Grand Slam match of 1995 purely because I was splashed all over the place for my outburst against the Scots. I admit to enjoying the limelight.

But this is different, almost mind-altering. I used to be flattered by the attention. I can no longer go out for a quiet meal without being bothered, and even if people are perfectly nice – sometimes they are, sometimes they are not – then it is still a bother. You can work on portraying the most forbidding body language, the best scowl, but they sail on straight past your exterior. They do not take the hint.

Also, I realize people will be cynical, and that some will believe those who live with high profile should not complain when the profile comes back to haunt us. That is harsh. I never thought that I would ever have to complain about all the attention. But there were times before and after the World Cup when I felt near the end of my tether, trying to insist that I was not a god, not a celebrity, but a rugby player, a better player than some, but not so much better that I was suddenly from another planet. Dying for one quiet, un-interrupted beer in one pub. For me, the fame is no longer the best bit of being an international, if it ever was. It is the worst bit.

But I realize that I am still well in credit for what rugby has provided. The full richness of a rugby career, of course, does not come solely, or perhaps even chiefly, from life as an international player. For me, the colours have been sketched in by playing for Nottingham University and the Nottingham club, by touring every major rugby country in the world, and a few others as well, in a variety of jerseys and parties. And there is nothing more colourful I suppose, indeed there is probably nothing so lurid, as the colours and jersey of Harlequins, my club for the past five seasons.

People asked me when I joined Quins in 1990 what I could possibly have in common with them. Perhaps they are not, ostensibly, my type of club with their rather louche, laid-back, Oxbridge and even lordly outlook, their seemingly easy acceptance of the fact that they continually come up short, and that their generations of highly talented teams have so rarely won trophies.

If you have ever stood at the top of Richmond Hill and looked down at the wonderful sweep of the Thames beneath, at the view across to Twickenham with the stadium itself in the right background, then you would know why I joined. The alternative when I arrived in London was to join Wasps, and good club though they are, perhaps with a philosophy nearer to mine, it was no contest. If you have ever fumed in the awful traffic gridlock around Sudbury, where they play, then you would understand even better. To live in Richmond and district is infinitely more appealing, and I rented a flat up on the terraces in Richmond when I first came down. Harlequins it was.

That is not to say that it has not been a frustrating experience, because we have been under-achievers. And since Harlequins are unquestionably, among other clubs and the general rugby public, the least popular club in the game, it has never been an easy ride. We had to fight desperately hard in season 1994–5, when I was captain of the team, to avoid the unthinkable – relegation from Division 1. And we had to fight our way on into the teeth of the realization that everyone was desperate for us to disappear. I am proud to say that we did not oblige them.

In fact, when I joined Harlequins my perception of them was already different from the general image. I had played against them for a long time but noticed a change around 1988. Dick Best had begun to crack the coaching whips, they had some illustrious players, and they did win the Cup in 1988. They had talent in the backs as ever, with Jamie Salmon and Will Carling in the centre, with the potentially devastating Andrew Harriman on the wing. But they were no soft touch in the pack either – they had Mick Skinner, Paul Ackford, Neil Edwards, Richard Langhorn. Southern softies they weren't.

Of course they are well connected, of course I understand the jealousy and frustration of clubs who lose players to Quins because we can put together a highly lucrative package with our city contacts. There was a great deal of adverse comment last season when Mick Watson, the No. 8 from West Hartlepool, joined us. He had been a lorry driver up in the North-East and now, suddenly, he was a trainee broker. But there are no sinecures. Once Harlequins have effected the introduction you are on your own, you have to perform. If you are in a job where tens of thousands of pounds change hands every day then passengers are not welcome on board. Peter Winterbottom became a Eurobond dealer when he joined Quins. Previously he had been a farmer. But he became extremely successful, was being regularly head-hunted. No passengers.

And only in the upstairs sanctum of the clubhouse do you really sense their traditions. There is a group photograph of eight MPs who were also members of Quins, and from the honours boards you gain some sense of how many Quins have become president of the RFU. To be frank, the upper-class areas of the club have never affected me. I have always simply ignored them and got on with the playing.

And I have found club rugby extremely rewarding. You spend a lot of time with your club colleagues. Some of them may go on to win caps, but for others this is their pinnacle and they apply themselves accordingly. That must be respected. When we beat Wasps in a semi-final of the Cup in 1993, Alex Snow, the Quin's lock, expressed surprise that Jason Leonard and I were so overtly delighted with the victory, considering that we had achieved so much with England. But this was an achievement gained with people you played alongside every week.

Some of my England colleagues miss out on that. Will Carling has never made club rugby a huge part of his life, and last season even players like Jeremy Guscott and Victor Ubogu missed league matches because of ancillary commitments. Will's relationship with Harlequins is quite obviously a difficult subject, and if he is honest he would admit that Quins comes low on his list. A lack of commitment is difficult for someone of my mentality to accept, but although he has never been an influential player when in Harlequins colours, I admit that Will has chosen a par-ticular route, prefers to keep total commitment to the England cause. Who is to say that his decision is right or wrong for him or the country as a whole?

But it has been a problem for Harlequins captains. It was a problem for me, it was a problem for Andy Mullins, my predecessor. It can be difficult for keen young players of high promise who are desperate to do well with the club, are prepared to sweat blood, but then find themselves eased out when Will becomes available. But he is a class player and a player of huge profile, so if he was dropped by Quins it would raise a whole different set of problems and attract the wrong attention. It would not be a question of a kind of quiet gee-up gesture lasting one week, because it would be massive news. That may seem to be a rather negative reason for selecting him.

I was once dropped by Salmon after a defeat at the hands of Bristol, when he claimed my attitude had not been appropriate. I was annoyed that I should have been victimized after a poor team effort, and I pointed out to Salmon that other people in the club were seriously falling short of pulling their weight. But I do not feel that my commitment to my club and to the philosophy of club rugby in general can ever be questioned.

It is, of course, a telling fact that we have never won the League and have never looked like doing so. Perhaps a typical result in the League life of Harlequins came three seasons ago against Bath. In the first half we played some brilliant rugby. We shattered their aura of invincibility, and at one stage led by a margin of 18–0. In the second half we lost Troy Coker, who was sent off, allowed Bath back into the game and had to settle for a draw.

Our critics always claim that our poor League form shows a lack of real sustained commitment, and that deep down we do not care enough. There is a grain of truth in that because, if you have a high-flying career in the City, it is not always possible to arrive for training at Quins feeling refreshed, on time and eager to put yourself through the mill, especially after negotiating the rush hour. At training, there are always people missing due to work commitments. In the end, we have never won the League because day to day it has never meant enough to enough players.

And social life at the club is fragmented, probably not as fervent as it is at other clubs. The club premises are not so much of a focal point to people who are scattered all over London. Whereas the Stoop Memorial Ground was a ten-minute trip around the corner for me, it was a monstrous trip for the likes of Mick Skinner, who came from Blackheath, and for others battling their way out of London.

We have reached three Pilkington Cup finals in my time. In 1991, having beaten Wasps, we met Nottingham in the semi-final. I was thrilled that my old club had battled their way through. I certainly felt sorry for them that we won – after extra time. In the last minute of normal time, Simon Hodgkinson had a penalty attempt from 40 metres, the kind of kick he would normally have put over. He missed, and Nottingham ran out of steam in extra time; we went on to beat Northampton in the final. In 1992, after a heroic performance by a weakened team, we lost in extra time to Bath with a dramatic last-second drop goal from Stuart Barnes, not the greatest moment of my career. And in 1993 we reached the final again. I was injured and missed the match, and we were beaten by Leicester. Two Cup wins is the sum total of our silver-tinged achievements.

The 1995 relegation battle was desperately fraught. We had been badly affected all season by a lack of effective locks, and by goal-kicking of quite staggering dreadfulness. As the relegation battle warmed up, I had to work hard in team meetings to keep the lads from freezing, from panicking. We had to concentrate on playing our game and to try to forget the parlous state of our League position.

We had to play Northampton, fellow strugglers, at the Stoop at the end of the season to keep our hopes alive, and we did beat them. It meant almost as much to me as winning an international, Northampton lost chiefly because the tension froze them almost solid. Later, we were dragged back into the mire at West Hartlepool where we lost to a last-minute try after we had a perfectly good try disallowed. Further evidence of the sad decline of English refereeing. In the end, we had to go to Gloucester for the last League match of the season. If we won, we stayed up. It was also an emotional occasion because at the time I had decided to retire and so it was to be, as I thought, my last club match.

In a sense to have to go to Gloucester loomed as a dire assignment. But for me it was something to be enjoyed. If my philosophy of club rugby can be encapsulated then it is properly encapsulated at Kingsholm. I love the place. Over the years, I have taken some fearful stick from Gloucester followers, especially those packed into the notorious Shed, the popular side. But I always felt that they were passionate about rugby, that the stick gave everyone a good laugh, rather than being malicious. I respected that. At Murrayfield the jibes are personal and bitter. At Leicester, too, I have found that the stick is pointed and humourless. 'Call yourself a solicitor. You're an animal.' Gloucester is different and the ordeal there is vastly to be enjoyed.

They took the lead in the early stages, and as I ran back to half-way, the Shed were all singing 'going down, going down, going down'. But we scored some tries, we played some good stuff, we kept our nerve when an ominous Gloucester revival took place in the second half, and we held on to win. It was a fantastic feeling. At the end I walked over to the Shed and waved. They all gave me a cheer, and even if I got nothing like the ovation afforded their hero, Mike Teague, who was retiring that day too, I got an ovation which touched me deeply.

A Division 1 title is something which I have never won. I

often used to wonder what it was like to play for Bath, with their passion and their pool of talented players, with their long run of glamorous success in both Cup and League. At one stage of my career I thought about moving out of London, and I received two offers from companies in Bristol. It would have been the ideal base to join Bath, and briefly I contemplated doing so. I knew full well that if I did, of course, it would have meant a major tooth-and-nail confrontation with Graham Dawe, the Bath hooker. It would have meant slogging it out with Dawesy twice or three times a week for the whole season.

Then I was offered the job in London with Edward Lewis. So my dreams of the League title receded. Perhaps it was a good thing, because I have had more than enough on my plate ever since. To add a full-scale battle with Graham to the mix might have tipped everything over the edge.

But in general, it would be supremely churlish to feel that my career had fallen short. It has provided me with the whole range of experience and emotion available to a sportsman, especially to a player in such a wonderful, global game.

On the night before we played Gloucester, I sat in an emotional state in my single room in the team hotel, just outside the city. I believed then that it was to be my last serious rugby match in Europe. I did have other painful things on my mind of a domestic nature, but for the moment I looked back on my rugby. I reflected that I had been in an England team that had beaten all the major rugby nations, that I had played in the Hong Kong Sevens, the Middlesex Sevens, the County Championship final, the British Lions, the Cup final. I had played at every level of the England ladder – for the Barbarians (an overrated experience, but at least I have gone through it), the Divisionals, the Penguins, the British Lions, the lot. I have not played for Bath, but I have played for everyone else. I do begrudge some of the disruption caused by fame. But if I had my sporting time over again, of all the things it would have been in my power to change, I would not change one.

EPILOGUE

Strange meeting

Even if England had won the World Cup, 1995 would not have been a happy year for me in any way. As season 1994–5 drew to a close, I decided that I would retire from all senior rugby, club and country, at the end of the World Cup. I was then thirty-three and as far as I was concerned, the decision was irrevocable.

The competing commitments had become ridiculous, for a start. I heard that I was to be made an equity partner at Edward Lewis and, as I have explained already, that means a substantial increase in responsibility and commitment. The unseen cost to players, their families and wives and their careers, is something that has always been glibly dismissed by the defenders of amateurism, but the pressure on me had become enormous. The burdens on wives and families of leading players, and the sacrifices demanded of them, especially if they have children, are heavy indeed.

You also realize how much you have excluded from your life, apart from personal relationships. I can hardly remember when last I have been able to indulge a love of literature, or when I have been able to do anything outside rugby that could possibly be called cultural, apart from my wine column in *Today*.

But none of these were insuperable, or the greatest sadness. It was not a pleasant time, quite apart from the demands of the Five Nations programme and the onerous preparations for the World Cup, and the emotion of a unique and rather anxious family matter which I explain in this final chapter. In July 1995, in the quiet period after the World Cup, it is fair to say that the overriding sadness of the period came to light when Penny, my wife, and I decided to separate and to seek a divorce. I did not add much to the bald statement of facts for the newspapers which contacted me, and it was hardly a comfortable experience to see that the profile of rugby and of myself had got so out of hand that some papers deemed the story was worth front-page pictures of Penny and me at our wedding, because I did not believe it was a matter of public interest, or of interest to the public.

All I said in public was that it was incredibly sad, and quite obviously it had a cataclysmic effect on both our lives. It did mark the end of one struggle in particular – Penny is a busy GP and it is fair to say that, in our lives together, we were ships in the night. We had only two holidays together in all the time we lived together and one of those was our honeymoon. It took a Herculean task of arrangement and forward planning months in advance, even to try and sort out a weekend away or to accept an invitation to a dinner party.

It was when Penny and I made the decision to go our separate ways that I first reconsidered my decision to stop playing rugby, partly because the decision had been made in an attempt to try to effect some kind of repair. The truth was that my sporting heart did not lie in the original decision. I remember talking to Eddie Butler, the former Wales No. 8, about retirement. He told me that he stopped enjoying it, so he stopped playing. Neat and simple.

But the truth is that I had not stopped enjoying it. I had not reached that stage. I always thought that the benchmark would be when I didn't care if we had lost or when I didn't feel like going out and fighting someone. I was concerned, too, that all the surplus adrenaline I would have inside me would have nowhere to go, and that I would have to work hard to channel it in positive ways.

During the World Cup campaign, after I had the meeting with Jack Rowell and Jack had confirmed that he would choose the England team in 1995–6 on merit, not with a so-called youth policy, I decided to play on. There was also the fact that none of the young hookers around in the game seemed anywhere near ready to step into the full England team. One or two may have the talent, but none, it seems to me, has anything like the record of solid achievement and the requisite experience. Peter Wheeler, John Pullin, Graham Dawe and myself all had years of first-class rugby under our belts when we arrived in the England squad.

I made public the decision to play on during the tournament's knock-out stages. Naturally the year had been desperately difficult, and emotionally extremely painful. It now needs a huge amount of clever shuffling of available time, to keep providing 100 per cent effort to my team and to my clients and company, but I have convinced myself that it can be done. The best news on that count is that there is no tour in the summer of 1996, a sorely needed break for all England players, and indeed for all British players. It means that I can make long-term plans in work, that I will be not be disappearing for the spring.

Plans to diversify, to catch up on lost time and pursue other interests, and perhaps to enter rugby coaching, are all now in abeyance. And I believe my surplus energy and my attitudes are still the same as they have always been. Perhaps it is relatively surprising that I still have a vast appetite when I should be rather tired. Yet if it was apposite to call me Pit Bull years ago, then it still applies. I have no explanation why I should still be, well, angry. It is just the way I am, and I still haven't found the right psychoanalyst to explain it.

And if I need confirmation that I had made what was the right decision, then it was provided by New Zealand. Facing their Haka, and the glowering and implied threats, facing down Mike Brewer as he advanced on us, made me realize that I am still addicted to the thrill and the confrontation of rugby, the theatre and the threat, just as I had been when I first played the contact sport, just as I had always been when facing down the volatile French on wild days in Paris.

My parents had never kept from me the fact that I was adopted. They told me practically as soon as I was old enough to grasp what it meant. I was grateful to them for that and for so many other things. I have always regarded them as true parents in every sense and will always do so.

Of course, I had often wondered who my natural parents were, though for many years I had no desire to find out. The desire did begin to grow in my late teens and early twenties, but I was aware that my parents were not wholeheartedly in favour of me setting out on the trail to find them. They knew people who had done the same and who subsequently had bad experiences – perhaps the rediscovered natural mother wanted nothing to do with them, perhaps a meeting had been set up but had gone badly. Both experiences would be profoundly distressing. My parents felt that it was all a fraught question, which could leave you open to long-term consequences. They wanted to be sure, they wanted me to be sure. The subject dropped for some years.

Last year, when I was approaching my mid-thirties, I was studying the obituary columns of a newspaper. I realized that, if I assumed that my natural mother was in her early twenties when she had me, then she would be passing her mid-fifties at the time. In the columns there were people who had died in their fifties. I thought how sad it would be if she died while I was still mulling over the decision whether to attempt to contact her. It pressed home a sense of urgency. It was not a question of trying to trace my roots, or a quest for knowledge, or because I felt that there had always been something missing from my life. It was simply a curiosity, perhaps an attempt to discover some of the origins of my aggression, and where my personality traits came from. You heard people say, to others: 'You're just like your father.' I had no-one on whom to blame my inherent character aspects!

My parents knew a few details. I had a birth certificate, and they also knew that my natural mother had been a teacher in Birmingham. That was about it. But in our office we were always using private detective firms to trace people, for a number of reasons. I gave one of the firms the name. Within two days they rang me in the office. They had the full name of my natural mother and told me her address and her phone number. They had also discovered that my natural mother had retired from teaching and that my maternal grandfather had been a steelworker in Sheffield.

I sat on the information in the office for around a week, in a mental turmoil. It was an extremely difficult time. I knew that the whole affair could turn out to be wounding, knew that I could face a second rejection. If you make contact and it goes wrong, you can hardly change your mind and take the contact back, and say forget it. But if you don't, then you will always have the nagging curiosity to deal with, the episode with no end.

Obviously, what I could not do was ring up out of the blue. It would have been a terrific shock, and I did not know my natural mother's situation. It may have been an episode she wanted to forget. There may have been people around her who knew nothing about me.

Ultimately, I went to Richmond Council's adoption department and spoke to social workers. They usually spend months tracing natural parents when they are approached by adopted children, and monitor an adoption register. You can put your name on it if you are interested in tracing your natural relations, and if two names on it coincide, they take steps to put the people in touch. This time all the tracing work had already been done, and I went to see a social worker for a compulsory interview. She tried to uncover my motivation, to ensure that I was not harbouring fanciful hopes. She agreed a strategy – she would write a bland letter to my natural mother saying that someone wished to get in touch and would she ring the social worker on this number. If someone in the household saw the letter, then she could pretend that it had come from, say, an old pupil she had taught.

The social worker rang me back in a couple of days. She

gave me some more details. My natural mother had been married for over twenty years, though not to my natural father. To my amazement, I discovered for the first time that I had a full brother and sister. And the social worker said that my natural mother would like me to ring her.

I did. I found she had a strange mixture of accents, part Yorkshire and part Birmingham, that she was from near Sheffield; I had spent much of my life surreptitiously trying to hide my roots in Birmingham to uphold my Yorkshireness, and now I found my family was from Yorkshire all along.

It was a very odd conversation. Neither of us knew what to say. I gave her some details of my life and what I did. I told her that I played rugby. She replied that she didn't know anything about the game. When I explained to her that I had played rugby more than fifty times for England, she kept very quiet. We both agreed that there was no point in dragging out the process any longer. We arranged to meet and that she would come down to my home in Twickenham the next week.

My emotions on the Sunday morning she was due to arrive were not so much mixed as in turmoil. When the time came, would I be upset or emotional, and what were the circumstances in which she sent me for adoption? I was also acutely aware that I did not want to hurt my parents, I did not want them to feel for one moment that the action of finding my natural mother was in any way a reflection on what they had done for me, and I did not want them to feel they might be replaced in my affections if things developed later. If they had been really upset I would not have taken things this far. I consoled myself with the thought that it was something I had to sort out for my own benefit.

I sat in the front room of our home. Penny was out. I looked out of the window as people walked down the street, and whenever a woman who looked to be in her fifties walked past, I wondered if it would be her. Eventually, a woman walked past the window and then stopped at the gate, then came up the path. I knew it was her. I opened the door. I had not seen my natural mother for thirty-three years. The first thing that struck me was how attractive she was.

The meeting was extremely charged. There were long silences, because when discussing weighty matters of the kind we talked about, you can hardly fill in the awkward silences with talk about what you did last week, how bad the weather has been or what a nice room it is. She explained the circumstances. I had been her first child and my natural father had been a dentist, who had left soon afterwards. She had been an unmarried mother in Birmingham in the Sixties, a time and place where single parenthood was not socially acceptable at all, and not economically feasible either. She was starting out on her teaching career, she did not have the wherewithal not to work, so she had me adopted.

She asked me eventually whether I could forgive her. I told her that I did not believe it was my place to be a judge, because I did not know all the circumstances, but if it was my place, then yes, I could. I told her that I could not have had a better placement than with Ralph and Dorothy Moore, which made her feel better. I told her how everything had turned out for me. She told me about my brother and sister. My brother, Gary, had gone to university in London and my sister, Natasha, had gone to university in Sheffield. She revealed that neither of them knew about me. She had not wanted to make a difficult situation worse. She had to go back and tell them.

Subsequently I met my brother, who looked only vaguely

like me. He did follow rugby, had played hooker at school and he knew exactly who I was. He was absolutely staggered to find that I was also his brother.

Neither side is pushing things at the moment, and perhaps I am wary of some kind of psychological fall-out somewhere down the line. We are all taking things very slowly. I speak to my natural mother occasionally on the phone and we meet occasionally. She has learned a lot about rugby and watches the games on the television. I don't know if she has told anyone about me from outside the circle of her immediate family.

People in the same position who are contemplating tracing their natural parents must be prepared for a full spectrum of caution and emotion. Both the act of adoption and of subsequent tracing are heavy events, both are done in painful circumstances. For me, the experience of tracing my natural mother has been both traumatic and rewarding. But at least it has answered the outstanding questions in my life.

MATCH-BY-MATCH STATISTICS

1. MAJOR INTERNATIONALS

Lions Tests

01.07.89	v Australia	L	12–30	Sydney
08.07.89	v Australia	W	19–12	Brisbane
15.07.89	v Australia	W	19–18	Sydney
26.06.93	v New Zealand	W	20–7	Wellington
03.07.93	v New Zealand	L	13–30	Auckland

England major internationals

04.04.87	v Scotland	W	21–12	Twickenham
23.05.87	v Australia	L	6–19	Sydney
30.05.87	v Japan	W	60–7	Sydney
08.06.87	v Wales	L	3–16	Brisbane
16.01.88	v France	L	9–10	Paris
06.02.88	v Wales	L	3–11	Twickenham
05.03.88	v Scotland	W	9–6	Murrayfield
19.03.88	v Ireland	W	35–3	Twickenham
23.04.88	v Ireland	W	21–10	Dublin
29.05.88	v Australia	L	16–22	Ballymore
12.06.88	v Australia	L	8–18	Sydney
16.06.88	v Fiji	W	25–12	Suva
05.11.88	v Australia	W	28–19	Twickenham
04.02.89	v Scotland	D	12–12	Twickenham

18.02.89	v Ireland	W	16–3	Dublin
04.03.89	v France	W	11–0	Twickenham
18.03.89	v Wales	L	9–12	Cardiff
13.05.89	v Romania	W	58–3	Bucharest
04.11.89	v Fiji	W	58–23	Twickenham
20.01.90	v Ireland	W	23–0	Twickenham
03.02.90	v France	W	26–7	Paris
17.02.90	v Wales	W	34–6	Twickenham
17.03.90	v Scotland	L	7–13	Murrayfield
28.07.90	v Argentina	W	25–12	Buenos Aires
04.08.90	v Argentina	L	13–15	Buenos Aires
19.01.91	v Wales	W	25–6	Cardiff
16.02.91	v Scotland	W	21–12	Twickenham
02.03.91	v Ireland	W	16–7	Dublin
16.03.91	v France	W	21–19	Twickenham
20.07.91	v Fiji	W	28–12	Suva
27.07.91	v Australia	L	15–40	Sydney
03.10.91	v New Zealand	L	12–18	Twickenham
08.10.91	v Italy	W	36–6	Twickenham
19.10.91	v France	W	19–10	Paris
26.10.91	v Scotland	W	9–6	Murrayfield
02.11.91	v Australia	L	6–12	Twickenham
18.01.92	v Scotland	W	25–7	Murrayfield
01.02.92	v Ireland	W	38–9	Twickenham
15.02.92	v France	W	31–13	Paris
07.03.92	v Wales	W	24–0	Twickenham
14.11.92	v South Africa	W	33–16	Twickenham
16.01.93	v France	W	16–15	Twickenham
06.02.93	v Wales	L	9–10	Cardiff
06.03.93	v Scotland	W	26–12	Twickenham
20.03.93	v Ireland	L	3–17	Dublin
27.11.93	v New Zealand	W	15–9	Twickenham
05.02.94	v Scotland	W	15–14	Murrayfield
19.02.94	v Ireland	L	12–13	Twickenham
05.03.94	v France	W	18–14	Paris
19.03.94	v Wales	W	15–8	Twickenham
04.06.94	v South Africa	W	32–15	Pretoria
11.06.94	v South Africa	L	9–27	Cape Town

12.11.94	v Romania	W	54–3	Twickenham
10.12.94	v Canada	W	60–19	Twickenham
21.01.95	v Ireland	W	20–8	Dublin
04.02.95	v France	W	31–10	Twickenham
18.02.95	v Wales	W	23–0	Cardiff
18.03.95	v Scotland	W	24–12	Twickenham
27.05.95	v Argentina	W	24–18	Durban
31.05.95	v Italy	W	27–20	Durban
04.06.95	v W. Samoa (as replacement)	W	44–22	Durban
11.06.95	v Australia	W	25–22	Cape Town
18.06.95	v New Zealand	L	29–45	Cape Town
22.06.95	v France	L	9–19	Pretoria

* Brian is the most-capped British hooker, having played five Tests for the Lions and sixty-three for England – sixty-eight in all, as well as making one other appearance in the scrum as a replacement forward in the World Cup against W. Samoa.

* Since coming into the England side against Scotland for the 1987 Calcutta Cup match, he has never missed an England Five Nations match. In all sixty-eight of his major internationals, he has never had to be replaced during a match.

* Brian was England's hooker in their five highest scores posted in major internationals: 60–7 v Japan (1987); 60–19 v Canada (1994); 58–3 v Romania (1989); 58–23 v Fiji (1989); and 54–3 v Romania (1994).

* He has been on the losing team only four times in his twenty-six major international appearances at Twickenham.

2. MOORE ON TOUR

Lions

10.06.89	v Western Australia	W	44–0	Perth
17.06.89	v Queensland	W	19–15	Brisbane

24.06.89	v New South Wales	W	23–21	Sydney
01.07.89	v AUSTRALIA	L	12–30	Sydney
08.07.89	v AUSTRALIA	W	19–12	Brisbane
15.07.89	v AUSTRALIA	W	19–18	Sydney
23.07.89	v ANZAC XV	W	19–15	Brisbane
22.05.93	v North Auckland	W	30–17	Whangarei
29.05.93	v New Zealand Maoris	W	24–20	Wellington
08.06.93	v Southland	W	34–16	Invercargill
16.06.93	v Taranaki	W	49–25	New Plymouth
19.06.93	v Auckland	L	18–23	Auckland
26.06.93	v NEW ZEALAND	W	20–7	Wellington
03.07.93	v NEW ZEALAND	L	13–30	Auckland

England

17.05.88	v Queensland Country	W	39–7	Mackay
22.05.88	v Queensland	W	22–18	Brisbane
29.05.88	v AUSTRALIA	L	16–22	Brisbane
05.06.88	v New South Wales	L	12–23	Sydney
12.06.88	v AUSTRALIA	L	8–28	Sydney
17.06.88	v FIJI	W	25–12	Suva
14.07.90	v Banco Nación	L	21–29	Buenos Aires
24.07.90	v Cuyo Selection	L	21–22	Mendoza
28.07.90	v ARGENTINA	W	25–12	Buenos Aires
04.08.90	v ARGENTINA	L	13–15	Buenos Aires
07.07.91	v New South Wales	L	19–21	Sydney
14.07.91	v Queensland	L	14–20	Brisbane
20.07.91	v FIJI	W	28–12	Suva
27.07.91	v AUSTRALIA	L	15–40	Sydney
21.05.94	v Natal	L	6–21	Durban
28.05.94	v Transvaal	L	21–24	Johannesburg
04.06.94	v SOUTH AFRICA	W	32–15	Pretoria
11.06.94	v SOUTH AFRICA	L	9–27	Cape Town

* Since becoming an international in 1987, Brian has been involved in eight summers of rugby. There was the World Cup in 1987, England to Fiji and Australia in 1988, Lions to Australia in 1989,

England to Argentina in 1990, England back to Australia and Fiji in 1991, a summer off in 1992, Lions to New Zealand in 1993, England to South Africa in 1994, and the World Cup in 1995.

* His only score on tour was a try on his Lions debut against Western Australia in Perth in 1989. He was captain of England in the match against the Cuyo Selection in Mendoza, Argentina, in 1990.

3. OTHER REPRESENTATIVE MATCHES

For England XVs in non-cap matches

11.10.86	v Japan	W	39–12	Twickenham
03.01.87	v The Rest	W	10–9	Twickenham
01.05.90	v Italy XV	W	33–15	Rovigo
07.09.91	v USSR	W	53–0	Twickenham
05.09.92	v Leicester	W	18–11	Leicester

For England B

17.04.85	v Italy	W	21–9	Twickenham
02.01.88	v England XV	W	13–7	Twickenham
07.11.92	v South Africa	L	16–20	Bristol

For the Midlands Division

06.12.86	v London Division	L	9–13	Wasps
13.12.86	v Northern Division	L	16–22	Gosforth
20.12.86	v S & SW Division	W	18–10	Leicester
05.12.87	v S & SW Division	L	9–12	Bristol
12.12.87	v London Division	W	25–9	Leicester
19.12.87	v Northern Division	L	15–23	Northampton
29.10.88	v Australia	L	18–25	Leicester
03.12.88	v Northern Division	L	9–27	Otley

| 10.12.88 | v S & SW Division | W | 16–14 | Nottingham |
| 17.12.88 | v London Division | L | 6–27 | Imber Court |

For the London & SE Division

01.12.90	v Northern Division	W	43–8	Stoop Mem Gd
08.12.90	v Midland Division	W	25–24	Stoop Mem Gd
15.12.90	v S & SW Division	D	12–12	Gloucester
05.12.92	v Midland Division	W	26–16	Wasps
12.12.92	v S & SW Division	L	24–26	Gloucester
19.12.92	v Northern Division	L	20–24	Stoop Mem Gd
16.10.93	v Northern Division	W	22–21	Gosforth
23.10.93	v New Zealand	L	12–39	Twickenham
30.10.93	v Midland Division	W	23–14	Leicester

For the Barbarians

| 28.12.87 | v Leicester | L | 30–48 | Leicester |
| 25.11.89 | v New Zealand | L | 10–21 | Twickenham |

For the Four Home Unions

| 22.04.90 | v Rest of Europe | W | 43–18 | Twickenham |

LEAGUE APPEARANCES IN COURAGE CLUBS CHAMPIONSHIP

For Nottingham

1987–8

05.09.87	v Moseley	W	21–12	Home
12.09.87	v Sale	W	17–0	Away
26.09.87	v Orrell	D	12–12	Home
30.09.87	v Coventry	W	20–15	Away

10.10.87	v Bath	W	25–15	Home
17.10.87	v Waterloo	L	9–10	Away
24.10.87	v Gloucester	L	9–17	Away
31.10.87	v Bristol	L	3–16	Home
14.11.87	v Leicester	L	13–22	Home
28.11.87	v Wasps	L	9–17	Away
01.04.88	v Harlequins	L	8–34	Away

1988–9

10.09.88	v Rosslyn Park	W	18–9	Away
24.09.88	v Bristol	W	10–6	Home
08.10.88	v Waterloo	W	18–9	Away
22.10.88	v Leicester	D	12–12	Home
12.11.88	v Wasps	L	9–15	Home
19.11.88	v Liverpool St H	W	22–15	Away
26.11.88	v Orrell	L	6–12	Away
11.03.89	v Bath	L	16–22	Away
08.04.89	v Harlequins	W	12–0	Home
22.04.89	v Gloucester	L	6–13	Away

1989–90

14.10.89	v Saracens	W	25–12	Home
28.10.89	v Leicester	L	6–15	Away
11.11.89	v Wasps	L	12–16	Away
18.11.89	v Bedford	W	47–16	Home
13.01.89	v Moseley	W	22–6	Away
28.04.90	v Gloucester	W	12–3	Home

For Harlequins

1990–1

22.09.90	v Wasps	L	12–18	Home
06.10.90	v Nottingham	W	19–6	Away
13.10.90	v Rosslyn Park	W	18–6	Home
20.10.90	v Saracens	W	39–7	Away
27.10.90	v Liverpool St H	W	41–12	Home

10.11.90	v Bath	L	3–23	Away
17.11.90	v Northampton	W	21–6	Home
23.03.91	v Leicester	W	15–12	Away
30.03.91	v Bristol	W	38–16	Home

1991–2

21.12.91	v London Irish	W	39–3	Away
04.01.92	v Bath	D	18–18	Home
11.01.92	v Northampton	L	14–25	Away
29.02.92	v Bristol	L	0–16	Away
20.04.92	v Orrell	L	7–10	Home

1992–3

19.09.92	v Bath	L	6–22	Away
03.10.92	v West Hartlepool	W	12–9	Away
31.10.92	v London Irish	W	47–24	Home
09.01.93	v Orrell	L	16–18	Away
13.02.93	v Bristol	W	16–0	Home
27.03.93	v Leicester	L	0–23	Away
03.04.93	v Rugby	W	35–14	Home

1993–4

11.09.93	v London Irish	W	30–15	Home
18.09.93	v Wasps	L	15–18	Away
25.09.93	v Bristol	L	15–20	Home
09.10.93	v Northampton	W	15–7	Home
13.11.93	v Leicester	W	10–3	Away
20.11.93	v Orrell	L	20–21	Away
04.12.93	v Bath	L	12–14	Home
15.01.94	v Wasps	W	22–17	Home
29.01.94	v Bristol	L	16–20	Away
12.02.94	v Newcastle Gosforth	W	12–6	Home
26.03.94	v Leicester	L	13–25	Home
09.04.94	v Orrell	L	13–20	Home

1994–5

| 10.09.94 | v Sale | W | 20–19 | Away |

17.09.94	v Wasps	L	26–57	Home
24.09.94	v Bristol	L	14–19	Away
01.10.94	v West Hartlepool	W	20–10	Home
08.10.94	v Northampton	W	23–16	Away
15.10.94	v Leicester	L	13–40	Home
05.11.94	v Gloucester	L	10–14	Home
07.01.95	v Sale	D	15–15	Home
04.03.95	v West Hartlepool	L	8–10	Away
25.03.95	v Northampton	W	10–9	Home
15.04.95	v Orrell	L	28–10	Away
29.04.95	v Gloucester	W	28–17	Away

* Brian played three seasons of league rugby under Alan Davies at Nottingham before transferring to Harlequins in 1990. He has scored two League tries – both for Harlequins: against Liverpool St Helens in 1990 and Wasps in September 1994. He captained Nottingham in 1988–9; Quins in their 1994–5 season.

RFU CUP APPEARANCES

For Roundhay

1980–1

| 24.01.81 | v Leicester | L | 3–34 | Home |

For Nottingham

1981–2

| 23.01.82 | v Sale | L | 9–15 | Home |

1982–3

22.01.83	v Liverpool	W	27–13	Away
26.02.83	v St Ives	W	20–3	Home

1983–4

24.09.83	v Solihull	W	29–3	Home
03.12.83	v Newark	W	34–2	Home
14.02.84	v Stourbridge	W	18–3	Home
25.02.84	v Moseley	W	10–3	Away
10.03.84	v London Scottish	W	22–16	Home
24.03.84	v Bath	L	3–12	Home

1984–5

26.01.85	v Northampton	W	15–3	Home
23.02.85	v London Welsh	L	11–12	Home

1985–6

25.01.86	v Southend	W	25–12	Home
08.03.86	v Wakefield	W	26–7	Away
28.03.86	v Wasps	L	13–13	Home

(Wasps won on away team rule)

1986–7

24.01.87	v Lydney	W	32–3	Away
14.02.87	v Wasps	L	10–25	Away

1987–8

23.01.88	v Waterloo	L	6–19	Away

1988–9

28.01.89	v Bedford	W	6–3	Away
25.02.89	v Harlequins	L	9–15	Away

1989–90

27.01.90	v Rosslyn Park	W	30–9	Away

336

| 10.02.90 | v Orrell | W | 12–6 | Home |
| 24.02.90 | v Gloucester | L | 16–26 | Home |

For Harlequins

1990–1

24.11.90	v Clifton	W	56–4	Home
26.01.91	v Gloucester	W	15–13	Away
23.02.91	v Rosslyn Park	W	24–12	Home
06.04.91	v Nottingham	W	22–18	Home
04.05.91	v Northampton	W	25–13	Twickenham (final)

1991–2

08.02.92	v Wasps	W	20–9	Away
22.02.92	v Rosslyn Park	W	34–12	Away
04.04.92	v Leicester	W	15–9	Home
02.06.92	v Bath	L	12–15	Twickenham (final)

1992–3

20.11.92	v Blackheath	W	72–3	Home
23.01.93	v Wakefield	W	47–18	Home
27.02.93	v Waterloo	W	21–14	Away
10.04.93	v Wasps	W	14–13	Away

1993–4

18.12.93	v Basingstoke	W	52–3	Home
22.01.94	v West Hartlepool	W	23–15	Home
26.02.94	v Sale	W	26–13	Home
02.04.94	v Bath	L	25–26	Home

1994–5

17.12.94	v Saracens	W	9–5	Home
28.01.95	v London Irish	W	40–15	Away
25.02.95	v Wakefield	W	13–8	Home
01.04.95	v Bath	L	13–31	Home

*Only twelve defeats – one of those on away team rule – from forty-four Cup matches in fourteen years is an impressive record. At Harlequins he reached two finals, winning in 1991 and losing in 1992. Injury ruled him out of the 1993 final. He has only played in three Cup defeats for Quins in twenty-one matches.

Statistics compiled by John Griffiths

INDEX

Note: Brian Moore is referred to as BM in sub-entries.

win over Wales at Twickenham
150; least satisfying 280; match
against Scotland, Twickenham
(1995) 4–5, 114, 138, 142, 161,
182, 308; merchandise 135;
some people had achieved goals
by winning 171; sporting grief
of the one that never happened
118; Wales searching for 173
Grant, Derrick 104, 279
Gray, Chris 70, 117
Green, Martin 98, 100
Greenwood, Dick 78–9, 91
Gregan, George 285
Griffiths, Mike 113
Grimsdell, Alan 94
Grindle, Mick 70
Gulf war (1991) 129
Guscott, Jeremy 112, 113, 115,
141, 154, 155, 162–3, 222, 224,
290, 295; absence from England
team 165, 169; arrogance 190,
201; first international 111;
highly effective 138; missed
league matches because of
ancillary commitments 311;
pace and skills 147; Playervision
involvement 244, 257; public
attention 306; regarded by BM
as a bit flash 215; scoring
drought broken 277; talent 303
Gutteridge, Neil 45

Hadley, Norm 274
Halifax 18, 21–2; answer to the
Partridge Family 25; Illingworth
20; Piece Hall 21–2; RUFC 37,
41; rugby league team 36;
Schools team 36
Halifax Town AFC 35–6
Hall, Jon 90, 94

Hall, Mike 111, 193, 197
Hallett, Tony 257
Halliday, Simon 76, 77, 147, 162,
252
Hamilton (New Zealand) 207–8,
225
Hands, David 205
Hardy Hansons 58
Harlequins 76, 84, 107, 338; BM
joins 69, 233; epitome of the
soft South 18; least popular club
in the game 309–10; lurid
colours and jersey 309; many
have become RFU president
311; MPs who were members
311; newspaper report of BM's
involvement in controversial
match 13; problem for captains
311–12; pub incident after
match against 7–8; scrum-half
out for a good time 80–1; social
life 313
Harriman, Andrew 107, 310
Harris, Sid 47
Harrison, Mike 93, 103
Harrogate 46
Hartill, Mark 197
Hartley, Gary 70, 73
Hastings, Gavin 115, 190, 201,
204, 211, 213, 223, 226;
changing–room preparation for
Lions match 193; easy penalty
miss 142–3; momentous Scots
victory in Paris 278; no love lost
between Carling and 214
Hastings, Scott 162, 190, 193, 201
Hawkes Bay 225
Headingley 40, 46–7
Hendrie, Paul 36
Herridge, Colin 136
Heslop, Nigel 133

for natural mother 321–5;
thought about moving out of
London 315
Moore, Catherine (BM's adoptive
sister) 18, 19, 25, 50, 51
Moore, Dorothy (BM's adoptive
mother) 18–20, 23–4, 25, 51,
92–3, 320–5
Moore, Elizabeth (BM's adoptive
sister) 18, 19, 25
Moore, Gwen (BM's adoptive
sister) 19, 28
Moore, Paul (BM's adoptive
brother) 19, 20, 25
Moore, Penny (BM's wife) 17, 23,
150, 318–20, 324
Moore, Ralph (BM's adoptive
father) 18–20, 23–4, 324
Mordcll, Bob 38
Morgan, Derek 86
Morgan, Willie 36
Morris, Dewi 11, 110, 147, 148,
155, 162, 224, 276, 292; furore
over Nike advertisement 249;
one of the best matches for
England 160
Morrison, John 68
Moscato, Vincent 149
Moseley 70, 80
Mougeot, Christophe 148
Muhammad Ali 36
Mullin, Brendan 190, 197
Mullins, Andy 311
Murdoch, Rupert 217, 257
Murphy, Kevin 96
Murrayfield 112, 114, 117, 119,
142–3, 151, 169–71; All Blacks
murder Scotland 165; Calcutta
Cup (1988) 279; English
revenge 130; ghosts of (1990)
125; huge influence behind the

scenes 183; invective 278;
personal and bitter jibes 314;
slaughter of 166
Myreside 117

Nadi 136
Napier 225
Natal 266, 271
Naylor, James 37, 42
New South Wales 106, 137, 196–7
New Zealand 96, 191, 202, 264,
276, 285, 292–6, 298; BM's first
match against 76–7; British
teams always stitched up by
match itinerary 165; defeat
against 141; despatched with
ease by Australia 143; favourites
to beat England 292–3; fitness
91; game of critical importance
140; Haka 166, 167, 222–3, 293,
294, 320; Lions tours 159, 164,
179, 207–27; Maoris 222–3;
nightmarish spell against 298–9;
personal goal of BM to take on
139; plan to shut down 112;
player sent home in disgrace
from tour of 267; racist abuse
during match 12, 167;
rewarding players 257; RU 218;
uncomfortable times against
302; Universities 76
New Zealand Cavaliers 237–8
Newark 229, 235
Newcastle (Australia) 206
News Corporation 257
nicknames 3–4, 57, 122, 124–5,
182, 195
Nike 249
Noriega, Patricio 287
Norster, Bob 99, 191–2, 194, 197,
200, 238–9

Index compiled by Frank Pert